Beyond Death and Jail

Beyond Death and Jail

Anti-Blackness, Black Masculinity, and the Demonic Imagination

Ronald B. Neal

LEXINGTON BOOKS
Lanham • Boulder • New York • London

Published by Lexington Books
An imprint of The Rowman & Littlefield Publishing Group, Inc.
4501 Forbes Boulevard, Suite 200, Lanham, Maryland 20706
www.rowman.com

86-90 Paul Street, London EC2A 4NE

Copyright © 2024 by The Rowman & Littlefield Publishing Group, Inc.

All rights reserved. No part of this book may be reproduced in any form or by any electronic or mechanical means, including information storage and retrieval systems, without written permission from the publisher, except by a reviewer who may quote passages in a review.

British Library Cataloguing in Publication Information Available

Library of Congress Cataloging-in-Publication Data

Names: Neal, Ronald B., 1973—author.
Title: Beyond death and jail: anti-Blackness, Black masculinity, and the demonic imagination / Ronald B. Neal.
Other titles: Anti-Blackness, Black masculinity, and the demonic imagination
Description: Lanham: Lexington Books, [2024] | Includes bibliographical references and index. | Summary: "Beyond Death and Jail explores death and the institutional machinery of policing, surveillance, and containment which breeds it. It seeks to explain why homicide, accompanied by an apparatus of jails, detention centers, prisons, and criminal courts haunts segments of America's Black population, Black boys, Black male youth, and Black men"— Provided by publisher.
Identifiers: LCCN 2023052589 (print) | LCCN 2023052590 (ebook) | ISBN 9781498572729 (cloth) | ISBN 9781498572736 (ebook)
Subjects: LCSH: African American men—Social conditions. | African American boys—Social conditions. | Racial profiling in law enforcement—United States. | Discrimination in criminal justice administration—United States. | Masculinity—United States. | United States—Race relations—Religious aspects.
Classification: LCC E185.86.N398 2024 (print) | LCC E185.86 (ebook) | DDC 305.38/896073—dc23/eng/20231213
LC record available at https://lccn.loc.gov/2023052589
LC ebook record available at https://lccn.loc.gov/2023052590

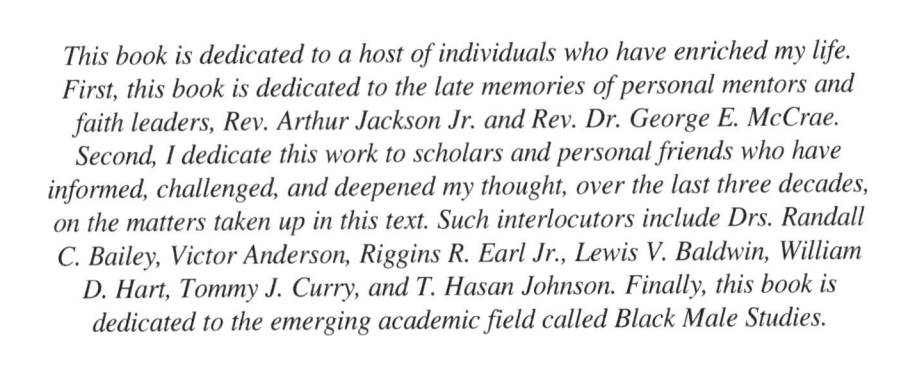

This book is dedicated to a host of individuals who have enriched my life. First, this book is dedicated to the late memories of personal mentors and faith leaders, Rev. Arthur Jackson Jr. and Rev. Dr. George E. McCrae. Second, I dedicate this work to scholars and personal friends who have informed, challenged, and deepened my thought, over the last three decades, on the matters taken up in this text. Such interlocutors include Drs. Randall C. Bailey, Victor Anderson, Riggins R. Earl Jr., Lewis V. Baldwin, William D. Hart, Tommy J. Curry, and T. Hasan Johnson. Finally, this book is dedicated to the emerging academic field called Black Male Studies.

Contents

Introduction		1
1	The Death of a Nation: Black Masculinity and the Failures of Black Leadership	5
2	We Don't Need Another Savior: Intellectuals, Activists, and the Myth of the Black Messiah	27
3	The Thrill Is Gone: The Obama Era and the Obsolescence of Black Orthodoxy	45
4	The Demonic Imagination: Black Masculinity and the Abominations of Religion and Theology in the United States	67
5	Who's Afraid of Black Men?: Black Women and White Saviors	85
6	Legal Misandry: The Prosecutor Who Is Afraid of Black Men	111
7	Detox: Purging the Demonic	133
8	The Saga Continues: Cruel and Unusual Punishment, State-Based Fatherhood, and the Rage for Order in the United States	151
Conclusion: Shut Up and Dribble		173
Bibliography		175
Index		187
About the Author		191

Introduction

February 26, 2022, marked the tenth anniversary of the murder of Trayvon Martin, a seventeen-year-old teenager who was killed at the hands of a citizen in Sanford, Florida. This date captured an event that not only highlighted a life that would have reached the age of twenty-seven were he still alive, but it also marked a period of social and political dissent, in the past ten years, only comparable to the political convulsions of the 1950s and 1960s. This ten-year period was one of homicide, the killing of Black citizens, most of which were Black and male, at the hands of private citizens and law enforcement, which sheds new light on the long-standing problems of anti-Blackness and its mortal consequences in the American Republic. From 2012 to 2022, the American nation and nations around the world were spectators to a Decade of Death. This decade spawned the movements of protest, most notably, Black Lives Matter, a social and political response to homicide. This book is concerned with death and the institutional machinery of policing, surveillance, and containment that breeds it. It seeks to explain why homicide, accompanied by an apparatus of jails, detention centers, prisons, and criminal courts, haunts segments of America's Black population, Black boys, Black male youth, and Black men. It addresses the limitations and failures of activism and theories of social justice and institutional transformation which, over a decade, were presented as solutions to mortal expressions of anti-Blackness in American society. This book asks readers to think critically and think anew about the nature and logic of anti-Blackness in the United States. It asks readers to reconsider and reimagine strategies of thought and action which are at present taken for granted as necessary, normative, and infallible instruments for long-standing social change. At the heart of this book are the perplexing problems which plague Black masculinity in America and the extent to which such problems are as old as America itself. *The Decade of Death (2012–2022)* resuscitated these problems which had been suppressed, ignored, and trivialized (for decades) prior to the murder of Trayvon Martin in 2012. The profundity and magnitude of the vexing state of Black boys, Black male youth, and Black men reached a crescendo in May 2020 with the spectacled murder of George Floyd, an adult Black man who was horrifically executed as it was recorded and later uploaded to the Internet, at the hands of Minneapolis police officer. The killing of George Floyd which set off a long summer of protest in the United States and across the world, in 2020, rendered explicit a specific predicament that plagues no other population in the United States. This book treats this matter not as a generic problem of racism but as a feature of anti-Blackness that is specifically Black and male. Essentially, this book asks readers, especially those committed to antiracism and social justice, to return to the drawing board and start over. Current methodologies and theories of antiracism and social justice simply do not work.

The first chapter of this book deals with a crisis of imagination as it exists among that class of Black Americans who have lived and worked as intellectual leaders within America's power elite over the last four decades. It deals with an economy of ideas related to social justice and antiracism, which have been propagated from the classrooms of elite colleges and universities since the 1980s. The second chapter of this book deals with the limitations and shortcomings of messianic politics and activism. It engages the problem of a Black Messiah or the rise of a leader or a set of leaders who are expected to overcome the conundrum of anti-Blackness overnight or in a single generation. The third chapter of this book builds on chapter 2. It specifically addresses the Obama presidency and the suffocating obsolescence of redemptive suffering as it is applied to homicide, the killing of Black Americans. The fourth chapter of this book deals with religious studies and academic theology and the extent to which these fields have evaded and contributed to the problems that haunt Black masculinity in the United States. It specifically outlines an imaginary, religious, and theological, that is, demonic, with respect to Black masculinity in the United States. The fifth chapter of this book is concerned with the dominant mode of gender ideology in the United States and the extent to which such ideology has bifurcated Black America along the lines of male and female and how such a division has worked for the last forty years in service of ruling-class White interests. What drives this division is an entrenched fear of Black men as a population. The sixth chapter of this book takes on the criminal justice system, specifically the role of the criminal prosecutor and the relationship between the criminal prosecutor and Black men. This chapter deals with the dynamic of fear and the extent to which the fear of Black men as a group informs the treatment of Black men by criminal prosecutors. The seventh chapter of this book is concerned with the fear of Black men as a group as it plagues American society and plays itself out in insidious ways in Black American cultural life, specifically family life and family formation. It calls for an outright purging of this imaginary within and outside Black American culture. The final chapter of this book is concerned with the future of law and order in the United States. It addresses the haunting specter of cruel and unusual punishment as an expanding force in relation to all of the concerns taken up in this book. It calls for a vigorous re-engagement of the prison industrial complex (PIC) and areas of criminal justice reform and prison abolition which have been minimized or ignored.

The title of this book was born in 2012, with the murder of Trayvon Martin at the hands of a private citizen. However, the concerns of this work predate Trayvon Martin's death and have lived with me long before he was born in 1995. This book is a product of lived experiences, questions, intellectual wrestling, and scholarly struggle which have characterized my entire adult life. This book is written from the standpoint of an academic intellectual, a scholar of religion, a Black man, who has spent over three decades vexed by the problem of death and jail with respect to Black boys, Black male youth, and Black men. I approach these matters critically, concerned about the efficacy of activism and intellectual work, as one who spent his late teens and all of his twenties working with churches, nonprofit organizations, and a variety of activist groups, at a time when activism and intellectual work did not have the currency they do at this moment. Today, prison abolition and criminal justice reform receive much media attention and are debated among the Power Elite. What many know today as Woke culture did not exist. Antiracist politics was not popular nor was it considered "cool." I worked in the shadows and on the fringes as many did at the end of the twentieth century, especially the decade of the 1990s. I approach the matters of this book from the standpoint of a GenXer, a generation, especially those in my cohort, young Black men, who were haunted by death and jail. Many of us did not expect to see the age of twenty-five. Many of us considered ourselves fortunate when we lived to see the age of forty. I do not pretend to be a detached investigator to all that has taken place over the last decade. Nor do I pretend to be the final authority on where we go from here. However, as I intimated earlier, my primary objective in this book is to "disturb the peace," to unsettle in a responsible and provocative fashion those methodologies of thought and action that were paramount during *The Decade of Death (2012–2022)*, especially as they are forwarded by elite activists and intellectuals. This book takes a critical look at one decade in particular and the last half-century and looks at the American Republic and says, "We can do better!!!"

Chapter 1

The Death of a Nation

Black Masculinity and the Failures of Black Leadership

During the first term of the two-term presidency of Barack Obama, America's long and arduous history of anti-Black American racism took a major turn. In what is perceived as a high point in American history, the tenure of America's first Black president unleashed events that will plague the United States for decades to come. The presidency of Barack Obama opened a new chapter of struggle and dissent in relation to anti-Blackness in the United States.[1] Intellectually and at the level of ideas, it was the publication of Michelle Alexander's *The New Jim Crow: Mass Incarceration and the Age of Colorblindness* which pointed to a new state of affairs from the standpoint of twenty-first-century America.[2] The publication of Michelle Alexander's *The New Jim Crow* marked the end of an era. *The New Jim Crow* encapsulated an epoch of death, jail, and destruction which was integral to the political, economic, and cultural life of the United States at the end of the twentieth century and the first decade of the twenty-first century. *The New Jim Crow* popularized a subculture of mass concerns, grassroots activism, and intellectual activity which mainstream America was not privy to. *The New Jim Crow* exposed levels of anti-Black racism in the United States which had been ignored and suppressed by America's power elite. The content of *The New Jim Crow* places a light on the mechanisms of surveillance and incarceration which at the time were decimating the ranks of the most neglected and despised Black American populations in the United States. Focused on America's decades long War on Drugs, it popularized the rise and expansion of America's prison industrial complex (PIC). What is more, it gave voice to a set of experiences connected to the long history of anti-Blackness in the United States which cofounds the creed of exceptionalism in America. As the pages of this chapter and book unfold, the persistent force of anti-Blackness will be framed as a religious problem. The religious category of the *demonic* will be employed to articulate its horrid manifestations. The *New Jim Crow* and the tentacles of the PIC represent ground zero for engaging the *demonic* in relation to Black America. Shortly after its publication, the thesis of *The New Jim Crow* was illustrated through dramatic events of anti-Blackness captured by then-emerging social media. In 2012, the scourge of policing and death that Alexander wrote about was given life in the murder of a seventeen-year-old Black male youth from Miami, Florida, Trayvon Martin. Trayvon Martin who lost his life in a fight and struggle with a private citizen as he walked through a highly policed White space in Sanford, Florida, became the avatar for the rebirth of the centuries-long struggle, undertaken by Black Americans, against America's legacy of anti-Black racism.[3]

From the tragic murder of Trayvon Martin on February 26, 2012, at the hands of a private citizen, to the anniversary of his death on February 26, 2022, a time span of ten years, the American public and the rest of the world have been spectators to a theater of death whose victims are mainly but not exclusively Black men and boys. These deaths have exposed a host of social, economic, and political problems, rooted in American history, which the decision-makers and ruling-class elites deliberately ignored.[4] That is, such elites chose not to put forward positive legal, educational, and economic interventions that would harness terrorist and genocidal activity directed toward Black men and boys. Ten years of spectacled deaths have not only revealed the complicity of the powerful over time, it made explicit deficits by way of political ideology and grassroots activism which insufficiently accounts for and engages wanton murder. In other words, the political responses to the spectacle murders of Black men and boys, beginning with Travyon Martin, reflected an impoverished social imagination. These political responses from grassroots activists to journalists to academic intellectuals displayed a crisis of imagination. Traditional civil rights advocates who have touted voting and electoral politics as ultimate responses to death and genocide and journalists and academic intellectuals who push post-modern ideologies, particularly, intersectional feminism, as final solutions to historical problems have been found wanting. In light of the above, one must ask, what accounts for this state of affairs and overall crisis of imagination? The deliberate refusal to acknowledge and address, at the level of politics, activism, and ideas, that an American condition of death and jail exists whose main targets are Black men and boys. This has been the case for close to fifty years. Since the late 1960s, the facts that support the presence of this condition have been deliberately ignored. The resurgence of activism (Black Lives Matter) with the murder of Trayvon Martin in 2012 and the responses to the murders of Black men and boys since that time, especially the horrific spectacles of execution of George Floyd in May 2020, have amplified a vacuum of imaginative thinking and activism which is serious about an American condition of death which primarily affects Black men and boys. The need for a new wave of imaginative thinking is paramount. A new imperative is necessary given the gravity of death and jail and anti-Black racism in the United States. The weight of death and jail and anti-Black racism demands new norms and new methodologies. However, a prerequisite for a reinvigorated imagination is a highlighting of limited thinking, a crisis of imagination, which is and has been an impediment to the condition of death and jail, which afflicts Black Americans. However, the concerns of this book are demographically specific. Its focus is on Black men and boys who are the main targets of death and jail in the United States. Fifty years of impoverished thinking are addressed as new thinking is advanced.

THE PROBLEM

What I am calling a crisis of imagination is generational in nature. In the pages that follow, I outline theoretically what this looks like. For now, the best starting point for this endeavor is the early 2000s and the intellectual climate of that period which speaks volumes to these concerns. In the early 2000s, there was an intellectual atmosphere where morbid assessments of Black men and boys echoed assessments of the entire Black male population more than a century earlier. These assessments ran parallel with a slow and gradual acknowledgment of the PIC and its ravages with respect to Black men and boys in the United States. These late twentieth-century approaches to Black men and boys were driven by pathological thinking and the unexamined belief that Black men and boys are defective problems to be fixed, reprogrammed, or removed from public view. These approaches advanced what constitutes a *demonic imaginary*. What drives this imaginary is the assumption that the plight of Black men and boys is largely self-inflicted or self-induced and that social structures are secondary and even tertiary to the condition of their lives. As the twenty-first century began, the writings of elite journalists and academics promoted this point view. Among those writers was Ellis Cose, an elite Black American journalist who was then an editor at *Newsweek Magazine*. Cose produced news features as well as a book which was a part of this genre of writings. In 2002, Cose published, *The Envy of the World: On Being a Black Man in America*, which was the culmination of his articles and news features on Black men at the end of the 1990s and the beginning of the 2000s.[5] A slim book on Black men and boys, *The Envy of the World* sought to address an ongoing crisis, at the dawn of a new century, among Black men and boys. In 2002, when *The Envy of the World* was published, Cose was among a handful of Black men whose writings about Black men and boys were carried by a national publication. With a pragmatic outlook on the relationship between Black men and boys and the United States, *The Envy of the World*, stood out as a sober assessment of the prospects of Black men and boys in America. It was a work of tough love or "compassionate conservatism" to invoke the popular political parlance at the time. Ellis Cose was not identified with political conservatism or any brand of right-wing politics. However, Cose wrote in a long tradition of Black self-reliance whose most famous representative was Booker T. Washington, offering practical wisdom to Black men and boys, on navigating America.[6] His perspective was not only informed by the tradition of Black self-reliance, it was born, in part but also not exclusively, from his own journey as a Black man in America. Despite its best effort to be a positive intervention, *The Envy of the World* did not stand out as an aberration, especially in relation to the most-trendy publications on Black men and boys which reveled in demonic accounts of the lives of Black men and boys. These accounts were in line with the then-superpredator ideology applied to Black men and boys, which was popular at the time.[7] Despite the well-intended efforts of Cose's work as an intervention, it was dismissed by feminist critics as an unimaginative response to the condition of Black men and boys in America. The most prominent feminist critic of Cose's book was the now-deceased, bell hooks, the Black feminist writer and theorist, whose writings on Black men and masculinity were widely circulated, hugely influential in colleges and universities, and popular among middle-class women. bell hooks took exception to Ellis Cose's outlook and approach to the lives of Black men and boys in *The Envy of the World* in her widely read 2004 book, *We Real Cool: Black Men and Masculinity*.[8] In *We Real Cool*, the work of Ellis Cose's did not meet her calculus of Black male existence nor did it meet the moral standards by which she measured the lives of Black men and boys. In *We Real Cool* not only was the perspective of Ellis Cose dismissed outright, so was the lived experience of Cose, as a Black man, which influenced his book.[9] In *We Real Cool*, a book with similar yet different aims as *The Envy of the World*, Ellis Cose is not the only Black male writer who is either dismissed or whose perspective on Black men is trivialized. This trivialization of the voices of Black men on the lived realities of Black men and boys was a part of hook's intellectual style and disposition toward Black men and Black masculinity. It was also consistent with the manner in which Black women of her generation, second-wave feminists in particular, engaged Black men in feminist thought. Such feminist thought contributed to an anti-Black male perspective, a long tradition in the United States which has had horrid consequences for the lives of Black men and boys. The pages that follow are concerned with troubling and overturning this tradition.

INFALLIBLE EXPERTISE

We Real Cool is the perspective of a Black woman, a feminist, on Black men and boys. As a book written by a Black woman, a feminist, on Black men and boys, it was consistent with a popular mode of writing at the time by Black American women on Black men and boys. When *We Real Cool* appeared in 2004, it stood as one more addition to a genre of literature produced in abundance since the 1970s, which gives unfettered and uncensored expression to Black American women's grievances in relation to Black men.[10] *We Real Cool* stands out as a work of a Black woman, a feminist, because it projects an authoritative posture with respect to its articulations of Black male existence in the United States. In *We Real Cool*, bell hooks wrote as an infallible expert on the dilemmas, conundrums, and trials and tribulations of Black men and boys. Writing as an expert, in an anthropological and psychological sense, on Black men and boys, *We Real Cool* traffics as an answer to the problems and challenges that Black men and boys face. Consider the following passages, taken from the preface of *We Real Cool*, where bell hooks speaks as an expert who addresses the necessity and imperative of feminist intervention where Black male existence is concerned. In this extended excerpt, hooks acknowledges the external force of anti-Blackness in terms of the historical and public perceptions of Black men which are beyond their control. Then she moves to an assessment of Black male existence which is plagued by internal forces, problems within the hearts or minds or souls of Black men which haunts their existence. However, the internal problems which she identifies, are the major preoccupation of *We Real Cool*.

> Seen as animals, brutes, natural-born rapists, and murderers, black men have had no real dramatic say when it comes to the way they are represented. They have made few interventions on the stereotype. As a consequence, they are victimized by stereotypes that were first articulated in the nineteenth century but hold sway over the minds and imaginations of citizens of this nation in the present day.

She goes on to say:

> Negative stereotypes about the nature of black masculinity continue to overdetermine the identities of black males are allowed to fashion for themselves. The radical subculture black maleness that began to emerge as a natural outcome of militant anti-racist activism terrified racist white America. As long as black males were deemed savages unable to rise above their animal nature, they could be seen as a threat easily contained. It was the black male seeking liberation from the chains of imperialist white-supremacist capitalist patriarchy that had to be wiped out. This black man potential rebel, revolutionary, leader of the people could not be allowed to thrive.

She concludes her expert assessment of Black male existence:

> Today it should be obvious to any thinker and writer speaking about black males that the primary genocidal threat, the force that endangers black male life, is patriarchal masculinity. For more than thirty years one aspect of my political activism has been working to educate a mass public about the impact of patriarchy and sexism in the lives of black folks. As an advocate of feminist politics, I have consistently called attention to the need for men to critique patriarchy and involve themselves in shaping feminist movement and addressing male liberation. In an essay written more than ten years ago, titled "Reconstructing Black Masculinity," I suggest that "we break the life threatening choke-hold patriarchal masculinity imposes on Black men and create life sustaining visions of a reconstructed masculinity that can provide black men ways to save their lives and the lives of their brothers and sisters in struggle." Yet despite this work and similar works by Michelle Wallace, Gary Lemons, Essex Hemphill, and other advocates of feminist politics, our work has not influenced the more mainstream writing about black masculinity that continues to push the notion that all black men need to do to survive is become better patriarchs.[11]

In *We Real Cool*, Black men and boys are problems which need to be fixed or corrected. Although bell hooks was an academic feminist, *We Real Cool* is not an academic book. Its conclusions about Black men and boys are not the fruit of empirical research. Rather, it is driven by popular myths and long-standing tropes related to the lives and Black men and boys. *We Real Cool* takes the most extreme expressions of Black male existence in America, the machinations of a minority, and renders them universal. There are aspects of *We Real Cool* that display insights on the sociological realities associated with Black male existence (as evidenced by the passages above). However, these kernels of truth are overshadowed by ontological speculation, apriori assumptions that cannot be empirically verified.[12] In every chapter of *We Real Cool*, hooks makes universal claims about the motivations, intentions, and overall internal constitution of the entire Black and male population which is unsubstantiated by data and steeped in speculation. Only an all-knowing deity can claim to know with no uncertainty the animating internal forces which overdetermines the lives of millions of people. As a work where ontological speculation is pervasive, *We Real Cool* is representative of how Black men and boys exist in the American imaginary. Twenty years since its publication, *We Real Cool* is a commentary on Black men and boys, written by a Black American woman, which is standard fare in an economy of voices on the lives of Black men and boys, especially as such voices are represented by Black American women.

THE CARCERAL STATE

We Real Cool is symbolic of the sociological and literary fact that there is no dearth of female voices/commentators on the lives and overall existence of Black men and boys. From poets to novelists to nonfiction writers to social scientists to filmmakers to journalists to gender theorists, we have, at minimum, fifty years of ideas, beliefs, assumptions, myths, projections, and pathology, in women's voices, on Black men and boys. Such voices constitute an economy, a profitable industry of conclusions, which makes demands on the lives and imaginations of black men and boys. At the time that hooks produced this book, the White American ruling class and its academic institutions, granted these female voices the authority and unquestioned legitimacy of the United Nations and the US Supreme Court. Empowered by the ruling class of White America, the weight of their voices is comparable to the Vatican and the Pope. Their voices and the authority they carry invoke, point to, and justify an entire world of jurisprudence and penology which currently determines the destinies/fates of Black men and boys. The American PIC is the enterprise and context through which such beliefs and ideas are granted legitimacy and authority. Recent revelations due to political movements under the banner of prison abolition and criminal justice reform have made it evident that myths, stereotypes, and metaphysical assumptions are all that is necessary in consuming Black men and boys through the edifice of prisons, jails, and detention centers.[13] Current scholarship and journalistic investigations related to the PIC has made it evident that no evidence, research, or critical thinking is required to send a Black man or boy to jail or prison for the duration of his life. All that is necessary is a belief, an assumption, or a myth to permanently alter the life of a Black man or boy. In the context of the United States, any random person can make a criminal claim or allegation toward a Black man or Black male youth and be guaranteed that such Black man or boy is punished to the highest extent of the law. In theory, the American legal system, with its courts, is designed to protect the innocent and the guilty to ensure that the innocent and the guilty are treated fairly. Where Black men and boys are concerned, the presumption of innocence until guilt is proven has no bearing. In the United States, Black men and boys as a population do not enjoy equal protection under the law. In very profound ways, the US Constitution, particularly, the Fourteenth Amendment, does guarantee full protection under the law for Black men and boys. From the perspective that is articulated here, it is impossible to fathom or grasp the gravity of this state of affairs without grappling with an American imaginary where Black men and boys exist as demons, as the embodiments of evil, as savages, and as criminals. This American *demonic imaginary* is the fundamental impediment to any and all efforts to engage Black men and boys as members of the human species, with the same rights, privileges, and dignities as the most privileged and powerful members in American society. To the extent that Black men and boys are imagined as demons in the ontological realm, they cannot experience justice in real world, the here and now.

BLACK MALE DEATH

What I have outlined above is the starting point of what I regard as a crisis of imagination. This crisis of imagination, specific to Black men and boys, is the consequence of a widespread consensus about the worth and disposability of Black men and boys.[14] What I regard as a demonic consensus is nurtured, promoted, and upheld across the ideological and political spectrum and across groups regardless of race, ethnicity, class, sexuality, and gender.[15] The American criminal justice system and the PIC is ground zero or the tip of the iceberg for engaging the disposability of Black men and boys. This starting point is necessary for grappling viscerally with perceptions and horrid treatments which impact Black men and boys beyond the confines of jail cells, detention centers, and prison walls. Black men and boys regardless of circumstance are imagined as potential inmates, inmates in training, or criminals who have yet to be caught for unspecified crimes and crimes that are attributed exclusively to Black men and boys. Before Black men and boys are even born, at the time of conception, they are haunted with this demonic criminal calculus. Due to the metaphysical underpinnings of the existence of Black men and boys, all Black men and boys are at risk for death and jail. Efforts to reduce or eliminate this vulnerability to social and literal death are at odds with a *demonic imaginary* and calculus which justifies the disposability of Black men and boys. Disrupting this *demonic imaginary* means overcoming the consensus which works deliberately to control, contain, silence, and exterminate Black men and boys. This disruption entails a confrontation with contemporary political ideologies across the political spectrum which revel in and profit from demonic accounts of Black men and boys. This also entails a disruption of silence in relation to those histories of Black male disposability which has been deliberately suppressed in the maintenance of demonic accounts of Black men and boys. There is simply too much at stake in terms of the ongoing loss of life and social death that goes unabated and unchallenged where the lives of Black men and boys are concerned. Because no other population in the United States is at a daily risk for death and jail, in the manner of Black men and boys, from the cradle to the grave, quietism or conformity to compulsory censorship is no longer a viable option in engaging these matters. In fact, censorship or quietism is one of the fundamental impediments to confronting problems pertaining to death, jail, and the lives of Black men and boys.

At the level of ideology, disrupting the demonic consensus means taking seriously the particularities of the existence of Black men and boys. This attention to particularity is what you find in the book, *Policing the Black Man*.[16] Edited by Angela J. Davis, this book is concerned exclusively with Black men and boys as objects and targets of hyper-policing and incarceration. In fleshing out a rationale for such a particular focus on Black men and boys, Davis gives credence to the concerns and objections of other groups, specifically, women, Latinos, LGBTQ+ people, and immigrants who are also impacted by state-sanctioned surveillance. Davis expresses great sensitivity and diplomacy to the circumstances of other groups.[17] However, the logic of diversity and inclusiveness does not adequately speak to the facts on the ground, that Black men and boys are at the worst end of policing and incarceration in the United States. To lump Black men and boys with women, Latinos, LGBTQ+ people, and immigrants without attending to very real differences in terms of numbers and forms of punishment flattens and erases a condition that is specific to Black men and boys in the United States. The case that Angela J. Davis makes for a particular focus on Black men and boys as objects and targets of policing speaks to a very real ideological problem. It speaks to the limitations of mainstream ideologies of diversity and identity politics which have not been friendly, over the last decades, to the specific experiences of Black men and boys. In fact, such politics, with a concern for women, Latinos, LGBTQ+ people, and immigrants, have set themselves in opposition to Black men and boys. In pointed terms, ideologies of diversity and inclusiveness have reveled in a *demonic imaginary* and calculus with respect to Black men and boys. The gravity of policing and containment, which Angela J. Davis addresses in *Policing the Black Man* questions the very efficacy of diversity politics and inclusiveness, where Black men and boys are concerns. Where this chapter is concerned, the policing of Black men and boys has been upheld and sustained by this very politics. To echo an earlier point, this evasion of the specific character of the lives of Black men and boys is not limited to the criminal justice system and the PIC. It exists within the realms of employment, education, health, and overall mortality. Ontological thinking regarding Black men and boys is what sustains it.

Ontological reasoning, as it is found in identity politics and creeds of diversity and inclusiveness, stands in the way of particularity, a specific focus on the conditions and circumstances that set Black men and boys apart from every population in the United States. Such ontological reasoning imagines Black men and boys as no different from ruling-class White men, sharing the same levels of dominance or male privilege as such men. Under these terms, no qualitative distinctions in terms of race, wealth, and psychology are made between ruling-class White men and Black men and boys. This is what you find in the writings of women, particularly gender theorists and feminists. These voices deny that Black men and boys are the most disadvantaged and disposable group in the United States. The denial exuded by these groups is founded on ontological not empirical grounds. Again, the late bell hooks is one representative among many who advance this mode of ontological reasoning. To echo what I stated earlier, bell hooks is very important because her writings and voice as a feminist are connected to an entire generation of women's voices where demonic accounts of Black men and boys have been pronounced. Again, at the level of ontological reasoning, hooks produced influential literature on Black men and masculinity. Her ontological thinking about Black men and Black masculinity speaks volumes about the *demonic imaginary* and political ideologies, steeped in diversity and identity, which characterized the late twentieth and early twenty-first centuries. As I indicated earlier in this chapter, at the heart of the ontological thinking that one finds in hooks is an omniscient and infallible disposition with respect to Black men and boys. Black feminists such as bell hooks write as irrefutable anthropological experts on the behavior and psychologies of Black men and boys. Writing and musing, arriving at conclusions about Black men and boys with virtually no engagement with the many voices and experiences of Black men, feminist accounts of Black men are conclusively demonic and tragic. Decades of scholarship by historians, sociologists, and economists are strikingly missing from such ontological assessments. A decidedly anti-empirical view of Black men and boys is upheld as authoritative and imperative. Again, her 2004 book, *We Real Cool*, symbolizes the type of ontological thinking and attitude that permeates Black feminism and popular feminism writ large.

The problem of ontological reasoning that you find in bell hooks and Black feminist literature has stood as a serious impediment to rigorous and empirical engagements with the conditions and circumstances that confront the lives of Black men and boys. More significantly, ontological thinking has quelled the political potential of critical examinations of Black men and boys. This has been achieved through the proliferation of women's voices since the 1970s and their concerns represented in the women's movement and the articulations of most feminist literature throughout American society and institutions The overall political thrust of the women's movement and feminism successfully suppressed political interventions intended to positively engage the lives of Black men and boys. In light of this phenomena, an unquestioned view of women, all women, as the most disadvantaged group in the United States became the written and unwritten law of the land. Enforced by corporations, universities, and the state, this view supported and maintained ontological thinking with respect to Black men and boys. Efforts to intervene on the part of Black men and boys were rendered bleak and improbable. Notwithstanding this state of affairs, the ontological reasoning which sustained this politics was not without its critics. As feminism became dominant at the end of the twentieth century, it was mainly a handful of sociologists and creative thinkers (Black men) who questioned assumptions and beliefs about Black men and boys that stood outside of history. Among these critics are the sociologists, Robert Staples and Orlando Patterson, and the novelist and nonfiction writer, Ishmael Reed.

DISSENT FROM FEMINIST ACCOUNTS OF BLACK MEN AND BOYS

The work of the late sociologist Robert Staples is paradigmatic for the critique of ontological thinking with respect to Black men and boys during the late 1970s and the decade of the 1980s.[18] With the onset of the 1990s, it is the work of sociologist, Orlando Patterson, which took a form of historical criticism, evident in Staples' work, to another level.[19] During the 1980s and 90s, the novelist and nonfiction writer, Ishmael Reed, added a literary dimension to this effort.[20] Where the subject matter of this book is concerned, it is the ontological criticism of Orlando Patterson which is most pronounced. For the purposes of this chapter and throughout the rest of this book, Patterson's work will be invoked as a major voice of dissent and critique.

At the end of the 1990s, Orlando Patterson's ontological criticisms of Black feminism appeared at a moment of unprecedented advancements for select groups of Black Americans located in the American middle class. This includes significant representation on the part of Black American women, upwardly mobile professionals. At the same time, as some Black Americans prospered, many Black Americans, especially Black American men, experienced no upward thrust. Changes in the American economy, a shift from industrialization to technology and information, destroyed the employment prospects of huge sectors of Black Americans, especially Black men. Simultaneous with this shift was the expansion of underground markets driven by crime, particularly the drug markets, which seduced significant numbers of unemployable Black men. Crime markets fueled by poverty and the collapse of legal work resulted in escalated violence and incarceration among Black Americans, especially, young Black men. In light of these conditions, coupled with long history of struggle and deprivation of Black Americans, rooted in the history and legacy of slavery, Patterson, forwarded the most incisive critique of ontological reasoning with respect to the lives of Black men and boys of the 1990s. Patterson raised questions about the claims of gender theorists pertaining to the perceived advantages that Black men and boys have in American society. For Patterson, Black men and boys possessed no advantages over women in American society. Patterson viewed Black men and boys, writ large, as a population in crisis with no special privileges. Unsurprisingly, the Black feminist, bell hooks, was among the feminist and gender theorists and voices who took exception to Patterson's ontological critique of feminist theory.[21] More than two decades later, the debate set off by Patterson about the status of Black men and boys in the United States remains relevant and unresolved. In light of *The Decade of Death (2012–2022)*, more ontological criticism is warranted in relation to any and all efforts to censor or repress the facts attendant to the condition of Black men and boys in the United States.

HIGH-BROW FAILURE: THE POSTMODERN THEORETICAL IMPOTENCE OF AN ENTIRE GENERATION

The criticisms articulated above are preliminary considerations of a much larger problem that must be overcome. This problem has to do with decades of theoretical musings, mainly on the part of academics whose theoretical interventions are intended to guide and inform social change. The late feminist bell hooks is just one academic from an influential generation whose work fits this bill. There are many others including Patricia Hill-Collins, Kimberly Crenshaw, Tricia Rose, Michael Eric Dyson, and Cornel West. All of these figures came of age and rose to prominence as theories derived from Marxist thought, British and German Cultural Studies, and French postmodernism became popular and normative in colleges and universities across the United States and the Western world.[22] These theories were wedded to feminist studies across the humanities and the social sciences and informed the enterprise of Women, Gender, and Sexuality Studies. All of the Black American intellectuals whom I have mentioned have, at one level or another, accepted and participated in these schools of thought. The philosopher and religious thinker, Cornel West is the most famous of these academics. More than anyone, his notoriety as an elite scholar and public intellectual personifies those efforts to use high-brow academic theory to interpret and ameliorate the socio-political challenges which Black Americans face. With a career that spans forty years, West is also indicative of the shortcomings, limitations, and overall failures of academic theory (postmodernism in particular) to adequately engage and transform the negative circumstances that afflict Black America, particularly Black men and boys. After decades of theoretical musing, it is necessary to acknowledge and confront the impotence of these interventions with respect to the Black American situation. In other words, in what ways have British,

French, German, and Italian theories of society, culture, and justice impacted, in a positive and transformative way, the Black American situation in the United States? What are the merits and value of these theories in terms of domestic policy, economic policy, criminal justice policy, and policies that purport to be just and fair? What is there to be said about the relationship between such theories and *The Decade of Death (2012–2022)* spawned by the murder of Trayvon Martin in 2012? The argument that I make here is that the above theories have been impotent in making the United States a more humane, just, and democratic society, especially as they relate to anti-Black racism. These high-brow theories have not had the kind of long-term impact of the movements of the 1950s and 1960s. The forms of enlightenment that these schools of thought claim to offer have not penetrated the larger public in ways that undermine anti-Blackness in America. More dramatically and ironically, these theories have functioned in the reverse direction. Rather than making society more humane, they have reinforced and amplified old prejudices. Such prejudices are born out in way Black men and Black masculinity have been understood in the past and is taken up in the present. These postmodern theories have contributed to the perpetuation of anti-Blackness rather than its eradication. Demonic accounts of Black men and boys are at the heart of these postmodern theories of American society.

HIGH-BROW THEORY IN A WORLD WITHOUT BORDERS

It should be noted that the high-brow postmodern theories in question have been shielded from intense intellectual and public scrutiny. They have largely been protected by the walls of academia and activist subcultures which are well guarded. The late feminist, bell hooks, despite being prolific in literary output, lived and died, without serious academic and popular criticism of her work. She was largely a celebrated feminist academic who was protected from intellectual interrogation.[23] What is true about bell hooks is also true about the other figures mentioned above with the sole exception of Cornel West. Cornel West is the only high-brow scholar from this generation whose corpus of theoretical writings, and even his political activism outside of academia, has been held up to rigorous microscopic scrutiny. At least two academic books of criticism exist which vigorously criticize his theoretical commitments and political activism.[24] Additionally, the level of criticism that Cornel West has endured has included a university president, namely, former Harvard University president, Larry Summers, who publicly criticized the merits of his work as teacher and scholar. Larry Summers, an economist by training, publicly criticized Cornel West's commitment to scholarship and teaching despite West's sizeable corpus of academic writings and his professional rank at Harvard University as a University Professor.[25]

If a high-brow academic such as Cornel West is a worthy candidate of vigorous critique, then it stands to reason that other high-brow critics, particularly those from his generation, are also worthy of rigorous microscopic interrogation. In the 2020s, the walls of protection need to be lifted from those critics who theoretical commitments have not undergone the kind of intense examination as has Cornel West. In light of what has been stated in this chapter about the late bell hooks, this means that the kind of analysis and critique of Black Men and Black masculinity, which was a concern in her work, should be extended to her theoretical musings and to the musings of others who work in a similar vein. The influence of the high-brow postmodern theory in question now spans four decades. The long-tenure and influence of postmodernism in academia is more than worthy of critical scrutiny, especially in light of *The Decade of Death (2012–2022)* and political movements such as Black Lives Matter, guided by postmodernism, which seek to counter anti-Blackness in the United States.

In light of the above, what exactly is the verdict when one considers more than four decades of high-brow postmodern musings on the part of academics who became prominent during the 1980s and 1990s? What we learn is that such high-brow musings have not enlarged our understanding of the most perplexing social dilemmas that plague the vast majority of Black Americans and the United States today. During *The Decade of Death (2012–2022)*, this was radically illustrated with the Black Lives Matter movement. From the standpoint of this chapter and book, Black Lives Matter proved to be a failed political endeavor. This movement failed politically in large part because the bulk of the language and thinking connected to its activities were generated behind the protective walls of academia, far removed from the lived experiences of the most disenfranchised Black Americans in the United States. Its leadership was uncritically informed by high-brow theory postmodern theory which has influenced academia since the 1980s. After a decade of political activity, the impotence of these lofty theories has been exposed in real time. As I write this chapter, American cities such as Baltimore, Maryland, Ferguson, Missouri, and Chicago, Illinois, among the focus of Black Lives Matter activism, are not better off today than they were prior to the murder of Trayvon Martin in 2012. Massive changes in law and policy have not taken place and radical transformations to the economy have been elusive. For example, Black Lives Matter activists made vocal demands to realign police departments by calls to *Defund the Police* and calls to eliminate cash in local city jails. These activist demands have been met with great resistance by local, state, and federal authorities. The PIC or the carceral state remains intact despite popular efforts to end mass incarceration. More significantly, the influence of high-brow postmodern theory which elevated concerns about gender and sexuality made no visible and lasting difference in the lives of millions of unincorporated Black Americans in American cities. For this reason, it is necessary to critique and even look beyond high-brow postmodern theory.

MASS INCARCERATION AND THE FAILURES OF THEORY

At the outset of this chapter and at various points throughout, I've pointed to the work of Michelle Alexander whose 2010 book *The New Jim Crow* popularized public concerns about mass incarceration and the PIC. As I have indicated earlier, prior to the publication of this book, activists and scholars who worked on the problem of policing and prisons worked in the shadows of activism and academia. Unlike the high-brow postmodern theorists whom I have discussed, they did not possess mainstream appeal. Because of the nonpopularity of scholarship and activism dealing with policing and the PIC, it was shunned by those enamored with high-brow postmodern theory and mainstream status. In fact, the postmodern theory, intersectional feminism, was conceived and advanced, independent from the problem of policing and prisons. Prisons and policing were *not* the concerns of intersectional feminism when it was born in 1991. As prison abolitionists and criminal justice reformers worked in obscurity, public voices in popular culture emerged which took up the slack. In the late 1980s and early 1990s, rap music and emerging hip-hop gave public expression to the social conditions, disenfranchisement, and anti-Blackness that were evident in the burgeoning HIC. Through graphic records and music videos, rap artists painted compelling pictures of the lived experiences of Black male youth and young Black men who were entangled in the criminal justice system, particularly its web of jails, detention centers, and prisons. With the popularity, growth, and spread of hip-hop the facts of death and jail articulated by artists were inescapable themes in this genre of art and entertainment. The popularity and spread of hip-hop unofficially facilitated the work of activists and scholars concerned with mass incarceration. It helped in laying the groundwork for the work of Michelle Alexander which marks the point where concerns about mass incarceration were no longer underground. The work of activists and scholars who focused on the PIC prior to 2010 and the popularity and growth of hip-hop both indict highbrow postmodern theory and exposes its failures over the decades. Hip-hop has produced many stories pertaining to death and jail, narratives which high-brow postmodern theorists have evaded. These narratives speak volumes about the condition of those aspects of Black America which have not been incorporated into the mainstream of White capitalism. One noteworthy example is Louisiana rapper Lil Boosie, whose experience with the PIC is among these narratives. In 2014, after spending six years in the Louisiana State Penitentiary (also known as Angola) and being acquitted of first-degree murder, Lil Boosie walked out of prison. He was one among a long line of celebrity Black men who found himself in the cross hairs of the PIC. Popularly known as the 2 Pac of the US South, Lil Boosie was the victim of ambitious state prosecutors who sought to convict him of murder by using his music, rap lyrics, as evidence that he committed a crime punishable by death.[26] An artist whose life and music have been tinged by the streets, Lil Boosie is a Black man whose forays into street crime have been widely condemned not only by the criminal justice system but also by politicians, journalists, religious institutions, and academics. Lil Boosie is among those Black men who was an object of the War on Drugs, the decimations of populations documented and politicized by Michelle Alexander and others. Due to his celebrity, support from the public, and his ability to pay a top-notch team of defense attorneys to fight deliberate prosecutorial misconduct, he was able to preserve his freedom and start his lifer over. Unfortunately, other Black men, with similar predicaments, were not able to fare so well. In the state of Louisiana, a young Black man who, due to the trifecta of poverty, ignorance, and the lack of opportunity, are vulnerable not just to the predatory streets of the Parishes of Louisiana but also to the predatory machinations of the law-and-order regime of the state of Louisiana. The Louisiana State Penitentiary (Angola) is the end game for young Black men who are powerless against prosecutors, judges, juries, and overall law enforcement which thrive on punishment without rehabilitation.[27] A storied penal institution, Angola is one of the oldest prisons in the United States. With origins in plantation slavery, a former breeding farm for enslaved people, it once had a notorious reputation of being the most violent and dehumanizing prison in the United States. A maximum-security prison, Angola has been the inspiration for Hollywood movies, documentaries, national and international journalism, academic articles, and countless books. Popular memoirs and autobiographies have been produced by inmates and administrators connected to this institution. What Angola represents in terms of the social, economic, racial, and political condition in the state of Louisiana is not the fodder high-brow postmodern theory. Men with life sentences, incarcerated men who are victims of sexual assault while in prison, men who are subject to intense levels of deprivation through solitary confinement, and men who are denied basic human rights and dignity, are far removed from the academic theorists who claim to be committed to deep forms of justice in America. Michelle Alexander's *The New Jim Crow* made explicit the enormous gap between middle- to upper-class elites, the classes from which high-brow postmodern theorists hail and the other class of citizens, most of which are Black and male who are vulnerable to the predatory carceral state. It should be noted that among the high-brow postmodern academics cited in this chapter, Cornel West is the only high-brow theorist of his generation who approximates a set of theoretical ideas (despite his embrace of postmodernism) which speaks to this condition. In fact, in the revised tenth anniversary edition of Michelle Alexander's *The New Jim Crow*, Cornel West addresses this state of affairs in the book's preface. His preface to this book demonstrates clearly why he is theoretically exceptional, and relevant where these matters are concerned. Though Cornel West is the exception, the postmodern rule is worthy of interrogation.

BEYOND POSTMODERNISM

In light of the concerns of this chapter, what I regard as the overall failure of high-brow postmodernism theory over the last forty years, it is necessary to rethink and reimagine theory along the lines of justice. The schools of high-brow theory which have already been listed do not go far enough in touching the most vexing social, economic, and political dilemmas that face the most vulnerable Black Americans in the United States, particularly the situation of Black men and boys. Such theories which are mainly ideologies of gender and sexuality are found wanting. Such theories which purport to be universal visions of justice have profound limitations. In this vein, it is necessary to pursue visons of justice that are not bound by identity as it popularly understood. To this end, theories and principles of justice are needed that do not begin and end with a particular group or identity. Also, principles of justice are needed that do not begin and end with the agency of a particular group or identity. In other words, principles and theories of justice are needed which is cognizant of the imperfections of all groups and identities and with such recognition pursues projects and visons of justice in an imperfect way. High-brow identarian theories do not function in this way. To repeat an earlier point, over the course of a decade, *The Decade of Death (2012–2022)*, such was the case with the movement Black Lives Matter. Unexamined high-brow theories of identity, postmodernism, crippled this movement. In very dramatic terms, this means checks and balances are necessary and without such scrutiny violence and harm, in terms of justice, are committed. The movements of the 1960s were largely impactful because robust theories of justice not bound by a specific identity or a particular group were implemented in service of social change and transformation. The articulations of a theory of justice by Martin Luther King Jr. and that of the Black Panther Party for Self-Defense, informed by traditions of human rights, domestically and internationally, were particular and universal in nature. In earlier periods, the abolition of slavery and the disruption of colonialism, in the United States and across the world, also took place without the constraints and limitations of any group or identity. This imperfect history of justice was undertaken by agents (such as the abolitionist John Brown in the United States and B. R. Ambedkar on the Subcontinent of India) of many backgrounds. What characterizes this history of justice is the existential commitment of those who sought a different set of human and social arrangements. In the quest for new theories of justice, there is a lot to learn from the history of justice in America and across the globe. There are major lessons in this history that can inform new theories of justice in the United States in the 2020s and beyond. One instructive chapter in this history is the struggle for justice in India during the first half of the twentieth century. This history of struggle is important because it impacted the struggle for racial justice in the United States during the 1950s and 1960s. Specifically, the quest to end British colonialism and the effort to abolish the caste system in India speaks to new thinking about justice in the United States.

TOWARD A NEW GENERATION OF THEORY

Overall, the problems of high-brow postmodern theory stated above constitute a prison of sorts, an intellectual prison. This intellectual prison is a world of limitations, restrictions, and reductions. Such a prison demands new kinds of intellectuals, intellectuals that engage in an uncensored fashion the current constraints and problems of the Black American condition, particularly the condition of Black men and boys. This type of engagement is a repudiation and transcendence of the work of late twentieth-century and early twenty-first- century high-brow intellectuals listed above. Every generation of every new century must think anew about the present condition which confronts them. High-brow theories are fallible tools that are subject to revision and even elimination. From this perspective, this means addressing those conditions that are disclosed related to the decade of death. Fortunately, such conditions have been revealed by the work of recent thinkers, new intellectuals who have emerged during the last decade. This new generation of intellectuals represent a departure from the high-brow thinkers criticized in this chapter. The new generation of intellectuals of whom I am speaking represent a provocative challenge to the intellectuals who preceded them. They stand apart from their predecessors by questioning past paradigms and the taken-for-granted assumptions connected to their mode of thinking. What stands out the most in their work is an empirical approach to the condition of Black people in the United States, particularly Black men and boys. In promoting empiricism, they rattle the cage of the intellectual prison. They break the chains and shackles of modes of high-brow thinking which have been fashionable and trendy for more than forty years. Again, the legal scholar, Michelle Alexander is one of these intellectuals. Others include the philosopher, Tommy J. Curry, the historian Stacey Patton, and the legal scholar James Forman Jr. In rattling the intellectual prison, they not only confront the legacy of anti-Blackness with respect to the dominant White population, they critically evaluate and criticize the imprint of anti-Blackness within the Black American population, a psychological and cultural stain, which has deleterious consequences on the lives of Black people in America. It is this latter impact which has heretofore not been taken seriously and has been avoided over the decades.

What is more, the significance of these new intellectuals listed here is the extent to which new vistas are opened for thinking not only about the Black American condition but also the agency of Afro-American in the twenty-first century. High-brow postmodern theories have almost exclusively focused on Black Americans as permanent victims of anti-Black racism at the expense of the agential capacities of the Black American population. Where such agency is concerned, Afro-Americans as agents in America involve the extent to which Black Americans are motivated and informed in relation to confronting the conditions they face. After *The Decade of Death* and the aftermath of the national activist movement Black Lives Matter, such agency is paramount and imperative. In what is now essentially a post-BLM moment, as of the writing of this chapter, the demand for Afro-American agency has increased exponentially. It is in the spirit of Afro-American agency that this book is undertaken.

NOTES

1. Michael Eric Dyson, *The Black Presidency: Barack Obama and the Politics of Race in America* (New York: Mariner Books, 2017).

2. Michelle Alexander, *The New Jim Crow: Mass Incarceration in the Age of Colorblindness*, 10th Anniversary Edition (New York and London: The New Press, 2020).

3. Sybrina Fulton and Tracy Martin, *Rest in Power: A Parent's Story of Love, Injustice, and the Birth of a Movement* (New York: Spiegal and Grau, 2017).

4. Ben Crump, *Open Season: The Legal Genocide of Colored People* (New York: Harper Collins Publishers, 2019).

5. Ellis Cose, *The Envy of the World: On Being a Black Man in America* (New York: Washington Square Press, 2002).

6. Booker T. Washington, *Up From Slavery* (New York: Signet Classics, 2000).

7. Nathan Robinson, *Super Predator: Bill Clinton's Use and Abuse of Black America* (West Somerville: Current Affairs Press, 2016).

8. bell hooks, *We Real Cool: Black Men and Masculinity* (New York and London: Routledge Press, 2004).

9. See the prefatory chapter, About Black Men: Don't Believe the Hype in *We Real Cool: Black Men and Masculinity*, pp. IV–VII.

10. Barbara Smith, Ed. *Home Girls: A Black Feminist Anthology* (New Jersey and London: Rutgers Press, 2000); Guy-Sheftall, Ed. *Words of Fire: An Anthology of African American Feminist Thought* (New York: The New Press, 1995); Patricia Hill Collins, *Black Feminist Thought: Knowledge, Power, and Consciousness* (New York and London: Routledge Press, 2000); Marita Golden, Ed. *Wild Women Don't Wear Blues: Black Women Writers on Love, Men, and Sex* (New York: Doubleday Books, 1993).

11. hooks, *We Real Cool: Black Men and Masculinity*, pp. xii–viv.

12. Victor Anderson, *Beyond Ontological Blackness: An Essay in African American Religious and Cultural Criticism* (New York: Continuum Publishing Company, 1995); Edward Farley, *Good & Evil: Interpreting a Human Condition* (Minneapolis: Augsburg Fortress, 1990).

13. James Braxton Peterson, *Prison Industrial Complex for Beginners* (Danbury: For Beginners, LLC, 2016). Bryan Stevenson, *Just Mercy: A Story of Justice and Redemption* (New York: Spiegal and Grau, 2014).

14. Tommy J. Curry, *The Man-Not: Race, Class, Genre, and the Dilemmas of Black Manhood* (Philadelphia: Temple University Press, 2017).

15. Ronald B. Neal, Troubling the Demonic: Anti-Blackness, Black Masculinity, and the Study of Religion in North America, in *The Routledge Handbooks of Religion, Gender, and Society* (Oxford: Routledge Press, 2022), Chapter 29.

16. Angela J. Davis, Ed. *Policing the Black Man* (New York: Pantheon Books, 2017).

17. See the Introductory chapter, Why Black Men, in *Policing the Black Man* (New York: Pantheon Books, 2017), VI–XXIV.

18. Robert Staples, *Black Masculinity: The Black Man's Role in American Society* (San Francisco: The Black Scholars Press, 1982).

19. Orlando Patterson, *Rituals of Blood: The Consequences of Slavery in Two American Centuries* (New York: Basic Civitas, 1998).

20. Ishmael Reed, *Airing Dirty Laundry* (New York: Addison-Wesley Publishing Company, 1993).

21. bell Hooks, Michele Wallace, Andrew Hacker, Jared Taylor, Derrick Bell, Ishmael Reed, Nathan Hare, Rita Williams, Cecilia Caruso, Carl H. Nightingale, Jim Sleeper, Elsie B. Washington, Yehudi Webster, Kenneth S. Tollett, Sr., and Cecil Brown, The Crisis of African American Gender Relations. Indiana University Press, Hutchins Center for African and African American Research at Harvard University, *Transition*, no. 66 (1995), pp. 99–175.

22. Michael Eric Dyson, *It's Not What You Know, It's How You Show It: Black Public Intellectuals in Race Rules: Navigating the Color Line* (New York: Addison Publishing Company, 1996), pp. 47–76.

23. In October of 2014, The New School of Social Research held a week-long symposium on the work of bell hooks. The presentations and symposium leaders,

such as Gloria Steinem, were largely in praise of her work as a nonfiction writer and prominent public intellectual. See The New School of Social Research. Press Release: Bell Hooks Returns for Third Residency At The New School, October 3–10 (2014), https://www.newschool.edu/pressroom/pressreleases/2014/bell_hook_oct.htm#.

24. George Yancy, Ed. *Cornel West: A Critical Reader* (Malden: Blackwell Publishers, 2001). Mark David Wood, *Cornel West and the Politics of Prophetic Pragmatism* (Urbana and Chicago: University of Illinois Press, 2000).

25. Cornel West, *Brother West: Living and Loving Out Loud* (New York: Smiley Books, 2009); *Democracy Matters: Winning the Fight Against Imperialism* (New York: Penguin Books, 2005).

26. Erick Nielson and Andrea Dennis, *Rap on Trial: Race, Lyrics, and Guilt in America* (New York: The New Press, 2019).

27. See Wilbert Rideau and Ron Wikberg, *Life Sentences: A Story of Rage and Survival Behind Bars* (New York: Times Books, 1992), Wilbert Rideau, *In the Place of Justice: A Story of Punishment and Deliverance* (New York: Alfred A. Knopf, 2010) and Albert Woodfox and Leslie George, *Solitary: Unbroken by Four Decades of Solitary Confinement. My Story of Transformation and Hope* (Chicago: Northfield Publishing, 2005).

Chapter 2

We Don't Need Another Savior

Intellectuals, Activists, and the Myth of the Black Messiah

During *The Decade of Death (2012–2022)*, journalist and writer Ta-Nehisi Coates came to prominence as a major voice on matters of race and anti-Blackness in the United States. Writing for *The Atlantic Monthly* during the Obama Era, Coates, similar to Michelle Alexander, author of *The New Jim Crow: Colorblindness in the Age of Mass Incarceration*, became, a go-to figure for the White liberal establishment in the United States.[1] Elevated as an expert on all things related to race and anti-Blackness in the United States, Coates became the object of messianic expectations and demands. Such messianic objectification was similar to that of the late writer and novelist James Baldwin, whose literary influence from the 1950s to the 1980s solidified his spokesperson status on the Black American condition in the United States. For most of his literary career, Baldwin was treated like a sage and magical figure by a White liberal establishment who was seemingly clueless about the gravity and depth of racism and anti-Blackness in America. This position was projected upon Ta-Nehisi Coates as he produced essay after essay on race matters and anti-Blackness during the Obama Era.

This chapter is concerned with the early stages of *The Decade of Death (2012–2022)* and the reintroduction of old problems, ideological and strategic, related to activists and intellectuals, which plagued prior generations. Such problems pertain to the dangers of messianic politics as it relates to the eradication of anti-Blackness in the United States. By the year 2015, messianic impulses and expectations were evident among activists and intellectuals as the movement Black Lives Matter had become a political phenomenon. The pages that follow deal with the problems and limitations of messianic politics. It is concerned with the uncritical elevation of messianic politics and its attendant demands as the means to overcome anti-Blackness in the United States.

I begin with Ta-Nehisi Coates because his popularity, intellectual work, and how it has been received by the public is fodder to what I consider the limits of messianic religion. In Jewish and Christian traditions, messianic religion is the religion of apocalyptic activism, the attempt to usher in a new world order, a Kingdom of God. A whole host of thinkers from the late Albert Cleage Jr. to Gayraud Wilmore to Rosemary Radford Ruether to Wilson J. Moses to Walter Raushenbush to Karl Marx have written about, promoted, and critiqued messianic religion.[2] At its best, messianic religion is utopian, the effort to redeem society, to eradicate, or to reverse all social maladies in a single lifetime. In considering the problems and limits of messianic religion, it is important to do so in light of new waves and new generations of activists, especially those that emerged during *The Decade of Death (2012–2022)*. The movement Black Lives Matter was the most visible expression of activism during this period. A movement that began as a hashtag on Twitter and Facebook in 2013, after the jury verdict (an acquittal) involving the murder of a Black teenager, Trayvon Martin (by George Zimmerman), morphed into a viable political enterprise. The voices and faces connected to this movement are young, led by Black Americans, mostly women, born during the Reagan era.[3] These activists are the children of the *New Jim Crow*, generations of young Black women, men, and children who have witnessed and experienced the ravages of the prison industrial complex (PIC), the law-and-order regime supported by the American ruling class. Emboldened by the deaths of Black Americans at the hands of law enforcement, police officers, and by extrajudicial murder, by private citizens, they possessed an activist zeal and commitment to justice not seen since the 1960s. Young and heroic, this emergent generation ended a decades-long period (at least thirty years) of dormant activism, energizing a young cohort of politically engaged young people under the age of thirty-five. As a movement, Black Lives Matter had the potential to effect longstanding change, in terms of anti-Blackness in the United States. However, it was confronted with problems, related to messianic religion, that are as old as the United States, challenges that no generation has ever escaped.

SKEPTICISM MATTERS

In the fall of 2015, Ta-Nehisi Coates published an important essay on mass incarceration in *The Atlantic Monthly*. On the cover of its October edition, a glossy image of a Black family stands out as the focal point of a feature story on the PIC, or what penologists call the carceral state. In what is clearly intended to provoke a national conversation, a Black American family ravaged by the American penal system and the American police state writ at large is the starting point for the lead article "Black Family in the Age of Mass Incarceration."[4] This important 2015 essay is one intellectual intervention among the many literary efforts of Coates to address one of the most vexing crises of our times. It is one effort from a Black writer who has used his public platform to engage subject matter that is too often relegated to the realm of the taboo: anti-Blackness in the United States and class. Ta-Nehisi Coates's public explorations of anti-Blackness have garnered him accolades, awards, and heated criticism. Having penned an impressive article on reparations in 2013, a *New York Times* bestselling memoir (*Between the World and Me*), and winning the McArthur Genius Award, Ta-Nehisi Coates established himself as a significant voice and interpreter of the vestiges of American history.[5] "The Black Family in the Age of Mass Incarceration" was a major intervention in a political moment where the visible nature of anti-Blackness was an inescapable fact of American public culture. Mass incarceration represents one of the most shameful institutionalized manifestations of anti-Blackness in our times.

Ta-Nehisi Coates is not a self-described Black Lives Matter activist. In fact, in terms of his own intellectual identity, he does not describe himself as an activist intellectual. Ta- Nehisi Coates is a Black American writer, a journalist, who has learned from and benefitted from the tumultuous Black history of messianic religion and activism in America, but such religion and activism are not reproduced in his work. Coates is a self-described atheist who has no place for religion, religious hope, or any kind of metaphysics in his thinking and writing about race and class in America.[6] His close reading of American history and the impact of this history on the present has made him skeptical of the ideologies of progress and their religious underpinnings. This has invoked a great deal of discomfort and disdain among readers of Coates for whom the *American Dream* and the creed of American optimism, and their efficacy as tenets of faith in America, are more important than the visible and invisible vestiges of American racism. *New York Times* writer David Brooks was a notable voice in rebuking Coates for giving up on the American promise of success for all, for ignoring the Disneyland/Disney World-like possibilities that America presents to the world. Another significant voice is Christian philosopher Cornel West, who chided Coates for having too little hope and not enough activist fire in his intellectual offerings. There are more critics including political scientist, Adolph Reed and the late Black feminist, bell hooks, both dissatisfied with Coates' posture toward anti-Blackness in America. For the most part, critics of Coates, who span the ideological spectrum, have been disenchanted with him for not playing the role of a hero, a messianic hero of ideals, of optimism, hope, and cosmic transformation.[7] In a loud chorus they seem to be saying, "Ta-Nehisi Coates, you are not doing the job that a Black man in your position is supposed to do, to present yourself as a 40-year-old Black Jesus who has a magical solution, a quick fix, to an American condition that has festered for close to four centuries."

It is through a deep study of American history, profound sociological sensibilities, and robust skepticism that Ta- Nehisi Coates resisted the demand to play the role of a redeemer with respect to the legacies of American racism. For many, this seems odd given the role that Black Americans have had to play, particularly elites, in being the moral conscience of this nation. It is a role that has deep roots in the history of the United States. One only has to revisit the antebellum period, the Reconstruction era, and the early twentieth century, to see how figures such as Sojourner Truth, Frederick Douglas, W. E. B. DuBois, and Ida B. Wells were messianic figures with respect to American racism. Being outspoken on civil rights, lynching, Jim Crow, terror, and death, they were stand-out figures, moral voices in the American wilderness. They all belong to a veritable tradition which had its most monumental impact during the Civil Rights and Black Power eras. The most visible and celebrated representative of this tradition and period is Martin Luther King Jr. Overall, a messianic tradition whose virtues are suffering, sacrifice, service, struggle, and death has made moral demands on all Black Americans, particularly the most elite among Black Americans.[8] In profound ways, the journalism and intellectual work of Ta-Nehisi Coates is informed by this tradition, yet in profound ways, it deviates from it. This departure from tradition is evident in a *Playboy* interview where Coates weighs in on the burdens of messianic religion. In Coates' own words,

> I want the notion of there having to be "the voice" of black folks completely obliterated. There is no one voice on climate change. There's no one person on sports. I think that allows for a kind of laziness among nonblack people who don't want to read other people's shit. It saves them from having to compare me with other writers who are not black. It allows them to say, "You're the king of the blacks over here."[9]

This quote speaks to the absurd demands and expectations that are imposed on Black elites, especially in times of intense racial crisis. Coates' words are a response to his critics and to supporters, Black and White alike, especially ruling- class Whites, who seek short cuts to racial justice in America. In other words, all of the work or labor necessary to overcome or topple the vestiges of race and class in America should not be concentrated in one heroic figure, group, or organization. For a Black man in a position such as Ta-Nehisi Coates, this means not assuming the role of a suffering gladly taking on a role that relieves power-wielding ruling-class Whites from becoming messianic figures themselves, a job which often, as history has proven, leads to death, martyrdom.

Ta-Nehisi Coates's refusal to be a Black messiah, a messianic moralist, was warranted and justified. The messianic role that Black Americans have been forced to play, historically, has been significant yet limited in overcoming ant-Blackness in the United States. Accordingly, no generation has devised a method to render the legacies of anti-Blackness obsolete. Black Americans have struggled in North America for four centuries, and we have yet to see the emergence of an American majority that is invested, economically, psychologically, and politically, in divesting itself from the lucrative market of anti-Black racism. More importantly, messianic religion at its most pronounced has invited death to those who have lived it out. Again, the most fertile period for this ethos was the Civil Rights era. This chapter is being written over a half century after the assassination of Martin Luther King Jr. More than fifty years after his assassination, we are confronted with the same conditions, informed by anti-Blackness, which drove his life.

Although messianic religion has played a necessary role in the struggle against anti-Blackness, it has been proven to be limited. No alternative tradition or paradigm has emerged to supplant it. For this reason, it remains the dominant tradition in America. The young, creative, and zealous ethos of the Black Lives Matter movement presented itself as an energetic embodiment of this messianic morality. Being central to the struggles of Black people in the United States, messianic religion has been the singular arena where the utopian imagination of African Americans has been exerted in creative ways. Again, messianic utopianism has been crucial to every instance of social advancement in the experience of Black people in America. The fact remains that the most politicized element within the Black population has responded to de jure and de facto anti-Blackness with messianic fervor. To reiterate what has been already said, under conditions of slavery and Jim Crow, Black American messianists championed a creed of struggle, sacrifice, suffering, freedom, and self-determination in the face of anti-Black terrorism and disenfranchisement, economic, political, and otherwise. Beyond the emergence of Black Lives Matter, the institutional legacy of Black messianic activism was recently dramatized in a profound way. The entire world was given a graphic window into the deep history and tradition of Black messianism, during the month of June 2016 in Charleston, SC, when a historic Black church with a deep record of messianic activism, *Emanuel African Methodist Episcopal Church*, became the target of domestic terrorism, resulting in the death of nine Black Americans (six women and three men). This storied church, led by a forty-year-old pastor/politician, Clementa Pinckney, was a living twenty-first-century symbol of messianic religion in Charleston, SC.[10] Because of its symbolic power and historical meaning, this church was targeted and terrorized in a methodical way by Dylan Roof, a twenty-one-year-old white supremacist. The martyrdom of nine Black Americans spoke volumes to the meaning of this tradition in the lives of Black Americans, to America, and the rest of the world.

CIVIL RIGHTS, BLACK POWER, BLACK LIVES MATTER, AND MESSIANIC RELIGION

In the twentieth century, the Civil Rights era marks the most recent and significant achievements of messianic religion in the United States. Political historians, including the late historians C. Van Woodard and Manning Marable, mark 1954 to 1968 as the second reconstruction of the United States.[11] It was during these years that messianic social activism in the United States had an unprecedented impact on the political and cultural imagination of North America. It was during this era that unprecedented changes in American law and public policy ushered in a new era of race relations in the United States. From the 1954 Supreme Court ruling in *Brown v. Board of Education* to the Civil Rights Act of 1964 to the Voting Rights Act of 1965, race relations were profoundly altered. However, it was the assassinations of Martin Luther King Jr. and Robert F. Kennedy in 1968 that marked a shift and gradual decline in grassroots organizing and civil rights-related protest activity. After 1968, a then-new wave and new generation of radical activists emerged, garnering much public attention as the civil rights groups which dominated the political scene were either dismantled or reconfigured as the decade of the 1960s came to an end. The organization that captured the public imaginations during this moment was the anti-imperial group *The Black Panther Party for Self-Defense*.[12] It is impossible to think about activism at the end of the twentieth century and the legacies of anti-Blackness, and the place of religion in it all without taking the cataclysmic decades of 1950s and 1960s into account.

It should be noted that significant differences exist between the activism that characterized the Civil Rights and Black Power eras and twenty-first-century activism, especially the decades-long dormant period covering the 1980s, 1990s, and the bulk of the 2000s. However, some similarities exist.[13] In terms of Black Lives Matter, especially in its early stage, much of the spirit and energy which drove this movement mirrored the spirit and energy which pushed the activism of the late 1960s. Being present in highly publicized protests against the deaths of Black people in 2014 in Ferguson, MO, and in 2015, in Baltimore, MD, a high level of messianic fervor was expressed which echoed the not-so-distant past. Mirroring the messianic activism of late 1960s, Black Lives Matter embodied its virtues as well as its excesses. In terms of virtue, when Black Lives Matter initially took off, it retrieved an uncompromising spirit of affirmative Blackness. Informed by the very best of the Black freedom struggle (collectivist thought), it, in a short period of time, remixed Black pride and Black consciousness.[14] In a manner which was public and verbal, it pointed out the unwillingness and failures of liberal to left-wing politics to effectively speak to the conditions that Black Americans find themselves in the twenty-first century. Moreover, through social media and public debates, it articulated the limitations and shortsightedness of assimilationist strategies in offsetting the legacies of anti-Black racism. Historically speaking, the liberal imagination has been limited when it comes to matters of life and death with respect to Black Americans. Historically, when liberalism plays a significant role in addressing anti-Blackness, especially at the level of law and politics, it does so when under pressure. In this regard, it is impossible to understand the actions of the US Supreme Court during the 1950s and all of the civil rights legislation passed during the decade of the 1960s, including the Civil Rights Act of 1964 and the Voting Rights Act of 1965, without thinking about the kinds of pressure that messianic activists placed upon the so-called "liberal state" during that era. The presidential administrations of John F. Kennedy and Lyndon B. Johnson were compelled, by messianic activists, to enforce the United States Constitution with respect to the civil rights of Black Americas.[15] Overall, Black Lives Matter was noteworthy in promoting an uncompromising affirmation of Black life in the United States. In profound ways, Black Lives Matters represented a profound litmus test of liberalism, particularly state-related neoliberalism. As such, it raised very important questions about the logic of neoliberalism, particularly its perceived commitment to inclusion and diversity, which has come to represent neoliberal politics.

As the catalyst for the re-emergence of a mode of politics which had been dormant for more than three decades, Black Lives Matter was emblematic of what is seemingly the near death of a dominant mode of Black politics which has been normative since the 1980s, the postcivil rights era. After the 1970s, an approach to race matters, informed by grassroots activism, wedded to systemic social conditions, ceded to a politics of racial and class assimilation alone. What was essentially an anti-imperial approach to anti-Blackness, found in the late stages of the Civil Rights Movement (at the end of Martin Luther King Jr.'s life) and the work of the Black Panthers, was displaced by a politics of identity or poststructuralist approaches to politics.[16] Politics more concerned with racial psychology, etiquette, and appearances (symbols) than with systematic social change displaced a critique of the American empire.[17] In very important ways, Black Lives Matter challenged this form of politics which has been promoted and sustained by Black elites and ruling- class Whites for close to four decades. This politics of compromise and assimilation, poststructuralist politics, was symbolized in the presidency of Barack Obama. It made his election to the Oval Office in 2008 possible and his re-election in 2012, and was characteristic of his style of governance and leadership. The politics tied to his presidency is the epitome of what was criticized via the Black Lives Matter movement. During his tenure as the forty-fourth president of the United States, Barack Obama was reluctant to address forthrightly and with candor, America's unresolved legacy of anti-Black racism; a legacy that manifests itself through education, economics, criminal justice, health, immigration, and foreign affairs. Under his presidency, it took horrific moments of domestic violence, state-sanctioned violence against Black men, Black women, and Black children to expose the weaknesses and limits of poststructural politics. Massive acts of domestic violence against Black people exposed the mythology of a color-blind/postracial America. Related to this now-disclosed racial fissure is the now-exposed American myth of progress. Overall, despite its relative youth, Black Lives Matter was an important political development because it has unapologetically called attention to and confronted a troubling politics of erasure, the aggressive effort to bleach out Black America, which characterizes the relationship between Black Americans and American political culture.

Overall, in its uncompromising affirmation of the lives of Black folk, Black Lives Matter, during its early stage, was an indictment of four decades of erasure, what I have identified as poststructuralist politics. It troubled a brand of politics which functions to erase the political and economic existence of Black Americans. This erasure is most visible in the *New Jim Crow* and the tentacles of the PIC. Widely documented by scholars such as Angela Davis, Michelle Alexander, Robert Perkinson, and Marie Gottschalk, the PIC has disenfranchised millions of Black Americans, thus erasing them from the rolls of citizenship in the United States.[18] The historic death match between law enforcement and Black Americans has only exacerbated this condition. To be effectively incorporated into and be recognized by the American mainstream, Black Americans are asked to bleach out and discard everything associated with the Black sojourn in the United States. To assimilate and compromise, to imitate the politics of a neoliberal Black elite such as Barack Obama or more dramatically, Oprah Winfrey, a figure instrumental in the presidency of Barack Obama. As far as assimilation is concerned, one has to *Oprahfy* oneself, becoming some abstract human being who has no past, no culture, or experience of struggle. This creed is integral to becoming mobile and successful in America. It is fundamental to the myth of the *American Dream.*[19] However, what neoliberals deem a politics of success is in actuality a politics of death. As a young movement, Black Lives Matter rejected the erasing and bleaching of Black America; it is through a deep disenchantment with assimilationist politics—the effort to *Oprahfy* and *Obamafy* Black America—that Black Lives Matter, built on the best of close to four centuries of the Black struggle in America.

THE DANGERS OF MESSIANIC RELIGION

As a young and energetic movement, Black Lives Matter was positioned to be a vanguard activist movement of our times. Like all young movements, the ability to maintain a disciplined focus on its objectives beyond election cycles and the machinations of mass media and political elites has the potential to impact the imaginations of generations. However, any vanguard movement must reckon with the psychological and political seductions that come with such status. What I am referring to are the temptations that come with being anointed a savior, a Black savior, a Black messiah. Similar to the twentieth-century movements that preceded it, the Black Power Movement, the Civil Rights Movement, and the movement led by Marcus Garvey, contemporary movements against anti-Blackness are vulnerable to the all-too-human problems that come with messianic status and celebrity. The most galling seduction and problem of such movements is the reduction of politics to singular methods, singular strategies, and singular personalities, to locate and umbrella all liberation efforts in one thing or person. In the twentieth century, every movement enacted by Black Americans has been thwarted, coopted, and shut down, due in part to a monistic or singular pursuit of social progress. Past movements have been limited by the cult of the one man show or, today, the one-person show. They have been stymied by the seductions and problems of persona or the cult that is erected around a personality, especially when such a personality is charismatic.[20] Because American popular culture and popular psychology have been shaped in profound ways by singular personalities, especially unelected charismatic celebrities, the possibility of social activists and movements to be swept away (by Hollywood) by personality and celebrity is great. Movements that are sustained solely by popular demand and popular personality have proven, in history, to be short-lived. The challenge of such movements is to engage in forms of organizing, strategizing, and politics that are not limited to the moment. There is an inescapable demand to tap into history and political culture and search for resources which lend themselves to longevity, a long game. In fact, it is unnecessary to go far in order to find models. The historic religions of the world are tremendous exemplars and resources in this regard and have a lot to teach justice movements, especially those which are young, that seek longevity. Religions that have a long history, which have been sustained over a long period of time, are instructive. The Abrahamic religions of Judaism, Christianity, and Islam are world traditions that are notorious for producing charismatic personalities. However, these traditions have sustained themselves for more than a millennium, apart from the presence of charismatic actors. Upon close examination, these traditions revel in institutionalized ideas and commitments, not personalities.[21] For this reason, Judaism, Christianity, and Islam remain alive and well. Charismatic personalities come and go, but institutionalized beliefs and commitments outlast a single lifetime. Ideas and commitments, not personalities, prevent a young movement such as Black Lives Matter from being a fleeting thing. In other words, a deep commitment to Black liberation, not predicated by the moment, will sustain movements against anti-Black racism into the future.

The problem of prisons, which began this chapter, is an important point of departure for thinking about the longevity of movements, particularly Black Lives Matter. The PIC presents a challenge, an imaginative challenge that messianic heroism alone does not address. The kind of imaginative challenge that it presents demands that one moves beyond the limits of the messianic imagination and activism. Clues to this are found in Ta-Nehisi Coates' essay on mass incarceration, *The Black Family in the Age of Mass Incarceration*, which invites frank discussion regarding the depths of mass incarceration (race, money, power, and justice). Ta-Nehisi Coates' essay is built on the work of historians, sociologists, and political scientists (whom I've already named) whose conclusions regarding the destructive effects of mass incarceration have been a part of a growing national discourse on the matter. The main virtue of this essay is the candor with which Coates points out the political actors, policies, and practices which have resulted in the largest prison enterprise in the world. Infused by the legacy of racism, conservative ideology, and corporate interests, there is a lot invested in the prison system in the United States. Much of the work that has been done, including that of Ta-Nehisi Coates, is significant. However, a national engagement with mass incarceration, driven by candor, is incomplete if it remains within the realm of sociology, history, politics, and economics. As I indicated earlier, Ta-Nehisi Coates is an atheist who has no interest in metaphysics or religion in addressing anti-Blackness in the United States.[22] He, like many secular intellectuals who do this work, gives no credence to forces outside the scope of history, which accounts for the problems they address. This is a limited position to hold in light of the influence of religion and metaphysics on the human imagination. This is a limited position to hold in light of the role that religion and metaphysics have played in America's racial situation. The religious and metaphysical imagination is very much a part of anti-Blackness in America. An engagement with religion and metaphysics is a necessary step in addressing mass incarceration.

THE DEMONIC: THE RELIGION OF MASS INCARCERATION

At the level of religion, metaphysics, and ideology, a phenomenon such as mass incarceration is an ontological problem.[23] What I am referring to is the problem of being in relation to Black people, that Black people, the most incarcerated people in the United States, being viewed outside the scope of the human, that the most incarcerated Black people in North America are transhuman. Far from new, this ontological problem serves as the underpinnings of anti-Blackness in American history. Mass incarceration is in large part a structural manifestation of anti-Blackness and its long history. The historical problem of anti-Blackness that is present in contemporary political culture is tied to deeply held ontological assumptions about Black people.[24] More dramatically, the ontological problem of mass incarceration is the problem of ontological evil. Mass incarceration exists and persists because it is predicated on the belief in inherent evil; that there are human beings, groups of people who are inherently abject, immoral, lawless, and destructive. Such human beings, who, according to this understanding, are tainted with inherent evil, must be punished, contained, and in many instances, exterminated. Where Black Americans are concerned, mass incarceration is a symbol of ontological evil. So, at the level of politics or activism, the prospect of making Black Lives Matter means engaging the metaphysical or ontological underpinnings of death and jail with respect to Black people. Beyond messianic heroism and activism, engaging and overcoming ontological evil is a necessary task in efforts of Black liberation.

Because this metaphysical element is missing from this discussion, it needs to be incorporated in every arena where the value of Black lives is under discussion. This metaphysical element ought to be addressed with vigor and candor. I call this ontological labor, the hard work of social change. The project of ontological labor is not without precedent. Whatever relative successes were achieved by the Civil Rights and Black Power eras, such achievements were in large part the result of ontological work and critique. In the 1950s and 1960s, the metaphysical structure that sustained white supremacy had to be challenged. If we go back further in time and consider the death of legal slavery, the demise of slavery through war, ontological deconstruction was a part of that effort. The fundamental ontological underpinnings of antebellum society had to be challenged in order to dismantle and outlaw the then-institution of slavery. After the Civil War, America had to re-imagine itself.[25] Ontological deconstruction is necessary and is most effective when done with candor. Ontological deconstruction is nonsensical without and apart from ontological candor. I will conclude this chapter by saying a little about what this means.

CANDOR

One of the unique features of this moment in history is the ubiquity and unique role of social media in illuminating and documenting race matters. Social media is instructive for thinking about ontological work. The Internet, including Twitter, Facebook, and handheld devices, was crucial to the Black Lives Matter movement. Today, the role that social media plays in engaging anti-Blackness is analogous to the role that Hurricane Katrina played in exposing the myth of postracialism close to two decades ago. Close to two decades after Hurricane Katrina, the United States is still grappling with its impact on the Gulf Coast and the United States writ large. Apart from the tragedy it wrought, Hurricane Katrina exposed the entire world to the vestiges of slavery and Jim Crow. Hurricane Katrina was important in exposing the myth that all lives matter in the United States; Katrina was a tragic pedagogical moment which taught the world which lives matter and which lives don't. Hurricane Katrina did more to disclose America's unwillingness to address its racial legacies than the last fifty years of journalism and sociological scholarship.[26] Hurricane Katrina and its aftermath were major instances where the belief, myth, and creed of a postracial America was tried and prosecuted. Prior to Katrina, there was a code of silence around anti-Blackness. In a word, race and class talk were taboo. If one revisits the media coverage of that moment, one will see that one young heroic voice was instrumental in breaking the silence. In that moment, hip-hop artist Kanye West, used his celebrity status to broach the ontological problem connected to Katrina. In what was supposed to be a scripted telethon for the survivors of Katrina, Kanye West went off script and famously stated, "George W. Bush doesn't care about Black people." In one sentence Kanye West cut through a great wall of polite talk and social etiquette which evaded everything that was happening in the Gulf Coast.[27] Although Kanye West did not use religious or metaphysical language, it was a moment of ontological candor. That Kanye West moment needs to be revisited and remixed. We can update this to include American political culture. Our current political landscape makes it ontologically difficult to conclude that all lives matter; that all lives are considered moral, virtuous, good, and in need of protection; that all lives are considered human and have equal worth or value. That all lives do not matter and are not deemed human is an ontological problem. The thesis that all lives *do not* matter needs to be articulated with vigor and candor. We are in a moment where ontological candor is an inescapable necessity. Bolstered by social media, the Black Lives Matter movement instigated the necessity of candor. More direct and frank treatments of anti-Blackness are needed. Ontological candor should be integral to discussions regarding the future of public policy discussion, including educational policy, health policy, employment, and policy discussions in relation to race, crime, policing, and prisons. Ontological candor demands that we move beyond our reluctance to talk about the lives of Black people in a forthright fashion. Everything that social media represents, by way of candor, is a necessary component of social change. An engagement with racial ontology is integral to long-range change. What I am positing is an intellectually and morally honest approach to these matters which have the gravity of life and death; that the destinies of Black people in America represent what's ultimately at stake.

CONCLUSION

Throughout this chapter, I have presented the virtues and limitations of messianic religion. Although the limitations of messianic religion have been pointed out as a reason to pause and examine its outcomes, there is something to extract from the best of this strategy and tradition. The best of the messianic tradition is its urgency about matters of life and death. Messianic religion places a high premium on the lives of Black people in America. Historically, it has championed, imperfectly, the idea and belief that Black lives matter. As it has been stated throughout this chapter, from the attack on the institution of slavery to the assault on lynching to the Civil Rights and Black Power movements to the twenty-first century Black Lives Matter movement, messianic religion at its best, concerns itself with those human conditions, tinged by anti-Blackness, that place artificial constraints on the dreams, aspirations, longings, and hopes of Black people in America. Again, such religion was and is fundamentally focused on those historical and material conditions in North America which symbolically, socially, and literally, kill Black people in America. The focus on matters of life and death means recalibrating concerns regarding human conditions, fomented by anti-Blackness. Those human conditions in North America which have created the PIC and the other-related complexes such as failing K-12 schools, unemployment, and overall social alienation, are the grounds for a politics of life and death. This politics includes a full-blown engagement with our capitalist system of social organization and its marriage to law, politics, and the media. Because American capitalism is bound to anti-Black racism, a politics of life and death can ill afford to ignore the relationship between the two. This theme is the legacy of those historic Black messianic activists whose affirmation of the lives of Black folk included the economic dimensions of Black existence in the United States. Overall, a politics of life and death with respect to the lives of Black folks means stripping messianic traditions of their metaphysical, moral, and psychological baggage. This means discarding the demand for a suffering savior, especially a solitary hero or heroine who is obligated to reverse history (the legacies of anti-Black American racism). This means renouncing the need to concentrate racial concerns in the hands of one group, organization, or entity. By stripping this tradition of its baggage and emphasizing its commitment to matters of life and death, this tradition is rendered mortal and brought down to earth. The focus on life and death makes the engagement with the lives of Black people in America an enterprise that is rooted in this world.

In the concluding chapters of his 1991 book, *Martin & Malcolm & America: A Dream or Nightmare*, the late Black liberation theologian, James H. Cone, ruminates on the limits of messianic religion. He points to and amplifies the mortal lives of Martin Luther King Jr. and Malcolm X as exemplars of the shortcomings of messianic leadership.[28]

> The "messiah complex" is a danger that pervades the leadership expectations of the African American community; for African Americans this complex involves looking forward to the coming of a "modern Moses" or a Christlike figure who will deliver them from the bondage of white racism. When we make Black Messiahs out of Martin and Malcolm, as if they alone knew how to achieve freedom, we will not be encouraged to complete their unfinished task but rather to wait for another savior to come and liberate us ... Messianic expectation also encourages "self-appointed men and women of God" to manipulate the African American freedom struggle for their own interests. In order to distinguish true prophets from false ones, it is important to identify a leader's shortcomings. Only false prophets shun criticism, because they do not want their real motives revealed. True prophets welcome the critical opinion of others because their primary concern is not their public acclaim but rather the cause of freedom for which they speak and act.[29]

In this quote, Cone clearly articulates the problems of messianic religion articulated throughout this chapter. It is a deliberate push back against the grandiose expectations and opportunism (baggage) that messianic religion invites. Martin Luther King Jr. and Malcolm X were once-in-a-lifetime messianic figures, committed to the life-and-death conditions suffered by Black Americans, were also limited human beings, mortal. Though both men were influential, historic, iconic, and celebrated, they were not above or immune to the vicissitudes of life and death, the consequences of messianic religion. Their legacies are historic paradigms for the promise and perils of messianic religion. The messianic ideals they lived out, positively affecting the lives of Black folk, also led to their demise. The anti-Black inequalities they fought against were the very conditions that shortened their lives. The mortal aspects of their lives and commitments are instructive for addressing race and class matters today, matters of life and death. In terms of anti-Blackness, the legacy of Martin Luther King Jr. points to those profane conditions that are external impositions on the lives of Black Americans. In terms of anti-Blackness, the legacy of Malcolm X points to those profane conditions that are both internal and external with respect to the lives of Black people in America. With respect to these historic figures, Black men, acknowledging the limitations of messianic religion while at the same time retaining its concern with life and death is a way of moving forward.

NOTES

1. Michelle Alexander, *The New Jim Crow: Mass Incarceration in the Age of Color Blindness*, 10th Anniversary Edition (New York and London: The New Press, 2020).

2. See Gayraud S. Wilmore's, *Black Religion and Black Radicalism: An Interpretation of the Religious History of African Americans*, 3rd Edition (Maryknoll: Orbis Books, 1998), Rosemary Radford Ruether, *The Radical Kingdom: The Western Experience of Messianic Hope* (New York: Harper & Row, 1970), Max L. Stackhouse, *Walter Rauschenbusch: The Righteousness of the Kingdom* (New York: Abingdon Press, 1968), Wilson Jeremiah Moses', *Black Messiahs and Uncle Toms: Social and Literary Manipulations of a Religious Myth* (University Park: The Pennsylvania State University Press, 1993), Jonathan Sperber's, *Karl Marx: A Nineteenth Century Life* (New York: Liveright Publishing Corporation, 2013), and Martin Kavka's, *Jewish Messianism and the History of Philosophy* (Cambridge: Cambridge University Press, 2004).

3. For accounts of the Black Lives Matter Movement and the Trayvon Martin case, see Keeanga-Yamahtta Taylor's *From Black Lives Matter to Black Liberation* (Chicago: Haymarket Books, 2016) and Subrina Fulton and Tracy Martin's *A Parents Story of Love, Injustice, and the Birth of a Movement* (New York: Spiegel & Grau, 2017).

4. See Ta-Nehisi Coates, The Black Family in the Age of Mass Incarceration, *The Atlantic*, October 2015, pp. 60–84.

5. See Ta-Nehisi Coates, The Case for Reparations, *The Atlantic*, June 2014, pp. 56–71, and *Between the World and Me* (New York: Spiegel and Grau, 2015).

6. Coates' atheism and biography are captured in Benjamin Wallace-Wells' essay for *New York Magazine*, The Hard Truths of Ta-Nehisi Coates, July 12, 2015.

7. See David Brooks' New York Times Op- Ed, Listening to Ta-Nehisi Coates While Driving White, *The New York Times*, July 17, 2015. Cornel West's public criticism of Coates appeared on social media via a Facebook Post that garnered a great deal of attention. In an interview in Playboy Magazine, with journalist, Bomani Jones, Coates discusses critics such as West and bell hooks, State of America: Ta-Henisi Coates, *Playboy Magazine*, July/August 2016.

8. See Moses', *Black Messiahs and Uncle Toms*; *The Golden Age of Black Nationalism, 1850–1925* (New York: Oxford University Press, 1978), Angela Y. Davis, *Women, Race, and Class* (New York: Vintage Books, 1983), and Herbert Robinson Marbury's, *Pillars of Cloud and Fire: The Politics of Exodus in African American Biblical Interpretation* (New York: New York University Press, 2015).

9. *Playboy Magazine*, July/August 2016, 53.

10. For an account of the historic significance of Emanuel AME Church see Bernard E. Powers Jr.'s *Black Charlestonians: A Social History 1822–1885* (Fayetteville: University of Arkansas Press, 1994). For an account of the Charleston 9 Massacre and its aftermath see David Von Drehle, Jay Newton Small, and Maya Rhodan, Murder, Race, and Mercy: Stories from Charleston, *Time Magazine*, November 23, 2015, pp. 42–68.

11. See C. Van Woodward, *The Strange Career of Jim Crow*, Commemorative Edition (Oxford: Oxford University Press, 2001), Manning Marable, *Race, Reform, and Rebellion: The Second Reconstruction and Beyond in America*, 3rd Edition (Jackson: University Press of Mississippi, 2007), and John Hope Franklin, *From Slavery to Freedom: A History of African Americans* (Columbus: McGraw-Hill, 2010).

12. For a recent history of the origins and development of the Black Panther Party for Self Defense see Joshua Bloom and Waldo E. Martin Jr.'s *Black Against the Empire: The History and Politics of the Black Panther Party* (Berkeley: University of California Press, 2013).

13. The Feminist Wire published two accounts of the history-specific nature of the Black Lives Matter Movement. One account is written by BLM founder, Alicia Garza, A Herstory of the Black Lives Matter Movement, October 7, 2014, https://thefeministwire.com/2014/10/blacklivesmatter-2/. The second account, Black Lives Matter/Black Life Matters: A Conversation with Patrisse Cullors and Darnell L. Moore, December 1, 2014, offers additional perspective by leaders in this movement. Both accounts highlight the roles of Black women and Black LGBTQ people in this new iteration of Black politics, https://thefeministwire.com/2014/12/black-lives-matter-black-life-matters-conversation-patrisse-cullors-darnell-l-moore/.

14. Keeanga-Yahmatta Taylor, *From #Black Lives Matter to Black Liberation* (Chicago: Haymarket Books, 2016).

15. See Taylor Branch, *Pillar of Fire: America in the King Years, 1963–1965* (New York: Simon and Schuster, 1998).

16. For an account of this shift over the last three decades, see Adolph Reed Jr., Nothing Left: The Long Slow Surrender of American Liberals, *Harper's Magazine*, March 2014. Also see Walter Benn Michaels, *The Trouble with Diversity: How We Learned to Love Identity and Ignore Inequality* (New York: Metropolitan Books, 2006), Eric Lott, *The Disappearing Liberal Intellectual* (New York: Basic Books, 2006), Nancy Fraser, *Fortunes of Feminism: From State Managed Capitalism to Neoliberal Crisis* (New York: Verso Press, 2013), and Houston A. Baker Jr., *Betrayal: How Black Intellectuals Abandoned the Ideals of the Civil Rights Era* (New York: Columbia University Press, 2008).

17. For a sociological and philosophical account of the quagmire of the assimilationist approach to race, see Orlando Patterson, *The Ordeal of Integration: Progress and Resentment in America's Racial Crisis* (New York: Basic Civitas, 1998).

18. See Angela Y. Davis, *Are Prisons Obsolete?* (New York: Seven Stories Press, 2003), Michelle Alexander, *The New Jim Crow: Mass Incarceration in the Age of Colorblindness* (New York: The New Press, 2010), Marie Gottschalk, *Caught: The Prison State and the Lockdown of American Politics* (Princeton and Oxford:

Princeton University Press, 2015), Robert Perkinson, *Texas Tough: The Rise of America's Prison Empire* (New York: Metropolitan Books, 2010) and Beth Riche, *Arrested Justice: Black Women, Violence, and America's Prison Nation* (New York: NYU Press, 2012).

19. Michael Eric Dyson's *The Black Presidency: Barack Obama and the Politics of Race in America* (New York: Mariner Books, 2016) and Kathryn Lofton's *Oprah: The Gospel of an Icon* (Berkeley: The University of California Press, 2011) give accounts of the assimilationist politics symbolized by Barack Obama and Oprah Winfrey. Shelby Steele's *A Bound Man: Why We Are Excited About Obama and Why He Can't Win* (New York: Free Press, 2008) makes insightful comparisons between Barack Obama and Oprah Winfrey and their appeal to white America.

20. Bloom and Martin Jr.'s *Black Against the Empire* captures the pitfalls of personality and celebrity with respect to the movements of the late 1960s and the 1970s.

21. One of the most popular scholarly voices which has consistently highlighted the persistence of the Abrahamic religions and their enduring appeal to the human imagination is Karen Armstrong. Her popular works, *A History of God: The 4,000 Year Quest of Judaism, Christianity, and Islam* (New York: MJF Books, 1993) and *Islam: A Short History* (New York: Modern Library Books, 2002) make this point.

22. Wallace-Wells, The Hard Truths of Ta-Nehisi Coates.

23. In general, what I mean by an "ontological problem" is what you find in twentieth-century existential literature. Jean-Paul Sarte's *Being and Nothingness* (New York: Washington Square Press, 1992) and Simone de Beauvoir, *The Second Sex* (New York: Vintage Books, 2011) are representative in this regard.

24. In recent years, this ontological problem with respect to Black people in the United States has been taken up by philosophers and cultural theorists. Important works in this regard are George Yancy's *Black Bodies, White Gazes: The Continuing Significance of Race* (New York: Rowman & Littlefield Publishers, Inc., 2008) and Alexander G. Weheliye, *Racial Assemblages, Biopolitics, and Black Feminist Theories of the Human* (New York: Duke University Press, 2014).

25. Louis Menand's, *The Metaphysical Club: A Story of Ideas in America* (New York: Farrar, Straus, and Giroux, 2001) explicates the ontological deconstruction that accompanied the Civil War. The demise of slavery and the addition of the thirteenth, fourteenth, and fifteenth Amendments to the US Constitution were the outcomes of this process.

26. For an account of the political and sociological impact of Hurricane Katrina on the United States, see Ronald B. Neal, *Democracy in 21st Century America: Race, Class, Religion, and Region* (Macon: Mercer University Press, 2012). Also, see New Orleans: Ten Years Later, *The Nation*, August 31/September 7, 2015.

27. See Mychal Denzel Smith, The Rebirth of Black Rage: From Kanye to Obama, and Back Again, *The Nation*, August 31/September 7, 2005.

28. James H. Cone, *Martin & Malcom & America: A Dream or a Nightmare* (Maryknoll: Orbis Books, 1991).

29. Ibid., pp. 272.

Chapter 3

The Thrill Is Gone

The Obama Era and the Obsolescence of Black Orthodoxy

In his groundbreaking 1971 book, *Is God a White Racist? A Preamble to Black Theology*, the now-deceased black philosopher William R. Jones posed a powerful challenge to Christian theology in the Western world.[1] Writing out of the North American context, in the decade following the assassination of Martin Luther King Jr., and the period that some historians described as the post–civil rights era, Jones put forward a set of questions that have not been resolved by those committed to a Christian approach to Black liberation. Since its publication four decades ago, White and Black Christian thinkers have dismissed it. Principally concerned with Christian beliefs regarding suffering, evil, and God, and their application of racial oppression, Jones offered a powerful dissent to what was taken as a normative account of suffering. Treated as a controversial work at the time that it was published and marginalized by the then-theological establishment, it questioned the underlying moral and theological logic of the civil rights movement and the overall messianic impulse of the Black freedom struggle.[2] That taken-for-granted logic pertains to the gravity of Black suffering and oppression in the United States, a multidimensional material condition that is understood in redemptive terms. The late twentieth-century Civil Rights movement, which was initiated and led overwhelmingly by Black southerners, was driven by a staunch commitment to redemptive suffering. Articulated profoundly in the orations, writings, and practices of Martin Luther King Jr., and reflected in the mission statement of the Southern Christian Leadership Conference (SCLC), it placed a moral and mortal burden on the shoulders of America's Black population.[3] Black Americans were asked to redeem the soul of America, to be its moral conscience and its sacrificial lambs. In accomplishing this task Black Americans must consent to a martyr's death. The assassination of Martin Luther King Jr., in 1968 and its subsequent effects embodied the intentions and relative social effects of this Christian ethic. In the decade after the assassination of Martin Luther King Jr., it was clear to William R. Jones that the very logic of redemptive suffering had to be interrogated and reassessed. Almost four decades later, with the rise of a new generation of Black liberationists, addressing the same conditions that produced the movements of the 1960s and 1970s, the normativity of death and salvation as a problem have re-emerged.[4]

Building upon Jones' work, this chapter is a continuation of the discussion regarding messianic ideology initiated in a chapter 2. It takes this discussion to another level by arguing that the logic of redemptive suffering is obsolete. The tradition of redemptive suffering which legitimizes and necessitates death is an impediment to imaginative thinking about Black Americans and its impotence in the face of unrelenting anti-Blackness. From the standpoint of this chapter, redemptive suffering is now an oppressive morality which does not erase that which it is intended to transcend, namely the legacy of White supremacy. Black redemptive suffering makes abominable moral and mortal demands on Black Americans.[5] It asks Black Americans to live out a superior and perfectionistic morality in relation to every group in the United States, especially White Americans. It asks Black Americans to sacrifice their lives, minds, and especially their bodies for the salvation of all. That Black Americans must give up ego, self, self-interest, and group well-being for the sake of the nation, is the basic end of this logic. Overall, Black redemptive suffering demands, in absurd ways, that Black Americans assume moral responsibility for erasing a history of race-related oppression and disenfranchisement, a historical condition that Black Americans had no hand in creating. All those who benefit from a history and inheritance of White racial supremacy are absolved from any responsibility in dismantling this historical condition.

THE EULOGY

With the most recent iteration of Black liberationist politics, Black Lives Matter, the absurdity of redemptive suffering was given graphic illustration with the involuntary deaths, compulsory martyrdom, of African Americans at the hands of private citizens and representatives of the state. One of the most chilling and dramatic illustrations of this took place on June 16, 2015, when nine African Americans were the object of racialized domestic terrorism. On this day, at Emanuel African Methodist Episcopal Church, nine African Americans were killed during a Bible Study at the hands of a gunman, Dylan Roof. How the relatives of those who were murdered responded to this act of terrorism and how it was consumed and interpreted in the public imagination speaks profoundly to the absurdity of the logic redemptive suffering. Moreover, the disturbing nature of this morality was further exacerbated by the then-president of the United States, Barack Obama, who performed the eulogy of the murdered nine.[6]

President Barack Obama's eulogy of the Emanuel 9 was one omission in a long line of anti-Black evasions which characterized his presidential leadership. It was one among many instances where anti-Blackness is reduced to psychical and individual moral lapse. That the actions of Dylan Roof were a product of a long history and ongoing set of human arrangements was not acknowledged. What is more, the gravity of anti-Black-related death was trivialized, as it is typically done through appeals to hope and calls for more virtue. In the end, what one has is another moment among many where the influence of Christianity on America's anti-Black condition is proven to be limited.

> God works in mysterious ways. God has different ideas. He didn't know he was being used by God. Blinded by hatred, the alleged killer could not see the grace surrounding Reverend Pickney and that Bible study group—the light of love that shone as they opened the church doors and invited a stranger to join in their prayer circle. The alleged killer could have never anticipated the way the families of the fallen would respond when they saw him in court—in the midst of unspeakable grief, with words of forgiveness. He could not imagine that.

Obama continues,

> The alleged killer could not imagine how the city of Charleston, under the good and wise leadership of Mayor Riley—how the state of South Carolina, how the United States of America would respond—not merely with the revulsion at his evil act, but with big-hearted generosity and, more importantly, with a thoughtful introspection and self-examination that we so rarely see in public life . . . Blinded by hatred, he failed to comprehend what Reverend Pickney so well understood—the power of God's grace.[7]

To place divine weight on the actions of Dylan Roof—to say that God used him for some good purpose—is to absolve him from culpability, lessening the gravity of his actions and future actions, on the part of others with the intent to kill Black people. Placing the massacre exclusively in the metaphysical realm of redemption frees the nation from reckoning with its anti-Black history. To say that Black-death is a part of some divine plan, which is good for the nation, is to normalize the killing of Black people; that Black people *must* be killed in order for the nation to advance. This ideology of suffering which has a long history is dangerous. It evades the real causes of anti-Black-death and only justifies the present and future killing of Black people in the United States.

NORMALIZING DEATH: THE MARTYR

As I have stated in chapter 2, the logic of redemptive suffering demands that Black Americans carry an enormous burden that no other group in the United States is forced to bear. Barack Obama's eulogy of Clementa Pickney bears this out. The picture that Obama paints of Pickney is one that is saintly, heroic, simple, and romanticized. It is a portrait of a suffering servant standing in the face of mind-boggling odds. Juxtaposed against the enormous social challenges suffered by poor and disenfranchised populations in the South Carolina Low Country and by the overwhelming opposition he faced as a politician, a Black Democrat and state senator in a majority Republican state, Pickney was described as a savior that the world needed. What is more, as Barack Obama articulated his leadership in exclusively messianic terms and connecting it to the Christian tradition that he belonged to, the African Methodist Episcopal (AME) Church, the necessity of messianic leadership was in no way extended to the State of South Carolina and the nation writ large. The messianic burden belonged exclusively to Clementa Pickney. Although President Obama cited the abysmal social conditions that plagued the state of South Carolina, conditions which demanded solid leadership, the state was not held culpable for rendering leadership toward such conditions. Obama's messianic omission stood in stark contrast to the standard response of US presidents to terrorism on US soil and other parts of the world. It was no way given the religious import that the September 11, 2001, terrorist attacks in New York City were accorded, and it was in no way perceived as the November 16, 2015, terrorist attacks in Paris, France.[8] In these latter instances, the response of the United States was clearly messianic. Unlike the Charleston Massacre, the messianic morality attached to these responses were oriented toward justice, not redemption. The deaths of thousands in New York City in 2001 and the deaths of hundreds in Paris in 2015 were not regarded as outcomes of a divine plan. They were perceived and responded to as unjustified evil. Because Clementa Pickney's death was viewed through the lens of a necessary divine plan, specific to Black Americans, his death was not afforded the moral and political weight of the death of those who were casualties in New York City and Paris.

It is a telling fact that the murder of nine African Americans in a historic Church took place in one of the least secular states in the least secular region in North America. The state of South Carolina is far from being a bastion of atheism and secular ideology. Like most of the US South and the rest of United States, religion, Christianity in particular, flourishes. A state where evangelical Christians are allied with political conservativism, the status of Christianity and the commitment of its adherents is no different from radical Jihadists in the Islamic world.[9] A state dominated by Southern Baptists,

South Carolina has one of the poorest records on civil and human rights in the United States. It is impossible to fathom such facts without accounting for the religious ideology and its propagating institutions on the dominant culture of the state. In terms of civil rights and the twentieth-century history of struggle and a much older history of struggle which resulted in a Civil War, it has led the way in the effort to conserve a Christian-based enterprise of White supremacy. Driven by a social ontology that is White, Christian, and Southern, it has sustained an uncompromising disposition toward matters pertaining to race. The dominant social ontology of South Carolina and the US. South writ at large, White, Christian, and Southern, is clearly what contributed to the actions of Dylan Roof at Emanuel AME.

There is much to be said about the manner in which African Americans in Charleston, South Carolina, and beyond, responded to the Massacre at Emanuel. It was a Christian response devoid of any anger, moral outrage, or demand for justice. It is telling that the Christian response came from children, those whose parents were on the receiving end of Roof's hate. Young utterances of forgiveness spoke magnitudes regarding the normalization and stoic acceptance of death and racial injustice. It was a response of the conquered Black Christian who is seemingly more interested in the moral status and salvation of the perpetrator of an anti-Black crime than with justice for a racial crime. This Christian response is comparable to and easily equated with Stockholm syndrome and the visible and psychological effects of colonization. More dramatically, it is comparable with the psychological effects of prison rape (among men) where a female gender identity is imposed on a male rape victim.[10]

The Black American response to the Charleston massacre is inexplicable apart from a very long history of Christian quietism and acquiescence. This is the history of passive Christian acceptance of anti-Black racism in America, a disposition of conformity to racial injustice with no grand demands for redress. This is the dominant Black American Christian tradition. It stands in contradiction and is often in opposition to a politicized stream of Christianity, generally labeled, prophetic. Often, these two traditions coexist in the same space. They are often at odds in the same space. Emanuel AME was one of those spaces.[11]

THE OVER-CHURCHING OF BLACK AMERICA AND AMERICA WRIT LARGE

The massacre at Emanuel AME Church raises many questions regarding the manner in which Black Americans, especially its victims, responded to this horrific event. How does one account for the manner in which Black

Americans called for forgiveness in relation to the person who initiated the massacre at Emanuel AME Church? How does one make sense of the response of the president of the United States, Barack Obama, who used redemptive logic to interpret this event, and to similar moments, during his tenure as president, when race-related deaths took place? The latter question is key to the former. President Obama forwarded a theological approach to anti-Blackness with respect to African Americans that was indicative of the influence of traditional Christian theology on the imaginations of Black Americans.[12] This influence is the consequence of the enormous impact of Christianity in the cultural life of Black Americans. As such, it is an over-determining force facilitated historically through institutions, namely, churches. With respect to Christianity, in the United States, Black Americans have held the distinction of being the most churched group in America. How Black Americans have imagined themselves and their sojourn in the United States has not escaped this fact. What I am calling the over-churching of Black America has not been lost on students and critics of Black American cultural life. Consider the sobering observations of cultural critic, Todd Boyd, who in 2003 made a similar assessment in his book, *The New HNIC: The Death of Civil Rights and the Reign of Hip Hop*. According to Boyd, Black churches play a pacifying and hegemonic role in the lives of Black Americans:

> In some ways, one could argue that the Black Church is ultimately not a threat to any of the larger sources of power in our society; it is a compliment. Though the church's influence reaches a large number of people, its politics of accommodation limits whatever potential impact the institution may have in altering existing power relations. If ever there was a situation in which Black people were being urged to stay in their place, it is the Black church that promotes this thought fully . . . The Black Church has not only bought into the system but become an integral part of the system itself . . . At this point in history, the Black Church has for too much influence on the affairs of Black people. Its often retrograde message tends to be immune to the sort of criticism that is often leveled at other forms of Black culture. One could even call the church a sacred cow because it often appears to be beyond the criticism that is leveled at other forms of Black cultural expression.[13]

For Boyd, the gravity of churches in Black American affairs is regressive and its influence has gone too far. In a word, Black churches stand as impediments to alternate forms of thinking that are potentially richer, more advantageous, and liberating than church-induced theological thinking. Boyd's words which were published in 2003 are still relevant at the time of this writing.[14] The most glaring public evidence for this assertion is the political career, and especially the presidency, of Barack Obama. From the moment that Barack Obama came to mainstream notoriety as a US Senator to his candidacy for and subsequent election as the forty-fourth president of the United States, his relationship to Black America was fundamentally theological. Barack Obama related to Black Americans as a Christian pastor would a congregation. Black Americans responded in kind. In this dynamic, the office of the US presidency, as a political entity was nonexistent. This relationship, which was a mirror of how Black Americans relate to ministers, pastors, elders, and Bishops, foreclosed any kind of scrutiny of President Barack Obama. It protected him with unqualified support. More importantly, it shut down critical thinking with respect to the life-and-death circumstances Black Americans endured under his presidency and continue to endure at this moment. Historically, an assault on critical thought has represented the underside of redemptive thinking and too much church in America. With respect to Barack Obama, who used religious charisma to great effect, his relationship with Black America symbolized the subordination of thought, in terms of too much church. Under these terms, charisma functioned as an assassin of critical thought that is married to and sanctioned by messianic ideology. As a charismatic figure who was understood in messianic terms, critical thought and the office of the presidency were mutually exclusive.[15]

BARACK OBAMA, THE OVER-CHURCHING OF BLACK AMERICA, AND AMERICAN RACISM

The extent to which the over-churching of Black Americans was embodied in the presidency of Barack Obama cannot be overstated. Redemptive thinking, bolstered by charisma, with respect to race, culminated with his election to the Oval Office. Theologically, his election as the forty-fourth president of the United States was perceived and treated as the climax of a grand narrative of historic events, the final death blow to anti-Black racism in America. Imagined as a messianic hero, voted into office by a white majority, Barack Obama was proof that a new chapter in America had been inaugurated. Not once did President Barack Obama downplay the messianic psychology and universe of expectations that come when one is anointed a savior. In fact the language, sonic delivery, themes of hope and victory, charisma and style drove this presidential arrival. Barack Obama positioned himself as an anti-politician and blurred any distinctions between a messianic prophet and a traditional politician. Unlike any presidential candidate in recent history, theology was the vehicle through which he articulated politics.[16] The Christian theological baggage that accompanied his run to the White House was amplified by the legacy of anti-Blackness in the United States. It was magnified by the fact that he ran as potentially the first Black president of the United States. Upon his election to the presidency, his theological approach to anti-Blackness was clear and consistent. In dealing with Black Americans, moralistic sermonizing, tied to sin and redemption, characterized his basic stance on anti-Blackness. By engaging anti-Blackness as a pastor or priest, consigning it to the private realm, regarding it as a problem of individual psychology, Barack Obama exacerbated a problem which theology helped to create. Herein lies the overall conundrum: this theological approach to anti-Blackness did not work. With the end of Barack Obama's two-term presidency, the inability of the first Black president of the United States, to be the redemptive world changer that it was purported to be, the pitfalls of messianic reasoning became more apparent. The subsequent backlash that came with the rise and election of his successor, Donald J. Trump speaks volumes to this fact.[17] With a two-term presidency that closed anti-climactically, and the limited racial fruit that it bore, the need to move beyond messianic reasoning is more urgent than ever. Black Americans should no longer be viewed as the redemptive agents of the United States. As a propagator and guardian of messianic reasoning, the Christian church should cease to be a starting and end point regarding matters of life and death where Black people in America are concerned.

DISMANTLING THE MYTHS OF HISTORY AND THE DE-NORMALIZATION OF BLACK DEATH

Moving beyond redemptive suffering and the Black messiah writ large means re-imagining social change and racial advancement in the United States. Such new thinking demands a deconstruction of death, specifically the ethic of martyrdom, the normalization of death. The prevailing romanticized view of martyrdom that afflicts the Black condition should be dismantled. This means re-imagining and placing into historical context racial struggles in the United States. A reexamination of history is the starting place for this endeavor.

In the most popular accounts of the Civil Rights era and in popular recollections, the heroic lives and deaths of messianic activists are lifted up as the driving force behind the political achievements which characterized that period. Whether this story is told through documentary film, major motion pictures, or the autobiographical accounts of those who lived through that period, little attention is given to larger world historical forces which helped produce a window and a moral economy which produced fertile ground for sacrificial messianic activists. In other words, limited attention is given to the spirit of the times and why messianic activism was relatively successful when it emerged after the 1950s, yet this messianic ethic did not exist on a grand scale in prior eras. In other words, the forms of messianism which emerged during the 1950s and beyond were unprecedented and specific to the late twentieth century.[18] In prior eras of messianic activity, as in the case of Marcus Garvey and the United Negro Improvement Association (UNIA) in the 1920s, it was effectively shut down by external and internal forces. Accordingly, there is huge distance between Marcus Garvey's era and the political context which saw a proliferation of grassroots organizations under the banner of racial justice after the 1950s. In fact, such groups could only exist after 1955.[19] For example, an organization such as the Southern Christian Leadership Conference which was founded in 1957 could not exist during the 1920s, 1930s, or 1940s. The reader should also know that it was prior to the social movements of the 1950s and 1960s, that iconic Black American activists such as Ella Baker and W. E. B. DuBois were compelled, due to the nature of their politics, to flee the base of their activism in the US South, along with thousands of Black migrants, who found refuge in American states and cities beyond the Mason-Dixon line. They lived and worked in southern environments which placed mortal limits on their activism.[20] Again, all of this happened before the political shifts of the 1950s including the US Supreme Court decision in *Brown v. Board of Education* (1954) and Montgomery Bus Boycott in 1955. In our popular recollections of the age of Jim Crown and the Civil Rights era, very little has been said or written about the fear, caution, threats of death, and actual terrorism which haunted the Black population in the United States South. Moreover, such remembrances omit the fact that early twentieth-century Black Americans such as Ida B. Wells and mid-twentieth-century Black Americans such as Thurgood Marshall, who risked their lives through heroic activism, did so with very little protection, fanfare, and celebration. Black activists of their ilk and those who engaged in activism in general were exceptions in the Black American population, not the rule. More significantly, few White Americans, particularly those who would regard themselves as liberal, progressive, or enlightened, joined forces with heroic Black Americans and actually risked their lives in confronting Jim Crow. During that period, the bulk of the White population was indifferent to and not empathetic toward the condition of Black Americans. All in all, there is much to be said about why heroic activism was not a pervasive norm, why pervasive fear among Black Americans would be interpreted by future generations (some not all) as cowardice. Lastly, there is much to be said and to be written about why most White Americans sat on the sidelines when it came to brutal realities of Jim Crow.[21]

Due to the historical silences in this regard, we have an unexamined tradition of heroic mythology that demands to be de-mythologized in the face of historical facts. World currents have to be acknowledged which have been evaded. We have not admitted that globalization during the 1940s encouraged and made possible messianic activism after the 1950s. The Cold War is the singular historical factor which has to be acknowledged, especially the threat and anxiety it fostered in relation to the spread of communism, particularly in the United States. Cold War anxieties pushed American politicians and businessmen to respond constructively to the problems of Jim Crow.[22] To be sure, martyrdom played a very important role in the confluence of events, but martyrdom alone did not reform American society. In a word, a close scrutiny of this history reveals that the relative achievements of this time period are the result of a plethora of forces. Today, what we essentially have is a monomythic view of social change that obscures and betrays the global facts that account for the reconstruction of a society. For this reason, heroic redemptive suffering alone should not stand as a sole morality necessary for the disruption of white supremacy.

MARTIN LUTHER KING JR.

For close to six decades, the face of Martin Luther King Jr., has represented the prophetic tradition that I referred to above. More than anyone, King's social activism and Christian love ethic has been held as evidence of Christianity at its best, Christianity concerned with race-related matters of justice. Often connected to a biblical tradition of prophets, the abolitionist tradition and the social gospel, Martin Luther King Jr. is imagined as a hero and exemplar with respect to Christian faith.[23] What often goes unspoken about Martin Luther King Jr. is that he was a member of a prophetic minority; that he was a once-in-a-lifetime figure, a personality that cannot be duplicated, in any era, on an assembly line. He was both an anomaly and an enigma. He accepted the call of a Christian martyr and opened himself up to death. He was criminalized and killed for the commitments he held and through his mature adult lifetime was a pariah within his social class. Availing himself to death, social and mortal distinguished him from most human beings, past and present who walk the earth. A Black American who was not above error, he transcended the most oppressive social tendencies of his time. Most human beings do not live such heroic lives and most do not live long enough to see such figures appear in their lifetimes. Although he was a product of the Christian tradition, Christianity alone cannot be credited for what he became and all that he pursued during his short lifetime. Martin Luther King Jr.'s quest for cosmic justice involved a radical engagement with the world which transcended Christianity.

WHY WE CAN'T WAIT

As I write this chapter, more than two decades after the dawn of the twenty-first century, there is virtually no public evidence that warrants confidence in the messianic Christian narrative and its ability and willingness to address the life and death conditions that affect Black people in America. There is no reason to hope or believe that the heroic vision of Christianity that drove the life and actions of Martin Luther King Jr. will somehow recalibrate itself and influence American Christianity and society writ large. All of the problems associated with Christianity that Martin Luther King Jr. outlined in his classic, *A Letter from a Birmingham Jail*, still persist.

> The contemporary church is often a weak ineffectual voice with an uncertain sound. It is so often the arch-supporter of the status quo. Far from being disturbed by the presence of the church, the power structure of the average community is consoled by the church's silent and often vocal sanction of things as they are . . . I am meeting young people every day whose disappointment with the church has risen to outright disgust.[24]

By and large American Christianity has resisted and has shown an indifference to social justice. American Christianity has an aversion toward the social gospel that is pervasive and all-encompassing. Despite the high visibility and verbosity of Christian elites, activists, and intellectuals, who fashion themselves as prophetic and progressive, their presence pales in comparison to the mainstream of American Christianity which is anti-prophetic and anti-progressive.[25] What is more, such elites are very far from being the mantle bearers of the legacy of Martin Luther King Jr. To reiterate what has been said earlier, since his assassination in 1968, no institution or personality has come close to embodying the kind of commitment to social justice that his life and death represented. At present, an elite minority of Christianity activists and intellectuals who are visible to have failed miserably in thinking beyond Christianity. They have failed in the task of being intellectually honest and engaging with candor, why the most dominant expressions of Christianity are reluctant champions of justice, particularly justice that confronts anti-Blackness. They have failed horridly at explaining why their respective visions of Christianity have not proven to be influential at a mass level. Christian elites who work on the margins assume at an apriori level that their outlooks on Christianity and social justice are normative, right, and necessary. Yet little reason, beyond social class, is given as to why only an elite few attempt to live it out. Moreover, no attention is given to the absence of any real movement or institutional apparatus that would sustain such a vision. Even when one factors schools of theology and university divinity schools, there is little ground for this movement to stand on. This is not just a matter of fact in the present. One can look to a prior era, the early twentieth century, when the social gospel was most prominent. From the standpoint of history, it is clear that this problem was evident when it was most popular. The impact of traditional Christianity on American culture impeded the influence of the social gospel. This includes Black Americans who participated in this movement prior to the Civil Rights era. An illustration of this is Benjamin Elijah Mays, a mentor of Martin Luther King Jr. and an elite Black educator and prominent champion of the social gospel during the twentieth century who saw very little institutional support (among American churches) for his commitments.[26] Mays belonged to an enterprise of Black churches and mainline denominational organizations which did not offer significant grounding for his gospel. Working outside of churches, as the president of a Black single gender (male) liberal arts college (Morehouse College), gave him the platform and space to articulate and live out his views. In recent times, the paucity of support for this form of Christianity was articulated by a prominent Black Christian intellectual, Michael Eric Dyson. A scholar and minister, Michael Eric Dyson has written extensively on the legacy of Martin Luther King. In a 2015 essay on the Christian philosopher, Cornel West, in the New Republic, Dyson weighed in on the idea of prophetic leadership (or messianism). Couched in relation to the Obama era, Dyson, with much candor talks about the institutional constraints, with respect to the Black Church, upon those who fashion themselves as prophets, those who champion a social gospel. Dyson's words are in response to Cornel West, who during the Obama era, publicly chided Black Christian elites such as Michael Eric Dyson and elite Black ministers, for not taking a prophetic stance toward Barack Obama's presidential policies.

> As an ordained minister and professor, I know the difference between the professorate and the pastorate, between prophets and scholars. When I utter progressive beliefs about equal rights for women or queer folk as a professor, I am sometimes lauded. When I was church pastor, not a prophet, something I have claimed to be—the same sermon that garnered praise from progressive scholars earned me much scorn from church officials and members and even cost me a pastorate when I tried to put my belief into action and ordain women as deacons.

Dyson continues,

> Most ministers are clerics attending to the needs of the local parish. Only a select few are cut from prophetic cloth. Yet nearly all the religious figures we recognize as prophets—Adam Clayton Powel, Jr., Jesse Jackson, Sharpton—were ordained ministers. Powell and King were pastors of local churches as well. To be sure, there are prophets who are not ministers or religious figures—especially women whose path to ministry has be blocked by sexist ideologies—but most of them have ties to organizations that hold them accountable.[27]

The prophetic Christianity or social gospel, promoted by Christian elites such as Cornel West and others, is a tenuous enterprise with limited to no institutional support. No institution (academic, church-related, or otherwise) is willing to commit itself to the moral/messianic demands of the gospel which the prophet espouses. The sobering reality is that American Christianity is too invested in the imagined and actual luxuries, rewards, and benefits that come with being a die-hard promoter and devotee of the American empire. This includes the Black American Christians whom figures like Cornel West believe represent the messianic future of American society. This messianic prophetic vision of Christianity, coupled with a romanticized view of Black Americans as American saviors, needs to give way to something else. There is much room for a more attractive and compelling vision of religion and justice, and a more realistic understanding of Black Americans. Hence, much is to be said about moving beyond Christianity and promoting a more complicated vision of social justice in relation Black life in the United States.

FURTHER HERMENEUTICAL AND EXISTENTIAL CONSIDERATIONS

Up to this point, if the argument put forward above has not been successful, then consider additional reasoning for thinking differently, in terms of religion about Black Americans. With the rise of the Black Lives Matter Movement, set off by the aftermath of death of Trayvon Martin in 2012, the limits of Christianity, were more than ever, placed on the world stage. Younger generations, born since the 1990s, have questioned Christianity as a guardian and authority, with respect to Black Lives. The activism of Black Lives Matter and that of young people writ large, threw into question the entire Black Christian tradition. Black Lives Matter ushered in the first wave of activism since the 1960s, where Christianity was not a source of sustenance and inspiration. In light of Black Lives Matter, it is a sobering fact that Black Christian elites and Black churches are not at the center of contemporary Black activism.[28] Much of this can be attributed to the disintegration of Black America, taken up in another chapter, whereby gaps exist (economic, educational, and moral) in Black America which has relativized morality authority in Black America.[29] These gaps have disrupted, existentially, the authority and status of Christianity in Black America. Black expressions of activism and outrage have brought this fact to light. This is particularly true with respect to the protest in Ferguson, Missouri, in 2014 over the death of Mike Brown at the hands of police officer, Darren Wilson. That moment in Ferguson, Missouri, in August 2014 was revelatory. Similar to Hurricane Katrina and its devastation upon the Gulf Coast, it exposed an oceanwide gap between the haves and the have nots in the United States. Where anti-Blackness is concerned, it offered a window into a class divide that now exists among Black Americans, a divide between unincorporated Black Americans and Black Americans who have been incorporated in the mainstream of American life, living comfortably in first world America. A divide that is specific to the post-civil rights era and to cultural rifts attributed to what black postmodernists call post-soul Black America, the political dissent among the residents of Ferguson, Missouri, mostly low-income Blacks, was evidence of a new state of affairs. Dissent in Ferguson, Missouri stood out because it was not led by traditional elites, educated Black Christian activists and spokespersons with connections to the White world. Dissent in Ferguson, Missouri was initiated and led by America's least wanted. Coupled with Hurricane Katrina, Ferguson was the second instance in a decade that leveled a blow to Black moral philosophy. It was a major instance, at an existential level which called for a reappraisal of ideas moral, religious, and otherwise which have dominated Black social thought. Because young Black people rejected, in profound ways, the Christian politics of the Black elite, there is a real need to rethink the entanglements of Christianity and the political existence of Black Americans.

Overall, there is huge gap between the life and death matters of Black Americans in the twenty-first century and the activism of elite Black Christians. This gap may be attributed in large part to those Christian traditions that were formed before the twentieth century. There is enormous distance between the extra-judicial and state-sanctioned killings of young Black men and women born after 1995 and the tradition of Christian activism of middle-class elites born before World War II. In other words, the moralism and politics that produced historical figures such as Booker T. Washington, Ida B. Wells, W. E. B. Dubois, Frederick Douglas, and Sojourner Truth are not translatable without difficulty into the twenty-first century. All of these figures and the histories that shaped their lives are instructive for thinking about the legacy of anti-Blackness in the United States. However, our contemporary context demands that such figures and the traditions they represented are contextualized. Because of the social and class differentiation that has taken among Black Americans over the last five decades, there is not a universal moral code or universally receptive audience to the moral philosophy that such figures embodied and espoused. In dramatic ways, Christianity does not function as a shared source of authority among most Black Americans and elite Christian figures command little to no real authority. In dramatic terms, we are talking about new generations of Black Americans who have lived outside of and have not experienced Christianity as an advocate on their behalf. Simply stated, Christianity does not function as a starting point for them. The early twenty-first century is unlike the early twentieth century where an elite Christian figure such as Booker T. Washington commanded the allegiance and attention of Black majorities. At the dawn of the twentieth century, Booker T. Washington was a moralist and authority figure who commanded the admiration of large number of Black Americans. Washington belonged to an era of Black leadership, where select black men and women were authority figures who had some connection to the Black majority.[30] Their fates were linked to the Black majority which gave them capital among the majority. Today, this idea of a common destiny among Black Americans, linked fates, does hold. It is virtually a romantic notion on the part of those who pretend that it is still alive.

WORLD RELIGIONS AND PHILOSOPHY

In a globalized world, one that is characterized by demographic shifts, connected by cell phone technology, computers, and social media, messianic reasoning should not determine, solely, how the Black American situation is understood. When a tragic death besets a Black American, especially when it is the result of terrorized violence, it should not be filtered through some creed of sacrifice, martyrdom. Black churches are no longer clearing houses for how such matters are engaged. The influence of Christianity has been relativized and diminished. In light of globalization, Christianity is one among the many religious traditions in the world. In light of the religions of the world and the many philosophies and ideologies that drape the global moral economy, more expansive understandings and more engaged thinking are needed to shed light on the life-and-death condition of Black Americans. The legacy of messianic reasoning, alone, is not enough in attending to the gravity of life and death with respect to Black Americans. Messianic theology, alone, in no way grapples with the enduring legacy of whiteness and white supremacy on the lives of Black people in American. More resources are needed. Elites, including intellectuals, activists, and politicians are needed who possess a broader moral vocabulary. With a 400-year history of Black Americans in the United States, the language of redemption has proven to be limited. Its primary function has been to normalize the deaths of Black Americans, when such deaths are expressed in a spectacled fashion.

In light of the above concerns, a close survey of the history of Black American religious thought reveals that Christian categories, alone, have not determined how Black Americans have understood themselves and their arduous condition in America. It should be remembered that the first Africans brought to North America as slaves were practitioners of Islam and traditional African religions. Many converted to Christianity over the course of time. Even with the gradual conversion to Christianity, on the part of Africans, during the antebellum era, Christian thought had to compete with the legacy of African traditional religion and its derivatives.[31] There was a very potent culture of conjure or magic that existed simultaneously with Christianity. I am referring to a phenomenon which has been widely documented by scholars, taken up by fiction writers, and depicted in popular film. Unlike the Christian tradition, there is no thought structure of sin and redemption. In this tradition, there is no intellectual apparatus that normalizes death, martyrdom. In this regard, the transatlantic slave trade cannot be viewed as some theologically necessary historical phenomenon intended for the salvation or good of the continent of Africa. No worldview is posited that regards entire populations, Black populations in particular, in redemptive terms.

In more recent years, Black American religious thinkers such as William D. Hart and Monica A. Coleman have made proposals that take Black American religious thinking beyond the Christian narrative.[32] In what Hart calls Afro-Eccentricity and what Coleman calls Third-Wave Womanist religious thought, they question and surpass the standard narrative of Black religion. By incorporating world religions and philosophies that are not typically associated with Black American Christians and promoting a skeptical and open outlook toward knowledge, ideas, and social problems, an expanded epistemology, a larger moral vocabulary, and a greater range of moral considerations are placed on the table.

In light of the efforts of Hart and Coleman, I propose a turn to additional resources and what that means. Thinking seriously about different possibilities by way of religion and philosophy means aggressively challenging an entrenched culture of xenophobia, ignorance, and fear that contributes to and reproduces a culture of African American death. The context of the Charleston 9 massacre, South Carolina, is appropriate in this regard. This context produced Dylan Roof. It is one context among many, with similar attributes, that is devoid of the possibilities of world religion and philosophy. Deeply mired in a tradition of Christian exclusivism, it hugs, kisses, and sleeps with the legacy of anti-Blackness in the United States. That Dylan Roof became a martyr for White Christian exclusivism at the age of twenty-one speaks volumes about the impact of this legacy across generations. When it is commonly presumed that members of young and emerging generations are naturally more sophisticated and forward-thinking and -looking than generations that precede them, figures such as Roof serve as a reality check. What is more, it is difficult to write such a figure off as an anomaly when the terrorist act that he committed occurred with a contemporary context of racialized violence. If he stands as an exception, it is to the extent his acts were articulated through an unapologetic verbal utterance of white supremacist ideology. Moreover, that publicly identifiable and vocal white supremacist organizations reside in South, Carolina should not be overlooked when considering the culture of xenophobia that pervades the state and similar states. White Christian exclusivism characterizes this world in the same fashion that Dutch Anglicanism has characterized Afrikaner rule in South Africa. This monolithic wall of whiteness is a great challenge to overcome. Again, because messianic reasoning has been limited in erasing white supremacy, multiple religions, philosophies, and ideologies stand as evolutionary possibilities.

At this point, a word of clarity is needed. What I am stating here is not a call for multiculturalism, diversity, or religious pluralism. What I am calling for is a cosmic and dynamic worldview that brings with it all of the virtues, anxieties, problems, and overall creative tensions that arise when cultures, regions, economic conditions, and most importantly ideas, intersect. In this regard, it is important to return to an American state such as South Carolina which is ground zero for the concerns of this chapter. A state that is racially polarized and ideologically and religiously homogenous like South Carolina can possibly change and become something else if and when it encounters something different. Consider, for instance, the subcontinent of India, a context where Hinduism, Buddhism, Islam, Christianity, and Judaism coexist. A context that is less than perfect, where internal tensions exist, but is dynamic in terms of the heterogeneous forms of thought and culture which thrive there. India's recent emergence as a global force to be reckoned with is unfathomable apart from the deep plurality which pervades the region.[33] Although Hinduism is the dominant religion, the plurality within Hinduism, in terms of deities, communities, and ontology, coupled with the ideas and ontologies of other world religions including Buddhism, Islam, Judaism, and Christianity, make it virtually impossible to reduce India to a single essence. Apart from Western myths and caricatures of South Asians, no group or person or religion is representative of all. In a closer look at the deep plurality which is there, the Western Gaze is disrupted with respect to the subcontinent of India. If one were to think about African Americans along these lines, then it makes it difficult to think about Black Americans in a monolithic way. It explodes the monomythic view of Black Americans which makes it easy to terrorize, criminalize, and kill Black Americans.

In this chapter, I have argued that orthodox thinking about Black Americans tied to the Christian tradition and Christian thinking about redemption has run its course and is obsolete. The persistence of this thinking is dangerous to the degree that it authorizes and justifies terrorism, death, and racial violence toward Black Americans. It renders Black American death as a normal and necessary function of history and a prerequisite for racial justice in the United States. This type of thinking quells dissent, protest, resistance, and rage with respect to the legacies of anti-Blackness in the United States. It absolves and renders innocent agents who enact terrorist violence against Black Americans. More significantly, it does not move the White ruling class and the dominant White majority in the United State to uproot and eliminate the structural and institutional impediments to full-blown African American advancement in the America. In light of the work of the late philosopher,

William R. Jones, whose book, *Is God a White Racist?*, was invoked at the start of this chapter, this argument in not new. However, I reassert this perspective in the face of recent history which gives Jones' thesis greater relevance. Moreover, the fact that a sitting US president, Barack Obama, appealed to this type of thinking during a period of resurgent violence toward Black Americans only heightens the absurdity of this thinking and the necessity of its repudiation. As I have indicted elsewhere, a crisis of imagination is indicative of this state of affairs. This orthodoxy must give way to new thought, a reinvigorated imaginary, where death is not a normal and necessary occurrence with respect to the futures of Black Americans.

NOTES

1. William R. Jones, *Is God a White Racist?: A Preamble to White Theology* (Boston: Beacon Press, 1998).

2. In the preface of the 1998 edition of his book, William R. Jones outlines how his book was received at the time that it was published. In his estimation, the then-theological establishment misrepresented the aims of his efforts and was disenchanted with his philosophical criticisms of Black liberation theology and Black American Christian thinking regarding redemptive suffering. According to Jones, his book was marginalized and suppressed due to his philosophical conclusions. In his own words, "Most Black theologians decided that IGWR was not a faithful trustee of liberation theology's philosophy and practice, nor of the black religious tradition. In fact, they found it a fraudulent traitor of these traditions. As a result of this criticism, IGWR was essentially removed from the theological market and consigned to the pariah status of Ralph Ellison's 'invisible man.'" See the entire preface in the 1998 edition of *Is God a White Racist?*, pp. viii–xviii.

3. The written works of Martin Luther King Jr. such as, *Stride Toward Freedom: The Montgomery Story* (Boston: Beacon Press, 1958), *Why We Can't Wait* (Berkeley: Signet Classics, 1964), and *Where Do We Go From Here: Chaos or Community?* (Boston: Beacon Press, 1968) are among the publications which articulate the Christian vision of the Civil Right Era.

4. I am referring to the rise of the anti-racist social movement, Black Lives Matter, which emerged in 2013. See Keeanga-Yamahtta Taylor's work, *From #BLACKLIVESMATTER to Black Liberation* (Chicago: Haymarket Books, 2016).

5. William R. Jones' pioneering critique of redemptive suffering set off a theological and philosophical debate that rages to this day. The most significant account of this debate is Anthony B. Pinn's work, *Why Lord? Suffering and Evil in Black Theology* (New York: Continuum Books, 1995).

6. See David Von Drehle, Jay Newton Small, and Maya Rhodan, Murder, Race, and Mercy: Stories from Charleston, *Time Magazine*, November 23, 2015, pp. 44–68. Also see Michael Eric Dyson, *The Black Presidency: Barack Obama and the Politics of Race in America* (Boston and New York: Mariner Books, 2016).

7. See the full text of President Obama's Eulogy for Clementa Pickney, https://www.cnn.com/2015/06/27/politics/obama-eulogy-clementa-pickney/index.html.

8. The US presidents George W. Bush and Barack Obama were swift in their condemnations and willingness to act, administratively, to acts of actual or perceived threats of terrorism, domestic, and international in scope. Islamic terrorism and US terrorism motivation by White Nationalism were not regarded equally in gravity and scope.

9. For an account of South Carolina, its religious orientation and socioeconomic position see Ronald B. Neal, *Democracy in 21st Century America: Race, Class, Religion, and Region* (Macon: Mercer University Press, 2012).

10. The colonial phenomenon that I have in mind is what you find in the work of Frantz Fanon, most notably, *Black Skin, White Masks* (New York: Grove Press, 1952). A clear description and articulation of the sexual dynamics of prison rape in a men's prison is the essay, The Sexual jungle, in Wilbert Rideau and Ron Wikberg, Ed. *Life Sentences: Rage and Survival Behind Bars* (New York: Random House, Inc., 1992).

11. The groundbreaking work of Cornel West, *Prophesy Deliverance!: An Afro-American Revolutionary Christianity* (Philadelphia: Westminster John Knox Press, 1982) is an articulation of late twentieth-century prophetic Christianity including its relationship to nonprophetic streams of Christianity and social thought among Black Americans.

12. See Amazing Grace: Obama's African American Theology in Dyson's *The Black Presidency*, 254–71.

13. Todd Boyd, *The New H.N.I.C.: The Death of Civil Rights and the Reign of Hip Hop* (New York and London, 2003), pp. 78.

14. Ibid.

15. The extent to which Barack Obama was protected from criticism and treated like a sacred figure immune to any scrutiny is reflected in the wok of Cornel West. Cornel West was among a handful of prominent Black American public figures who scrutinized the Obama administration and endured public backlash as a consequence of it. For West, the prophetic tradition necessitated a critical response to the Obama presidency. This is laid out in Cornel West and Christina Buschendorf, Ed. *Black Prophetic Fire* (Boston: Beacon Press, 2014).

16. For an account of how the 2008 presidential candidacy of Barack Obama was married to and fueled by redemptive/messianic impulses see Ronald B. Neal's, Savior of the Race: The Messianic Burdens of Black Masculinity; Jesus Traditions and Masculinities in World Christianity, *Exchange: Journal of Missiological and Ecumenical Research*, Vol. 42, No. 1 (2013). Also see Barack Obama's, *The Audacity of Hope: Thoughts on Reclaiming the American Dream* (New York: Crown Publishers, 2006).

17. The election of Donald J. Trump as the forty-fifth president of the United States in 2016 was a gross repudiation of Barack Obama's two-terms in the Oval Office. Such backlash was outlined one year after the 2016 election by The Atlantic Monthly. See The Trump Presidency: A Damage Report, *The Atlantic Monthly*, October 2017, Vol. 320, No. 3.

18. For a classic account of the messianic tradition in the twentieth century see Wilson Jeremiah Moses, *Black Messiahs and Uncle Toms: Social and Literary*

Manipulations of a Religious Myth, Revised Edition (Pennsylvania: The Pennsylvania State University Press, 1993).

19. Apart from Garvey' movement during the 1920s, the only organization which had longevity as an anti-racist organization was the NAACP. Using legal strategies and the US Constitution as the basis of its work, its approach was cautious and gradualistic, especially from the 1920s to the mid- 1950s. One significant account of the NAACP during this period is Carl T. Rowan's, *Dream Makers, Dream Breakers: The World of Justice Thurgood Marshall* (Canada: Little, Brown & Company, 1993).

20. The perils of Black activism prior to the 1950s is also documented by the biographer of W. E. B. DuBois, David Levering Lewis. See David Levering Lewis, *W.E.B. Dubois: The Fight for Equality and the American Century, 1919–1963* (New York: Henry Holt & Company, 2000).

21. The indifference of most White Americans to the condition of Black Americans during the first half of the twentieth century is expressed in Lillian Smith's classic work, *Killers of the Dream*. See *Killers of the Dream* (New York and London: W. W. Norton & Company, 1949).

22. The relationship between the Cold War, political liberalism, and Civil Rights during the second half of the twentieth century is articulated in Jason K. Duncan's, *John F. Kennedy: The Spirit of Cold War Liberalism* (New York and London: Routledge, 2014).

23. The myth of the martyr and messianic hero and all of the contextual problems it presents is personified in the life and legacy of Martin Luther King Jr. Among the rich body of published writings which have enshrined Martin Luther King Jr. as a heroic ideal worthy of perpetual emulation is the work of historian Vincent Harding. A scholar and activist who knew King personally, Harding's book *Martin Luther King: The Inconvenient Hero* (Maryknoll: Orbis Books, 1996) exemplifies the messianic impulse which has permeated Black American political culture.

24. James Washington, Ed. *Martin Luther King, Jr.: I Have a Dream: Writings and Speeches That Changed the World* (New York: Harper Collins Publishers, 1986), pp. 97–98.

25. One recent and sober assessment of the political state of Christianity in Black America is Walter Earl Fluker's, *The Ground Has Shifted: The Future of the Black Church in Post Racial America* (New York: New York University Press, 2016).

26. Neal, *Democracy in 21st Century America*.

27. Michael Eric Dyson, The Ghost of Cornel West, *The New Republic*, April 19, 2015.

28. The Black Lives Matter movement which began in 2013 was largely secular in its orientation and approach to activism. In fact, much of its leadership rejected established traditions and institutions dedicated to Afro American advancement which were connected to and informed by Christian traditions. In the emerging literature on Black Lives Matter, the absence of Christianity, as a source and influence, is what stands out. See Taylor, *From #BLACKLIVESMATTER to Black Liberation*. Also see Jelani Cobb, Where Is Black Lives Matter Headed? *The New Yorker*, March 14, 2016, pp. 34–40.

29. See Eugene Robinson, *Disintegration: The Splintering of Black America* (New York: Anchor Books, 2010).

30. Moses, *Black Messiahs and Uncle Toms*.

31. See Albert J. Raboteau, *Slave Religion: The Invisible Institution in the Antebellum South* (Oxford: Oxford University Press, 2004). Also see Peter J. Paris, *Virtues and Values: The African and African American Experience* (Minneapolis: Fortess Press, 2004).

32. See William David Hart, *Black Religion: Malcolm X, Julius Lester, and Jan Willis* (New York: Palgrave Macmillan, 2008) and Monica A. Coleman, Ed. *Ain't I A Womanist Too? Third Wave Womanist Religious Thought* (Minneapolis: Fortress Press, 2013).

33. See Kim Knott, *Hinduism: A Very Short Introduction* (Oxford: Oxford University Press, 2016). For a recent account of India and its emergence as a global economic force see Arundhati Roy, *Capitalism: A Ghost Story* (Chicago: Haymarket Books, 2014).

Chapter 4

The Demonic Imagination
Black Masculinity and the Abominations of Religion and Theology in the United States

Over the last half-century, a liberationist impulse has animated the fields of theology and religious studies. As of this writing, fields of thought, intellectual programs, and ethical projects bolstered by theology and religious studies have been devoted to groups identified as victims of systems of oppression in the United States. Women and LGBTQ+ people are the sole groups that are regarded in this way. An entire genre now exists, which began during the late 1980s and early 1990s, which focuses exclusively on these victims of oppression, and is now the most dominant in religion and theology. Beginning with groundbreaking texts in the early 1990s such as Delores Williams' *Sisters in the Wilderness: The Challenge of Womanist God-Talk*, to the late 1990s work of Kelly Brown Douglas', *Sexuality and the Black Church*, to texts published since the mid-2000s such as Traci West's *Disruptive Christian Ethics: Racism and Women's Lives*, and Keri Day's, *Religious Resistance to Neoliberalism: Womanist and Black Feminist Perspectives*, the victimization of women and LGBTQ+ groups has reigned supreme.[1] As this chapter is being written, the amplification of LGBT+ concerns found in works such as Roger A. Sneed's *Representations of Homosexuality: Black Liberation Theology and Cultural Criticism*, EL Kornegay's, *A Queering of Black Liberation Theology: James Baldwin's Blues Project and Gospel Prose*, and Pamela Lightsey's, *Our Lives Matter: A Queer Womanist Theology*, have heightened the priority that is now given to these victimized populations.[2] Unlike women and LGBT+ people, Black American men as a group have not been targeted by theology and religious studies as victims of systematic oppression. Black men are not imagined as a population where interventions are deemed necessary and given intellectual justification. In the five decades, where other special victims were prioritized, the fields of theology and religious studies have produced few works which take on the tumultuous condition of Black men in the United States. The kind of intellectual work and focus which takes on dramatic and reoccurring instances of Black male death such as the 2020 police-initiated execution of George Floyd, a deep symbol of elimination of Black men as a group, is nonexistent. While there is no dearth of works about Black women, Black LGBTQ groups, and even Black popular culture, only a handful of works broach the subject of Black men. Most of these works are reactionary and moralistic in nature. Such works include Garth Karimu Fletcher's edited volume, *Black Religion After the Million Man March* and his book, *Xodus: An African American Male Journey*, treat Black men as problems to be fixed, men in need of massive correction and rehabilitation.[3] These works largely treat Black men as victimizers of others, instigators and perpetuators of oppression. In a word, Black men as a group are treated as the villains of history. There are hardly any treatments of Black men that regard them as casualties of anti-Black racism in the United States. Interestingly, during *The Decade of Death (2012–2022)*, one exception to this general rule emerged. This is the work of womanist theologian and religion scholar, Kelly Brown Douglas. In 2012, with the murder of seventeen-year-old Trayvon Martin in Sanford, FL, at the hands of a private citizen, Douglas produced *Stand Your Ground: Black Bodies and the Justice of God*.[4] *Stand Your Ground* was a reaction to the event of Trayvon Martin's death, a moment which launched the movement Black Lives Matter. *Stand Your Ground* was also motivated by the fact that Douglas, who at the time, was the mother of a Black male youth from the same generation as Trayvon Martin. However, Douglas' interventive effort is anomalous in relation to the main currents of theology and religious studies in the twenty-first century. It is an exceptional text in the realm of contemporary theology and religious studies in general. It is also exceptional in relation to the Black woman-centered genre that she writes in, womanism. Apart from this anomalous effort, contemporary theology and religious studies have no way to account for a *demonic imaginary* and its relationship to the elimination of Black men.[5] There is no pervasive sensibility and more significantly, no genre, which addresses, in an uncensored fashion, the murders of Black men at the hands of law enforcement and that of private citizens. More importantly, there is no body of material in religion and theology which deals specifically with the overall condition of death and jail which haunts the lives of Black men and boys in the United States. This omission is significant, given that death and jail, including police murder, have represented a historical problem in the United States. With the advent of *The Decade of Death (2012–2022)*, new light was shed on this problem, as it impacts an emerging generation of Black boys and Black male youth, born near the end and at the beginning of the twenty-first century. The efforts of Kelly Brown Douglas in *Stand Your Ground*, exposed the dilemmas taken up in this chapter. This conundrum is tied to the present and to the consequences of history. A demand now exists for a full-blown engagement, in terms of theology and religious studies, with the beliefs and ideas that contribute to such spectacled Black male death. However, this work has yet to be undertaken. What I regard as gross indifference and the inability of contemporary theology and religious studies to account for the elimination of Black men is not an accident or an innocent omission. It is tied to an unspoken rule that authorizes resistance toward any engagement with the circumstances and conditions tied to the elimination of Black men in America. If contemporary theology and religious studies appear to be negligent and useless as a constructive tool and force in addressing the elimination of Black men, its lack of utility is by design. In the domains of religion and theology, there is great resistance to a constructive engagement with Black men by contemporary theology and religious studies. Such resistance is integral to and entangled with a *demonic imaginary* and what I regard as the abominations of religion and theology.

THE DEMONIC IMAGINATION: BLACK MEN, BLACK BOYS, AND BLACK MALE YOUTH AS THREATS TO OTHERS

A very graphic testament to the *demonic imaginary* and the abominations of religion and theology is found in the recent work of religious scholar and ethicist, Walter Fluker. Writing about Black men and Black male youth, at the level of religious analysis and philosophy, Fluker lays out the barriers and impediments to a robust engagement with the predicaments of young Black men in the United States. As an ethicist and religious scholar, who has produced works of scholarship in the fields of African American religious studies and Black Church studies, his treatment of Black men and Black male youth, in *The Ground Has Shifted: The Future of the Black Church in Post Racial America,* is a window into how Black masculinity, Black boys, and Black male youth have been imagined over the last half-century.[6] Writing as a scholar and activist who has been a part of interventive efforts to ameliorate the plight of Black boys and Black male youth, Fluker's treatment of Black boys and Black male youth is prefaced with disclaimers and qualifications. These disclaimers and qualifications serve as an apologia to readers of this work, those who may and will take offense to interventions, ethical and otherwise, which seek to positively address the condition of Black boys and Black male youth. In engaging these matters, he offers a prefatory apologia, a plea for forgiveness, for any unintended harm that he may have caused by devoting critical attention, an entire chapter in a book, to the plight and predicament of Black boys and Black male youth in the United States. In Chapter 9 of *The Ground Has Shifted*, Cultural Asylums and the Jungles They Planted In Them, his apologia states the following:

> We begin the discussion of the plight of Black youth, particularly young Black men, as a *common(s)* where Black churches and their many and varied interlocutors must congregate, conjure, and conspire. At the outset I want to be clear that this focus on young Black males is not meant to ignore, erase, or make nonspecific the incredible toll of systematic violence against black female, lesbian, transgender, and queer bodies. The focus on Black males in this chapter grows out of long-standing work in this area and is offered as one of the many challenges that churches and their leadership should address together.[7]

Walter Fluker's apologia is revealing. His prefatory disclaimers and qualifications regarding his focus on Black male youth revel in unquestioned popular assumptions about the nature of Black masculinity, which have permeated theology, religious studies, and academic thought for the last four decades. These assumptions are currently present in social justice activism, including the movement Black Lives Matter, which was led primarily by elites, and is imbued with ideas about gender, sexuality, and masculinity manufactured in colleges, universities, seminaries, and divinity schools. The underlying assumption is that some violence or erasure is done to Black women and LGBTQ populations by granting specific attention to Black men and Black male youth. The presumption is that there is something about the predicament of Black men and Black male youth that competes with, overwhelms, and obliterates the moral, ethical, and political claims and demands of these victimized groups. What is more, Fluker's sensitivity to these groups and his concern about not offending them, assumes that Black women and LGBTQ+ people do not have lobbies, organizations, spokespersons, and powerful allies among the White ruling class. It smacks in the face of contemporary realities and betrays the enormous impact that feminism, womanism, and LGBTQ+ politics have had on all institutions across America and the West writ large. Fluker's disclaimers and qualifications highlight deep fears related to Black masculinity which permeate the United States. His prefatory apologia is in many respects comical in light of the current state of religious studies and theology in the United States and across the Western world, where the interests of Black women, LGBTQ, and transgender people are represented, affirmed, and promoted, in ways which have no analog with respect to Black men and boys. The audiences to which Fluker addresses these matters represent a terrain in theological education and religious studies which do not privilege the interests and concerns, the overall predicament, of Black men and boys in the United States. In fact, seminaries, divinity schools, and departments of religion in colleges and universities in the United States have been actively hostile to interventions in religious studies and theology which in any way seek to alleviate the horrid condition faced by Black men and boys in the United States. If anything, Fluker's opening apologia is expressive of the *demonic imaginary* and is indicative of the hostility which exists on the part of special victims, Black women, LGBTQ, and transgender people and their interests, in relation to Black men and boys in America. The condition of Black men and boys is treated largely as an adversary and competitor which needs to be neutralized or eliminated completely from competition with these victim groups. In short, the population of Black boys and Black male youth present a threat and are dangerous to the interests of this group of special victims.

Despite Fluker's disclaimers and qualifications, he writes as a scholar who is concerned with addressing the unique predicament of Black men and Black male youth. He is concerned about possible interventions into a condition which some have deemed intractable and irredeemable. Although his efforts are intended to be responsive in a positive sense, his account of Black men and Black male youth does not go far enough in countering the barriers, impediments, stigmas, and myths which have permeated religion and theology, historically, with respect to Black men's relationship with America. Fluker's treatment of Black masculinity. takes on imaginative problems generated outside of religion and theology which cast Black masculinity in demonic terms. However, it does not grapple with the extent to which religion and theology proper have contributed to the demonic predicament of young Black men in America. More specifically, in light of his apologia, his treatment of Black masculinity. does not consider why contemporary religious studies and theology have a hostile posture toward Black men and Black male youth. Despite this limitation, Fluker's account is an unintended outline of the *demonic imaginary* with respect to Black men and Black male youth. He accurately paints a picture of Black men and Black male youth that is not distant from eighteenth-, nineteenth-, and twentieth-century accounts of Black men and Black male youth which render them savage and subhuman. Aided by the theories of the French postmodernist, Michel Foucault, he illuminates this picture of Black masculinity.

BLACK MEN, BLACK BOYS, AND BLACK MALE YOUTH AS SELF-CREATIONS

Notwithstanding Fluker's efforts at intervention, the fundamental limitation of his account is that it does not go far enough in grappling with the *demonic imaginary* and the abominations of religion and theology. As was suggested earlier, the *demonic imaginary* is implicated in a half-century of work in religion and theology. However, the severe limitations of religion and theology are not only found among academic elites and justice advocates such as the movement Black Lives Matter. It is also limited within the Black population itself. Very pointedly, Black Americans as a group have not been sufficiently motivated and invested in forwarding interventive efforts intended to address the challenges that Black men and Black male youth face. The only religious, theological, and cultural effort among Black Americans to address the predicament of Black men and Black male youth men is the Nation of Islam (NOI). For close to a century, the positive development of Black men and Black male youth has been a core part of the mission of the NOI.[8] However, the Nation of Islam has never represented the primary religious, theological, and cultural orientation of Black Americans as a group. The Nation of Islam is a minority within a minority. If Black Americans have not been motivated to address this condition it is in a significant measure due to the *demonic imaginary* or the *demon within* and its existence among Black Americans as a group. What this means is that the imprint of anti-Blackness is not solely external to Black Americans as a group, it has a robust life *inside* of Black America. Consequently, as a population, Black men and Black male youth are largely left to fend for themselves. As such, many are caught up in matrix of external and internal forces which contributes to their condition. To his credit, Walter Fluker addresses these forces which shape and condition the lives of Black men and Black male youth. However, the internalization of anti-Blackness, facilitated by economic and cultural forces, which is aimed at Black men and boys, throughout the duration of their lives, is absent from his analysis. For the purposes of this chapter, anti-Blackness as it related to Black men and Black male youth, is essentially anti-Black misandry (or the hatred of Black men). This anti-Black misandry is tied to and evident within an entire web of relations and relationships that bear on the lives of young Black men and Black male youth. The most powerful and important relational system where such misandry is evident is the family. Unfortunately, in Fluker's work, there is no engagement with family structures, compounded by structural realities, which make populations of Black men and Black male youth vulnerable to social death, prisons, and the asylums which Fluker says condemns them. In light of the *demonic imaginary*, it is very easy to assume and get the impression that Black men and Black male youth whose fates are tantamount to a caste-like condition exists in a vacuum, that huge social barriers are not erected to impede them from being incorporated into White capitalist America. These Black men and Black male youth are often imagined and treated like existential cowboys whose lives are completely of their own self-making. In a word, one does not have to account for a long tumultuous history, four centuries, where the full development of Black men and Black male youth as a group has never been taken seriously. More specifically, one can ignore the intense hostility faced by Black men and Black male youth in American society. For instance, for the last four decades, much has been made of absent and wayward fathers or deadbeat dads, who have been said to play no role apart from procreation in the positive development of Black men and Black male youth. However, there is no account of the condition of women, the mothers who birthed them in particular, who have been and are bereft of blueprints for socializing and bringing into young adulthood, Black boys, Black male youth, and young men who could effectively navigate White capitalist America. Along these lines, what does one say about those young Black men who are socialized into a bifurcated cultural and familial system where mothers and fathers are alienated from each other, by social policies and culture, where mothers and fathers exist in tension with each other, where the role of fathers is restricted, and mothers carry the weight and responsibility of raising children? How does the latter condition, the restrictions placed on fathers, impact, developmentally, Black boys and Black male youth? Should we treat these Black boys and Black male youth as automatons, utter self-creations whose entire existence is produced in a vacuum? For what I suspect are political reasons, Fluker broaches these questions yet does not address fully them in a manner which shines an important light on family formation with respect to Black men and Black male youth. For decades, such questions have been regarded as taboo and inappropriate in addressing the predicaments of Black men and boys. Since 1965, with the publication of *The Report on the Negro Family in the United States: The Case for National Action*, authored by late sociologist and late US Senator, Daniel Patrick Moynihan, intellectuals, professional academics, politicians, and activists, have actively censored and suppressed such lines of inquiry.[9] Although Fluker recognizes that external as well as internal forces are important factors in assessing this condition, he avoids saying anything explicit about cultural practices such as parenting, mothering in particular, which plays a role reproducing the vulnerabilities and precarious social status of young Black men and boys. For the purposes of clarity, parenting, alone, is not the sole determining factor in their fates. However, the manner in which Black masculinity is socialized through parenting is a variable that cannot be ignored. Attending to the *demonic imaginary* in relation to the internal force of family formation, is, in the twenty-first century difficult to avoid.

To put Fluker's work in greater context, what I am calling the abominations of religion and theology as it is reflected in Walker Fluker's account of Black men and Black male youth were particularly acute as the twentieth century came to a close and the opening decades of the twenty-first century. Such abominations were reflected in the manner in which religion and theology responded to the predicament of Black men and Black male youth during these years. As the late twentieth century came to a close, religious studies and theology were largely reactionary to a then-new generation of Black men and Black male youth whose emergence was impacted by major economic and political shifts in the United States as well as new configurations of Black American life since the 1980s. This era marked the rise of Generation X and that group of young Black men for whom hip-hop music and culture was the soundtrack of their lives. The generations who birthed and socialized this generation, the Baby Boomers and the Silent Generation, as well as the country at large, did not anticipate the postindustrial society and social fragmentation which the late twentieth century and early twenty-first century ushered in. The singular and most impactful occurrence which they did not foresee was the birth of the prison industrial complex (PIC) and hyper-incarceration and the mass surveillance of Black men and boys. As this chapter ends, I will say more about these factors. First, however, more must be said about the *demonic imaginary*, Black men, Black male youth, and the entanglements and constraints of race, power, and wealth in the United States.

AMERICA'S MOST WANTED AND THE SELECT FEW AMONG THE OPPRESSED

In light of the above, the question begs, why does the *demonic imaginary* persist? The *demonic imaginary* which produces the abominations of religion and theology is tied to the fundamental priorities of those who engage in scholarship and ethical interventions. As was indicated at the outset of this chapter, in terms of prioritizing specific groups, religion and theology have placed a high premium on those populations, special victims in particular, which are closest to the power-holding White ruling class. I call these populations, who are in close proximity to the power elite, *America's Most Wanted Victims*. For the purposes of this chapter, *America's Most Wanted Victims* are those Black Americans and those discriminated-against groups who are incorporated into the mainstream of White capitalist society. These groups have benefitted from political and economic liberalism. Civil Rights laws and corporate policies have engineered their status in mainstream White capitalist America. Black men and boys, as a demographic of millions, have not benefitted, as a group, from such incorporation. That parts of the Black American population and select groups with special victim status are targeted for incorporation and other populations (Black men and boys) are not, has not been lost on a minority of voices in religion and theology. One voice among this minority is the religious scholar and philosopher, Cornel West, a keen observer, critic, and public intellectual who has been very vocal about America's unwillingness to incorporate *all* victimized groups into the White capitalist mainstream of the United States. The selective incorporation of particular victim groups has been witnessed by him.

WEALTH, POWER, AND ANTI-BLACKNESS IN THE UNITED STATES

For over four decades, Cornel West has written effectively about religion and theology and the privileged interests of the White ruling class and its impact not only in the United States but across the world. This ruling class is implausible apart from the legacies of the Abrahamic religious tradition, especially as it is linked to empire and the creed of exceptionalism in the United States. As early as 1982, when West penned his groundbreaking book *Prophesy Deliverance: Afro-American Revolutionary Christianity* to his 2005 work, *Democracy Matters: Winning the War Against Imperialism*, West has outlined and critiqued the kind of religion and theology, a version of Christianity in particular, that supports and justifies White ruling-class interests.[10] In *Democracy Matters*, West classifies this ethos as Constantinian Christianity, the history and function of Christianity as an imperial religion. West associates this tradition of imperial Christianity with those who have disdain for powerless and disadvantaged groups. West's account of imperial Christianity is mainly concerned with politically active Christians, aligned with the state, who do their work through churches and grassroots organizations. Christianity that is largely in line with political conservatism is what he has in mind. In his account, Christianity that is wedded to political liberalism does not count as a Constantinian expression of Christianity. However, for the purposes of this chapter, the history and pervasive nature and popularity of imperial Christianity cannot be restricted to a single political orientation. From this perspective, the appeal of imperial Christianity cuts across race, class, gender, sex, nationality, and political ideology. Historically speaking, imperial Christianity has dominated the United States since the arrival of the first White settlers from England in the seventeenth century. For those who are not White and are not members of the White ruling class, imperial Christianity is a passport to the goods of the White ruling class. This imperial mode of Christianity is distinctively American in its expression and has promoted, across history, all of the myths that are associated with the United States, especially the myth of American exceptionalism or American greatness.

Cornel West's criticisms of imperial Christianity are an extension of a career-long critique of race, wealth, and power in the United States. Writing out of the philosophy of religion, such criticism coincided with movements in theology and religious studies driven by liberationist imperatives. Where theology is concerned, West forwards a religious vision of Christianity with a prophetic impulse which allied itself with Black theologies of liberation and theologies of liberation, worldwide, which sought massive changes to society.[11] In the United States, theologies of liberation fashioned themselves as distinct from dominant White theological traditions. Notwithstanding the fellowship which West had with these liberation theologies, West did not think theologies of liberation, including Black theologies of liberation and its derivatives went far enough. For West, liberation theologies were not sufficiently concerned with the entanglements of race, wealth, and power in the United States. In West's estimation, theologies of liberation did not go far enough in accounting for Black Americans who had not been incorporated into White capitalist America. To the degree that theology evaded the trinity of race, wealth, and power, and unincorporated Black America, such theologies were liberal and reformist in orientation, seeking to be included into the mainstream of White capitalist America and not transform it. In terms of social justice, such theologies, similar to imperial Christianity, were concerned primarily with *America's Most Wanted Victims*, the incorporation of select members of marginalized groups into America's power elite. Overall, in the early 1980s when West published his first book, he identified a problem that still plagues theology to this very day.[12] This problem also plagues religious studies. The failure of theologies of liberation to adequately grapple with the entanglements and restraints of race, wealth, and power limited their ability to adequately confront the predicament of Black Americans. This includes Black men, Black boys, and Black male youth. This omission speaks volumes to the concerns of this chapter which addresses the specific conundrums related to the lives of Black men, Black boys, and Black youth in the United States.

BLACK MASCULINITY AND AMERICA'S MOST WANTED VICTIMS

Cornel West's career-long concerns with race, wealth, and power are instructive for engaging the condition of Black men and Black male youth in America. In his large corpus of religious and philosophical writings, the problems of Black men and Black male youth are not a central part of his analysis and conclusions regarding race, wealth, and power in America. Yet the condition of Black men and Black male youth, if it is to be adequately engaged, must attend to race, wealth, and power in the United States. In doing so, it takes seriously the fact that Black men and Black male youth are not among *America's Most Wanted Victims*, those persons and groups who have been selectively incorporated into the machinery of the American empire and its creed of exceptionalism. The sociological and economic status of Black men and Black male youth mirror this fact. In this chapter, what I have referred to as the *demonic imaginary* is the misrepresentation and miscalculation of the sociological and economic status of Black men and Black male youth. This *demonic imaginary* is mired in the imperial ethos and the American creed of exceptionalism that produces and reproduces the selective incorporation of *America's Most Wanted Victims*.

More must be said about the *demonic imaginary* and the extent to which it produces the abominations of religion and theology. Such abominations involve the commitment of religion and theology to the lives and interests of *America's Most Wanted Victims*. The claims of theologies of liberation including Black liberation theology are false. Contrary to the liberation claims of liberation theologies, which place a high premium on those categorized as oppressed, such theologies are not principally concerned with *all* oppressed people or *all* groups of people who have been impacted by the legacies of anti-Black racism. To the contrary, the consequence of such theologies has been the incorporation of *a select few among the oppressed*, those who exist in close proximity to race, wealth, and power, *America's Most Wanted Victims*. Liberation theologies have functioned as a lobby for this select group of marginalized people. As I indicated at the outset of this chapter, Black men and boys, as a group, have never had and presently do not have a lobby, a set of established organizations, and support among the White ruling class in the United States. Since its earliest formulations, Black liberation theologies and their derivatives erred by conflating the status of millions and millions of Black men and boys with the relative enfranchisement of a handful of elite Black men across history. What is more, additional fallacies were committed as the status of all Black men and boys has been conflated with a small population of Black men and youth, mired in crime, a sliver of which are career criminals who engage in violent crimes, some being sociopathic in their behavior. In short, liberationists in religion and theology have reveled in and promoted an oppositional stance toward *all* Black men. Much of this opposition can be found in the literature produced, over the course of five decades, by liberationists, on Black men in politics and social and religious organizations. This includes civil rights organizations, activist groups, and Black churches. Their *demonic* interpretation of Black masculinity. indicted all Black men and boys. In the writings of Black liberationists and their derivatives, in relation to the historic leadership of Black churches, that of the Civil Rights and Black Power eras, and male leadership during the post-Civil Rights era, have misrepresented the overall status and existence of Black men and boys in America.[13] Although Black men and boys, tens of millions of people, have never been among *America's Most Wanted Victims*, they are not imagined as outsiders to America's status quo. Standing outside of *America's Most Wanted Victims*, Black men and boys, as a group, tens of millions of people, have been and are estranged from the trinity of race, wealth, and power in the United States. As a consequence of this *demonic imaginary*, Black men and boys have been left estranged, left to fend for themselves. Since the 1980s, one important and highly visible arena where this estrangement has been most evident is popular culture. As religion and theology ran from a creative engagement with the predicament of Black men and boys, Black popular culture, via hip-hop, exposed the world, through aesthetics, to the cumulative effects of the unincorporated condition of Black men and boys, and especially Black male youth in America. It was only with the rise of hip-hop, during the 1980s and 1990s, that Black masculinity became a provocative voice, a window and mirror which indicted the *demonic imaginary,* including misandry, and modalities of discrimination and exclusion suffered by millions of Black men and boys, especially Black male youth in the United States.

HIP-HOP AND ITS REBUKE OF RELIGION, THEOLOGY, AND AMERICA'S MOST-WANTED VICTIMS

As this chapter is being written, hip-hop has enjoyed five decades of popularity in the United States and across the globe. It has represented the preeminent voice of young Black men and Black male youth who are estranged from the corridors of power in the United States. For five decades, it has done more to highlight the predicament of Black male youth and young Black men in the United States than religion and theology. As such, it is a major cultural indictment of religion and theology in the United States. What is more, is that this has stood as a grand rebuke to *America's Most Wanted Victims.* Over the course of four decades, Hip- Hop has effectively held a mirror to all of the ills of the United States. From American cities such as Miami, New Orleans, Atlanta, and Memphis, Tennessee, portraits of estrangement have been vividly painted by hip-hop artists. Over the course of its five-decade run, hip-hop has produced many political voices which have rebuked the entanglements of wealth, power, and anti-Blackness in the United States. Rappers from Generation X such as KRS One and Chuck D (of Public Enemy) and rappers from the Millennial Generation such as Lupe Fiasco, J Cole, and Kendrick Lamar have spoken about the consequences of wealth, power, and anti-Blackness in the United States. In recent years, one prominent hip-hop voice among the many hip-hop artists whose witness is a testament to this fact is Atlanta-based rapper Killer Mike (Michael Render). An artist and activist of sorts, Killer Mike's vocation in hip-hop has placed a spotlight on the unincorporated condition of Black men and boys in America. During the presidential elections of 2016 and 2020, Killer Mike was catapulted to high levels of visibility as a popular voice of dissent among presidential candidates and voters.[14] Killer Mike gained the attention of Vermont Senator and US presidential candidate Bernie Sanders, who recruited him to assist in Sanders' quest to become the President of the United States. Bernie Sanders, a democratic socialist, and Killer Mike shared a set of socioeconomic concerns which addressed the condition of unincorporated Black America. As mentioned above, the class of politically engaged hip-hop artists including

Killer Mike is a prophetic testament to the facts of selective incorporation, *American's Most Wanted Victims*, those who are at a huge distance from the lives and circumstances of unincorporated Black men and boys in the United States. Killer Mike is a member of Generation X who grew up with hip-hop as its soundtrack. His music is an expression of the political and prophetic side of Generation X for whom hip-hop was their introduction and initiation into the Black American struggle for freedom. For Generation X, it was the life and legacy of Malcolm X which fueled their politics and dissent. Malcolm X is the foundation of those members of Generation X whose voices have been political and prophetic.[15] As foundational to Generation X rap, the life and legacy of Malcom X is a source of religious sensibilities, rhetoric, and political commitment devoted to unincorporated Black America. The voice of Malcolm X, coupled with kindred voices such as Muhammad Ali, James Baldwin, and Eldridge Cleaver, anticipated the cutting edges of rap music which emerged at the end of the twentieth century. Such voices, with genealogical ties to rap music, expose the abominations of religion and theology in the United States. Not only are the abominations of religion and theology indicted by rap music, but also the abominations of religion and theology point to the evasion of the forceful influence of Malcolm X in theology and religion. Unlike the legacy of Martin Luther King, Jr., whose legacy has been domesticated by religion and theology, the relationship between Malcolm X and theology and religion is fraught with tension and hostility. Unlike Martin Luther King, Jr., Malcolm X is not a widely celebrated figure and source in theology and religious studies. Malcom X is an American bogeyman, a voice of unincorporated Black Americans, who stands at a huge distance from these disciplines.[16] Because major gaps exist between the legacy of Malcolm X, as it is tied to Hip-Hop and *America's Most Wanted Victims* (and that such gaps do not appear to disappear anytime soon), it is necessary to flesh out a distinct perspective, a religious philosophy whose goal it is to engage and overcome the *demonic imaginary* as it bears upon the lives of young Black men and Black male youth. A new school of thought is called for which meets this challenge. Fortunately, over the last four decades, there have been some efforts outside of the mainstream trends in religion and theology which assists in this effort. Such efforts began at the end of the 1990s and the early 2000s, by a small group of thinkers in religion and theology, which has continued in a marginal fashion since that time. A small body of scholarship on religion and hip-hop, pioneered by Anthony B. Pinn, is instructive in this regard. In considering this scholarship, it is important to note that this marginal body of work is not specifically addressed to the predicament of young Black men and Black male youth.[17] It deals with rap music mainly as a cultural and aesthetic phenomenon worthy of religious and theological interrogation. This body of scholarship is significant because it ventures beyond the normative trends of theology and religious studies over the last four decades. It possesses religious and theological sensibilities informed by hip-hop which are valuable to a full-blown engagement with Black men and boys. This work is not controlled and animated by a *demonic imaginary* and is willing to entertain the depths of anti-Blackness in the United States which distinguishes it from mainstream models of scholarship in religion and theology.[18] It is the task of what lies ahead to employ these sensibilities as they relate to the *demonic imaginary* and the specific plight of young Black men and Black male youth. In other words, the epistemological orientation of what is now understood as hip-hop and the critical study of religion is a robust framework for this work.

BLACK MALE STUDIES: OVERCOMING THE DEMONIC IMAGINARY AND THE ABOMINATIONS OF RELIGION AND THEOLOGY

Hip-Hop and its engagement with religion and theology is just one necessary framework for moving beyond the *demonic imaginary* and the abominations of religion and theology. Other resources beyond contemporary religion and theology are needed. One such resource is the emerging academic genre of Black Male Studies. Black Male Studies is a new genre born during *The Decade of Death (2012–2022)*. Black Male Studies is a new intellectual development which addresses all of the concerns of this chapter and the overall aims of this book. Pioneered and led by the Black American philosopher, Tommy J. Curry, whose 2017 book, *The Man-Not: Race, Class, Genre, and Black Manhood* inaugurated this new field of inquiry and research.[19] The work of Tommy J. Curry is accompanied by Africana Studies scholars Serie McDougal III and T. Hasan Johnson. McDougal's 2022 work, *Black Men's Studies: Black and Masculinities in Manhood the U.S. Context,* and Johnson's 2023 text, *Solutions for Anti-Black Misandry, Flat Blackness, and Black Male Death: The Black Masculinist Turn*, advance this field.[20] Black Male Studies is a departure from normative trends in race, class, and gender studies over the last half-century. It is a multidisciplinary enterprise that is sensitive to and proactive about the diminishment of the plight and predicament of Black men, Black boys, and young Black men. It is attentive to the *demonic imaginary* and its presence across intellectual disciplines and society writ large. Black Male Studies is an invitation to rethink intellectual disciplines and reframe research and theoretical work on Black men and boys. That Black Male Studies was conceived and emerged during *The Decade of Death (2012–2022)* is important as it represents a necessary intellectual turn as countless cases of homicide with respect to Black men, Black boys, and Black male youth took place during this period. It should also be noted that its multidisciplinary sensibilities are accompanied by an empirical methodology. Through the employment of historiography, sociology, philosophy, and economics, Black Male Studies is a radical departure from more than a half-century of academic accounts of Black men and boys in the United States. It is a decisive move away from all of the problems which concern this chapter and book. Black Male Studies casts a specter of doubt on the history of scholarship in the United States which is tainted by anti-Black *demonic imaginary* as it pertains to the existence of Black men and boys. As this chapter and book are being written, Black Male Studies scholars are engaged in an excavation project which unearths those works of scholarship and historical materials which have been used to justify and legitimate the policing and containment of Black men and boys. The work of Black Male Studies is in many respects comparable to the work of prison abolitionists and those who seek to reform the U.S. criminal justice system.[21] In this regard, it is similar to the work of lawyers, legal scholars, and journalists who have brought public attention to judicial and prosecutorial error in relation to the PIC and criminal courts in the United States. This latter work has focused on deliberate judicial misconduct, on the part of judges and prosecutors, which have produced wrongful convictions and wrongful executions of Black men by the American criminal justice system. Prison abolitionism and criminal justice reform have been aided by DNA science and a reassessment of criminal indictments and sentencing for crimes applied to Black men. The contemporary prison abolition movement and the movement to reform the US criminal justice system question the very existence of the PIC, its logic and justifications. The orientation that drives prison abolition and criminal justice reform animates Black Male Studies. However, Black Male Studies go beyond prison abolition and criminal justice reform in its engagement with Black men and boys. It seeks to abolish *all* barriers and impediments to the study and engagement of Black men and boys.

In this chapter, the work of Walter Fluker as a scholar of religion and theology has served as a major representation of the *demonic imaginary* and the abominations of religion and theology when it comes to Black boys and Black male youth. His treatment of Black boys and Black male youth is one component of a larger set of concerns which animate his book, *The Ground Has Shifted*. This book is largely concerned with the future of Black churches or the Black Church in the United States, especially as the formations of Black America have been significantly altered over the last three decades. Black churches, which at one time constituted a central force in the lives of Black Americans, having the status of the Vatican and to a lesser degree a political party, no longer have that status and authority among Black Americans. Black churches are victims and casualties of changing times and the unprecedented fragmentation of the Black American population. Desegregation, secularization, globalization, technology, and ideological relativism among Black

Americans have marginalized its historic role in the lives of Black Americans. What is true about Black churches is also true about religion and theology in the United States. Religion and theology have declined in their influence in the United States. Similar to Black churches, religion and theology struggle to stay afloat in the midst of an ever-changing context. In light of the current status of Black churches and that of religion and theology, it is clear that their respective futures are implausible without revision and reconstruction. Such restructuring appears implausible without a new imagination for current times. For the purposes of this book and chapter, such imagination cannot appear without a full-blown repudiation of the *demonic imaginary*. To the extent that black churches, religion, and theology align themselves with projects of justice and *America's Most Wanted Victims*, they will be held suspect, as such alignments are restricted to a select few. The *demonic imaginary* limits their purported quests for justice. To the extent that this state of affairs remains the case, they cannot be viewed as robust and all-encompassing sites for justice in the United States. Notwithstanding the quagmire of Black churches, religion, and theology, the role that they have played in perpetuating the *demonic imaginary* should not be ignored. It has been impactful and remains undeniable. The imprint of the *demonic imaginary* has had far-reaching consequences for Black men and boys in the United States. It is exactly this imprint that this chapter and this book maintain is worthy of rebuke.

In the 2020s and beyond, the *demonic imaginary* is a vestige of the past that continues to haunt the United States. Its origins precede the twentieth and twenty-first centuries. However, its most recent manifestations over the last four decades are a barrier and impediment to theological and religious engagements with anti-Blackness in the present and the future. As such, it should be treated as an abominable stain on the history of theology and religious studies. It is a relic of an anti-Black American past which should be resigned to the museum of history.

NOTES

1. Delores S. Williams, *Sisters in the Wilderness: The Challenge of Womanist God-Talk* (Maryknoll: Orbis Books, 1996); Kelly Brown Douglas, *Sexuality and the Black Church: A Womanist Perspective* (Maryknoll: Orbis Press, 1999); Traci West, *Disruptive Christian Ethics: Racism and Women's Lives* (Philadelphia: Westminster John Knox Press, 2006); Keri Day, *Religious Resistance to Neoliberalism: Womanist and Black Feminist Perspectives* (New York: Palgrave Macmillan Press, 2016).

2. Roger A. Sneed, *Representations of Homosexuality: Black Liberation Theology and Cultural Criticism* (New York: Palgrave Macmillan, 2010); E.L. Kornegay,

A Queering of Black Theology: James Baldwin's Blues Project and Gospel Prose (New York: Palgrave Macmillan, 2013); Pamela Lightsey, *Our Lives Matter: A Womanist Queer Theology* (Eugene: Pickwick Publications, 2015).

3. Garth Kasimu Baker-Fletcher, Ed. *Black Religion After the Million Man March* (Maryknoll: Orbis Books, 1998); *Xodus: An African American Male Journey* (Minneapolis: Fortress Press, 1996).

4. Kelly Brown Douglas, *Stand Your Ground: Black Bodies and the Justice of God* (Maryknoll: Orbis Books, 2015).

5. What I am calling and referring to throughout this chapter as the demonic imaginary is outlined in a chapter I authored, "Troubling the Demonic: Anti-Blackness, Heterosexual Black Masculinity, and the Study of Religion in North America," *Routledge Handbook of Religion, Gender, and Society* (London: Routledge Press, 2021), Chapter 29.

6. Walter Earl Fluker, *The Ground Has Shifted: The Future of the Black Church in Post-Racial America* (New York: New York University Press, 2016).

7. See Fluker, Cultural Asylums and the Jungles They Planted In Them, *The Ground Has Shifted*, pp. 199.

8. See Sherman Jackson, *Islam and the Black American: Looking Toward the Third Resurrection* (New York: Oxford University Press, 2005).

9. See James T. Patterson, *Freedom Is Not Enough: The Moynihan Report and America's Struggle for Black Family Life in the United States from LBJ to Obama* (New York: Basic Books, 2010).

10. Cornel West, *Prophecy Deliverance: An Afro-American Revolutionary Christianity* (Philadelphia: Westminster Press, 1982); *Democracy Matters: Winning the War Against Imperialism* (New York: Penguin Books, 2005).

11. See Cornel West, Black Theology of Liberation as Critique of Capitalist Civilization, in *Black Theology: A Documentary History, Volume Two: 1980–1992* (Maryknoll: Orbis Books, 1993).

12. See Cornel West, Chapter 4, Prophetic Thought and Progressive Marxism, in *Prophesy Deliverance: An Afro-American Revolutionary Christianity* (Philadelphia: Westminster Knox Press, 1982).

13. The late James H. Cone and the late Delores S. Williams produced works under the guise of Black liberation theology which entailed a strident and persistent critique of Black male leadership in churches, denominations, and civic organizations during the after the political movements of the 1950s and 1960s. This mode of criticism has been standard within the genre of Black liberation theology and it persists to this day. The Black men under critique were elites whose status was unrepresentative of the majority of Black men found among the ranks of the lower and working classes who did not share their status as power brokers inside and outside of Black America. Representative books which include this critique are James H. Cone's, *Martin & Malcolm: A Dream or a Nightmare* (Maryknoll: Orbis Book, 1993) and Williams', *Sisters in the Wilderness*.

14. During the 2016 and 2020 elections, Killer Mike was very vocal about *The Decade of Death (2012–2022)* and its political consequences. He was recruited twice by Bernie Sanders who was a presidential candidate in those years. Killer Mike

was pivotal in Sanders' efforts to attract voters from the Millennial Generation and Generation Z. Killer Mike has been outspoken about his political views on numerous social media platforms. During the tumultuous summer of 2020, he was recruited by the then-mayor of Atlanta, Keisha Lance Bottoms, to assist in quelling violence as confrontations between protesters and law enforcement got out of control. The New Republic Magazine did a feature on Killer Mike and his politics in 2016. During the summer of 2020, as the United States was engulfed in protest, Killer Mike and his politics appeared in a story in Rolling Stone Magazine. See Bijan Stephen, Rebel Without a Pause: Killer Mike and the Return of the Politically Engaged Rapper, *New Republic*, January/February 2016, pp. 52–55. See Jamil Smith, Killer Mike's Battle Rhymes, *Rolling Stone Magazine*, Issue 1341, July 2020, pp. 36–38. It should also be noted that as an artist and rapper Killer Mike has been an outspoken defender of the First Amendment. As a prominent defender of the First Amendment, Killer Mike authored a foreword to a recent book on rap music and the United States Constitution. See Erik Nielson and Andrea L. Dennis, *Rap on Trial: Race, Lyrics, and Guilt in America* (New York: The New Press, 2019).

15. See Michael Eric Dyson, *Making Malcolm: The Myth & Meaning of Malcolm X* (New York and Oxford: Oxford University Press, 1995).

16. Largely due to a Christian bias in religion and theology in the United States, Malcolm X, who was Muslim, has been treated as an esoteric figure, a deviation from accepted norms. Scholarly treatments of Malcolm X by scholars in theology and religious studies such as the late James H. Cone, Michael Eric Dyson, Cornel West, and William H. Hart are reflective of his anomalous relationship to the dominant Christian narrative which is privileged in theology and religious studies. Among the aforementioned scholars, William H. Hart's treatment of *Malcolm X in Black Religion: Malcolm X, Julius Lester, and Jan Willis* (New York: Palgrave Macmillan, 2008), drives home the point that I am making here. In a word, unlike Martin Luther King, Jr., Malcolm X has not been domesticated and colonized for normative purposes.

17. Anthony B. Pinn, *Noise and Spirit: The Religious and Spiritual Sensibilities of Rap Music* (New York and London: New York University Press, 2003); *Why Lord?: Suffering and Evil in Black Theology* (New York: The Continuum Publishing Company, 1995).

18. Monica Miller, *Religion and Hip Hop* (New York and London: Routledge, 2013).

19. Tommy Curry, *The Man-Not: Race, Class, Genre, and the Dilemmas of Manhood* (Philadelphia: Temple University Press, 2017).

20. See Serie McDougal III, *Black Men's Studies: Black Manhood in the U.S. Context* (New York, Bern, Berlin, Brussels, Vienna, Oxford, and Warsaw: Peter Lang, 2020) and T. Hasan Johnson, *Solutions for Anti-Black Misandry, Flat Blackness, and Black Male Death: The Black Masculinist Turn* (Oxford: Routledge, 2023).

21. For a representative account of prison abolition and efforts to reform the criminal justice system which lends itself to the proposal that I am advancing here, see Joshua Dubler and Vincent W. Lloyd's, *Break Every Yoke: Religion, Justice, and the Abolition of Prisons* (New York: Oxford University Press, 2020).

Chapter 5

Who's Afraid of Black Men?
Black Women and White Saviors

In *Capitalism: A Ghost Story*, South Asian writer and feminist Arundhati Roy tells a sobering story about the nature and logic of capitalism in the twenty-first century. Concerned with the role of American corporate interests in remaking and exploiting societies across the world, she exposes the methods of the rich and the powerful in managing populations and resources for the purposes of social control. In her narration, the subcontinent of India and the capital transformation which has taken place in the context over the last five decades is the main object of her concerns.[1] India, which has emerged as a key player in the expansion of global capitalism, is now a new site for the extreme effects, unprecedented prosperity and extreme poverty, of the forces of capitalism on the world stage. In the work of capitalism in fomenting this condition is the neutralization and suppression of forces of dissent, protest, and resistance through benevolent means. Benevolent tools, such as nongovernmental organizations (NGOs), which target women, are a key feature of this work. Under the auspices of women's rights and human rights, women are absorbed into the machinery of capitalist interests in India. In Roy's account, the integration of women into this present iteration of capitalism in India has strong links to the integration of women and select aspects of Black America, since the 1970s, into the White capitalist mainstream of the United States. Similar to present-day India, the neutralization and suppression of dissent, protest, and resistance to the underside of capitalist domination was integral to this technique of capitalist control.

Capitalism: A Ghost Story speaks volumes to the concerns of this chapter. A socially engineered capitalist condition of extremes, bifurcation, exists in the United States, albeit with respect to America's Black population. Such bifurcation exists along the lines of male and female, Black women and Black men. It is an unprecedented condition in light of the 400-year experience of

Black Americans in the United States.[2] As I write this chapter, this condition is assumed to be the product of natural forces, a matter of freedom, choice, merit, and unfettered opportunity. Such assumptions reflect the weight and impact of the logic of American capitalism on the US imaginary. However, these assumptions betray and conceal a colonial reality of anti-Blackness under the auspices of women's rights, women's freedom, and women's empowerment. What I argue in this chapter is that this anti-Black deception is an evasion of the deep fissures of anti-Blackness and its social, economic, and political consequences in the United States. After *The Decade of Death (2012–2022)*, it is no longer feasible to ignore what is now a condition of extremes, fomented by White capitalist interests, which is played out through a divide between males and females in the Black American population in the United States.

The insights of Arudhuati Roy's *Capitalism: A Ghost Story* are instructive for engaging the role of capitalism or White capitalist interests in empowering American Black women over the last four decades. Such empowerment entails a lucrative market which includes corporations, academia, politics, popular media, and entertainment. Fueled by White interests, this market embodies and caters to the experiences, interests, concerns, and overall economic mobility and utility of Black women in America. Mostly college-educated middle-class Black women are the faces of this market. Over time, this market has produced its own ideology, myths, and icons which are present in magazines, movies, music, and self-help media. The most recognizable figure in this market is the hugely popular and successful singer and entertainer, Beyonce Knowles-Carter. The most popular American entertainer since the late Michael Jackson and one of the most influential personalities, next to Oprah Winfrey, Beyonce Knowles-Carter personifies an ideal of a fully developed successful Black woman. Next to Beyonce Knowles-Carter is the former First Lady of the United States, Michelle Obama. As an Ivy League educated corporate attorney, among the first-generation of Black Americans to be incorporated in the mainstream of White capitalist America after the civil rights movement, she is symbolic of a class of professional Black women whose presence and ascent in American life is unprecedented and ubiquitous.[3] Lifted up as an immaculate role model for Black women in particular and all women in general, she is a magnified representation of the successful professional Black woman. Both Beyonce Knowles-Carter and Michelle Obama have come to represent what is affectionately known in Black women's media as Black Girl Magic. Black Girl Magic is not fathomable apart from five decades of social advancements, in the United States, on the part of Black women, especially Black women who have been fully incorporated into the economic and educational mainstream of American life, or what I refer to as, First World America (First World Black American

Women). Although this phenomenon is assumed to be the product of natural forces, it is not sensible apart from the achievements of the Civil Rights Movement and the Women's Movement. Where the latter is concerned, liberalism and US feminism have been pivotal to the expansion of opportunity, for women, by way of higher education and the professions.[4] So Black Girl Magic exists as a by-product of substantive political and economic shifts which characterized the last decades of the twentieth century and the early decades of the twenty-first century. Black Girl Magic is a serious enterprise and beyond corporations, politics, popular media, and entertainment, it is tied to a full-blown ideology that nurtures and perpetuates its existence. Consequently, this Black woman enterprise is a profitable commodity that is bought and sold by American corporations, colleges and universities, and the corporate political establishment.

AHISTORICAL EXCEPTIONALISM: THE CULT OF THE SELF-MADE BLACK WOMAN

As I will demonstrate shortly, the commodification of Black American women has taken place through a decade-long process. Unique to the late twentieth century, this commodification process has given voice, through ideology, to the interests, concerns, anxieties, fears, hopes, and aspirations of Black American women. Popular writers, journalists, and academics have produced a substantive body of literature and popular culture which centers exclusively on Black American women. This literature includes Alice Walker, the late Toni Morrison, the late Delores S. Williams, Beverly Guy-Sheftall, Angela Davis, the late bell hooks, Patricia Hill-Collins, Kelly Brown Douglas, Tricia Rose, Monica A. Coleman, and countless others.[5] A recent iteration of White capitalist interests and Black women's empowerment or Black Girl Magic which concerns this chapter is given full articulation, ideologically, in a recent religious and political text by feminist and womanist Christian ethicist, Keri Day. Her 2016 book, *Resistance to Neoliberalism: Womanist and Black Feminist Perspectives* is the culmination of close to fifty years of intellectual work on the empowerment of Black women and their role and significance as political and moral agents in the United States and across the globe.[6] This book is a major instance of the incorporation of Black American women, professionally, politically, and intellectually into the mainstream of White capitalist America.[7] Framing Black American women as messianic political actors, it extends more than four decades of Black feminist and womanist thought into the twenty-first century. Published in the final days of the Obama era, *Resistance*, like Barack Obama's presidency, is presented as a work of social justice. Concerned with capitalism, activism, and religion within and outside of the Western world, it is a work that lends itself to the questions in this chapter pertaining to White interests and Black American women in the United States, particularly the empowerment of Black women through women-centered gender ideology and politics and the present status of more than forty million Black Americans, twenty million of which are not Black women. For the purposes of this chapter, the convergence of White interests and the empowerment of Black women have marked the bifurcation of Black America. In terms of the concerns of this chapter, White America has demonstrated, in terms of political and economic interests, an exclusive focus on Black American women as objects of empowerment and enfranchisement. Although Black America represents over forty million people in the United States, 13% of the US population, its efforts to address the consequences of 400 years of anti-Blackness in America, concentrate exclusively on Black American women. Over the last five decades, White Americans have exerted a preoccupation with Black American women which has produced unprecedented gaps, fissures, and fragmentation among Black Americans, a thick line of demarcation between Black American women and men. This condition is observable at the highest levels of White American society, with the White ruling class concentrating exclusively on the empowerment and enfranchisement of Black women. Over the last five decades, White America's incorporation of Black women in the mainstream of White capitalist America runs parallel and corresponds with the incorporation of White LGBTQ+ populations into the mainstream of White capitalist America. Keri Day's work is symbolic of decades of Black women's advancement in the United States and is fodder for discussing the merits, scope, and existence and/or nonexistence of Black America as a configuration of men and women.

HOW IT HAPPENED

What I am calling the bifurcation (or death) of Black America did not happen overnight. It was a gradual process that occurred over five decades. When this process of gender division began during the 1970s, it was not evident at the time that it would create unprecedented socioeconomic gaps between Black men and boys and Black women and girls. During the 1970s, no one could predict the emergence of an entire gender ideology and enterprise, married to these disparities, where Black women would be isolated and categorized as a distinct group, apart, in relation to Black boys and men. However, it was during the decade of the 1970s when this shift took place.[8] With the dawn of the 1980s, this bifurcation of Black America would gradually accelerate.[9]

The gradual process of bifurcation emerged after 1965 after the publication of Daniel Patrick Moynihan's government-commissioned Report on

The Negro Family in the United States: The Case for National Action.[10] Moynihan's report called attention to an economic crisis with respect to adult Black men in industrial centers of American society. He called for an economic program to be undertaken to alleviate the economic barriers to jobs in relation to Black American men across institutions. Subsequent to its release, Moynihan's report was read and interpreted as a government-initiated study and proposal that was hostile to the condition and predicament of Black American women.[11] At the center of Moynihan's findings was the dominant family formation among Black Americans, in America's industrial centers, which was led primarily by women. In contrast to the nuclear family, this woman-led family formation was treated by Moynihan as a cultural impediment to the development of the Black male population. It was held up as a factor which contributed to the dilemmas faced by Black men in American society. A family formation where men did not function as economic providers and authorities in the family life was regarded as hazardous to the full incorporation of Black Americans into White capitalist America. Moynihan's findings produced tumult on the part of White American ruling class, Black elites, women, and men, who then created and propagated an alternative to Moynihan's thesis regarding Black family structures prior to the 1970s. Black American women and men elites, bolstered by White ruling- class interests, took an opposite position which affirmed the role, authority, and dominance of women in Black family life. These elites promoted the positive role of the extended family and the leadership and influence of women in this family arrangement. In doing so, they identified matrifocality as the dominant impulse in Black American family life. The turn to matrifocality as a positive family arrangement was supported by liberal White women and men and feminists, who would attach it to the political interests of the burgeoning women's movement. Since the 1970s, matrifocality among Black Americans has been promoted as a major cultural advancement to be preserved and valorized perpetually.[12] More significantly, matrifocality was treated as a Black American gift to the West. This perspective mirrors the sentiments of W.E.B. DuBois who promoted what he termed the genius of Black folk, valorizing the positive aspects of Black American culture.[13] Since the 1970s, matrifocal defenders of Black American culture have overvalued and overrated the powers of matrifocal family structures.[14] In contrast to matrifocality, which I regard as romantic exaggeration, I view and treat matrifocality as a consequence of centuries of conquest and oppression. As such, it is a historical adaptation to conquest and oppression which is tied to the historical suppression of Black American men. To this end, if matrifocality (mother figures and women) has been prominent in Black American family life (and Black American social thought), it is in large part due to the historical barriers and obstacles faced by Black men as a group. If Black men as a group have been marginal as authority figures and shareholders in family power in Black American culture, much of it can be attributed to the economic, legal, and political impediments to Black men's ability to live out traditional masculine roles, norms, and expectations in the United States. The primacy of matrifocality or motherhood is less a product of a heroic and noble matrifocal tradition independent of historical circumstances than it is the effect of the economic and political suppression of Black men reflected in unemployment, underemployment, and overall disenfranchisement. The fact remains, despite more than half a century of protest to the contrary, Black men as a group are measured according to, stigmatized, and punished by traditional masculine standards. As a group, the inability of Black men to live up to such standards is what propels a matrifocal Black American culture. White Americans have demonstrated over several decades that it is more advantageous to throw marginal support behind this matrifocal enterprise than it is to remove all the barriers to the full-blown participation of Black men in American society. The welfare state, philanthropic initiatives, and affirmative action policies, which primarily target women, have been integral to the preservation of White interests in the United States. So the preservation of matrifocality among Black Americans is a useful tool in the perpetuation of White power in America. In a word, there is a happy marriage between matrifocality and the interests of ruling-class White society. Matrifocality among Black Americans does not alter, disrupt, or undermine White interests, and White supremacy in the United States. The marriage between Black matrifocality among Black Americans and White interests is relentless, damn near impenetrable, and enduring in the United States.[15]

After forty years of incorporation, White America maintains and perpetuates a freakish preoccupation with Black American women. Recent presidential elections in 2016 and 2020 have confirmed this state of affairs. In both instances, White Americans, mainly on the liberal to feminist to leftist spectrum, amplified the role of Black women as political saviors. Again, White America's obsession with Black American women emerged with the end of the civil rights era. Before and during the civil rights era, White America's treatment of Black American women was tied to its treatment of Black American men. Black American women and Black American men had different roles in relation to their domination in White American society. However, the fates of Black American women were tied to the fates of Black men. Such fates were conditioned by legalized segregation and Black America's overall exclusion from White society and the bulk of its resources. Black American women's engagement with the White world through work, mainly low-wage and low-status work, was constrained. There was a pervasive consensus among Black and White Americans that the worlds of Black people and the worlds of White people were separate, distinct, and unequal. Prior to the civil rights era, it was understood that this social and racial condition was permanent and inescapable. With the desegregation of American society, bolstered by unprecedented civil rights legislation, and the emergence of a White women-led women's movement, the overall status of Black American women (as a group) changed. The once low-status and low-wage segregated relationship that Black women had with White America disappeared and a new relationship, expanding the status of Black women (as a group), took its place. This new relationship began a process of division, bifurcation among Black Americans, which has reached unprecedented levels as I write this chapter. Again, it was a gradual process, slowly producing cleavages among Black Americans, men and women, over a fifty-year period. Simply stated, White America, through law, policy, and corporate incorporation, produced a state of affairs where matters pertaining to America's legacy of anti-Black racism begin and end with Black American women. As this chapter is being written, the relationship between White America and Black American women typifies White America's engagement with a legacy of anti-Black racism which spans 400 years. As such, this relationship has eliminated Black American men (as a group) from any and all assessments, calculations, and solutions that would overcome or reduce the social consequences of centuries and generations of anti-Black racism.

The achievements of the civil rights era are major factors in this bifurcated condition. However, the White women-led women's movement, aided by second- wave feminism, is the primary catalyst for the transformed relationship between White America and Black American women (as a group). White women-led women's movement, driven by second-wave feminism, replaced Anti-Black racism with sexism as the most profound source of inequality in the United States. Feminism and its emergent ideological focus on women, including a woman-centered and gender ideology, was integral to a nationwide shift away from anti-Black racism as America's core social dilemma. The fact that this shift occurred in relation to the social, economic, and political aspirations of the second most powerful group in the United States, American White women, is not lost when assessing the impact of the women's movement on American institutions at the end of the twentieth century and the first decades of the twenty-first century. The impact of the White women-led women's movement has been so profound that it is not hard to argue that it has produced the greatest social shifts in the history of the United States.[16] In the United States, we have witnessed more changes in law, politics, economics, and overall social life, under the guise of women's rights and gender justice than we have in the arena of racial justice. In contemporary America, the national focus on women over and against America's fragile and tenuous redress of racial inequality is what shapes and controls *all* justice efforts in the United States. It is within this context that White

Americans relate to Black American women as a shorthand means and shortcut to anything remotely close to racial justice. The status of Black American women as women (in America) is more profound and significant than their status as Black Americans (with a group history including Black men) who are also women. In White America's tenuous and modest approach to matters of racial justice, it has contributed to an exoticized and fetishized status with respect to Black American women. This exoticized and fetishized status is not only congruent with and subservient to ruling-class White interests; it classifies Black American women as a group apart, separate and distinct from non-Black American groups of women in America, and more significantly, it renders them separate and distinct from Black men. As I intimated earlier and will delineate later, as a consequence of this condition, Black American women now possess a tribalistic ideology and identity, an enterprise of Black women's empowerment and consciousness, that revels in their special status in relationship to White America.

As this chapter is being written, White America's incessant preoccupation with Black women has elevated Black American women as magical figures, cosmic agents of justice. This elevation has resulted in the death of Black America and has undercut four centuries of Black American struggle in the United States. What I am calling the death of Black America now produces high levels of Black American erasure which is violent and offensive in its expression. The death of Black America has relocated the once-Black American freedom struggle to one side of Black America, Black American women. White America's exclusive focus on Black American women has absolved White America, especially ruling-class Whites, from engaging the depths of anti-Blackness in the United States. White Americans are exonerated from the types of investments and risk-taking necessary to address the legacies of racism in America in robust and substantive ways. White America's incorporation of huge segments of the Black and female population since the 1970s is a shortcut, even a Band-Aid, with respect to ongoing experiences of discrimination, deprivation, and disadvantage in relation to the majority of the Black population. In twenty-first century America, in very specific ways, White Americans do not have to engage the other side of Black America, that side which is Black and male. In a word, the fetishizing of Black women by White America presents a one-dimensional and minimal strategy and approach to American racial legacies. This method of enfranchisement and empowerment pretends to be more than what it is. At the level of image and appearance, it purports to be enlightened and progressive. However, from the standpoint of this book and chapter, it is highly conservative and anti-progressive. Overall, the White American treatment of Black women as the face of Black America and its focus on Black women as the entrée points for engaging the centuries-long struggle of Black Americans against White supremacy is destructive, disingenuous, and racist. It has spelled a death sentence for Black America. Birthed in the 1970s, this White strategy, especially on the part of the White ruling class, has been exposed. With the last decade (2012–2022) of spectacled deaths and mass mediated protests in Black contexts, which have been witnessed the world over, the deliberate effort to ignore, marginalize, silence, and expunge the plight of the other side of Black America, which is Black and male, has been revealed. More significantly, due to global technologies, such revelations are worldwide.

THE WHITE AMERICAN CREATION OF TRIBALISTIC BLACK WOMANHOOD

The White-induced death of Black America has had a major impact on Black American women. This impact is psychological and ideological. The White fetish of Black women over the decades has produced a cult among Black women, a political sisterhood which is tribalistic in nature. This sisterhood, mainly among professional women, is egoistic and obsessed with its perceived sense of magical power. Because it is effectively used by White American society to advance ruling-class White interests on the level of politics, it regards itself as invincible and infallible.[17] What is more, like White Americans who fetishize Black women, this sisterhood sees itself as a progressive and redemptive force in American culture.

Essentially, what I am calling tribalistic sisterhood has produced an enterprise of political separatism in relation to Black American men. This sisterhood has severed its ties from the Black American tradition of linked fates. It is imbued with class preoccupations driven by upward mobility, careerism, and individual American success, which is radically distant from the lives of forty million Black Americans. The conditions and circumstances of unincorporated Black women and girls and the conditions and circumstances that affect the lives of the vast majority of Black boys are in no way accounted for by this professional class. The iconography of Michelle Obama, who is the archetype of the quintessential prototypical professional Black woman, and the imagery of Beyonce Knowles-Carter (and her Beehive) as the embodiment of unconditional sisterly solidarity are public markers of this tribalistic and separatist program. More significantly, they are the posterchildren for and revel in the meritocratic credo that pervades the United States. This tribalistic sisterhood is a purveyor of pervasive beliefs about the United States as a bastion of fairness and equality, that hard work and individual effort alone will guarantee and propel groups and individuals into American greatness. As such, those who give themselves over to this ethic will ascend to lofty heights, if not the pinnacle of American success. Those who do not ascend or fail to rise do so for a lack of effort and drive. This Protestant Ethic, American style, negates, minimizes, and in many instances erases a long history of prejudice, discrimination, and oppression tied to the American legacies of anti-Black racism.

THE BLACK BOGEYMAN

There is now a highly visible professional class of Black women whose newfound status as judges, mayors, university presidents, politicians, media figures, and academics presents new questions about the opportunity structure of the United States. More specifically, it presents profound questions in relation to standard narratives of prejudice, discrimination, and victimization. Among such questions is the role that Black men as a group play in the subordination and limits placed upon Black women. Stated another way, to what extent are the fates of Black women determined by Black men (as a group)? In light of *The Decade of Death (2012–2022)*, how far do we go attributing the fates of Black women to the sexism of Black men? In standard narratives of Black women's victimization, Black American men are presented as gatekeepers and curators of a system of male dominance which thwarts and impedes the fates of Black women. In such narratives, Black men are coupled together with ruling-class White men who manage and control the distributive resources in American society. Overall, Black men as a group are framed as immovable obstacles to the aspirations of women. American feminist ideology of all stripes has propagated this narrative consistently since the 1970s. Accordingly, the incorporation of women, through higher education and professionalization, across American institutions, has sustained this standard view of Black women. Although this point of view exists and persists, the gradual expansion of the professional class of Black American women which has been astonishing contradicts this perspective. What makes this perspective suspect are the class gaps that currently exist between Black women and men. By and large, the unprecedented expansion of this professional class of Black American women has not been accompanied by a similar phenomenon among Black men. This belief and notion that Black men as a group have stood and stand as stumbling blocks to the ascent of professional Black women, a highly visible population in the United States, is a myth fabricated by gender ideology. The enormous gap between this class of professional Black women and their Black male counterparts is hidden by standard narratives of Black women's victimization. Heretofore, the significant class differences that now exist between Black men and women have not been taken seriously. Such class differences have been immune to and protected from rigorous investigation. They are largely ignored in order to maintain narratives of Black women's victimization that treat gender and sex as ultimate determinants of the fates of Black women.

KAMALA HARRIS AND DENOMINATIONALISM

As was indicated earlier, recent presidential elections have elevated gender and gender ideology in ways that have eviscerated the deep wells of anti-Blackness in the United States. The 2016 presidential campaign of Hillary Clinton and the presidential campaign and subsequent victory of Joe Biden in 2020 are testaments to this condition. However, it was the latter campaign and electoral success of Joe Biden where Black women as magical figures and saviors were amplified. On this front, it was Joe Biden's selection of US Senator Kamala Harris as his running mate for Vice President which unashamedly and unapologetically advanced gender ideology through the spectrum of Black women as a necessary force in securing the presidency and advancing American democracy.[18] Kamala Harris, who identifies as a Black woman, made such identity integral to her candidacy as a potential and future Vice President. Harris made appeals to Black American voters which were anchored by her identification as a Black woman. Similar to Barack Obama, who invoked the Black American tradition of struggle when he ran for the US presidency in 2007, Kamala Harris attached herself to the historic struggles of Black Americans, especially the history of civil rights protest. On her way to the Vice Presidency of the United States, then-Senator Kamala Harris not only appropriated the history of Black American struggles in the United States, she also appealed to and garnered support from Black Americans by citing and amplifying her affiliations with Black American cultural institutions.[19] Kamala Harris is a college graduate of Howard University, a storied institution of higher education which is predominately Black. She is also a member of a Black American sorority. This sorority is a part of a tradition of Black organizations, sororities, and fraternities, which have existed for more than a century. These organizations, which thrive on college and universities in the United States, especially Historically Black Colleges and Universities (HBCUs), are no different in orientation and commitment from Christian denominations. Kamala Harris used her affiliations with Black American cultural institutions as currency in legitimating her candidacy as Vice President as well as the presidential candidacy of Joe Biden. Black American women were the major targets of her campaign. Her affiliation with these traditions and her invocation of her membership as a means of multiplying Black women supporters and voters spoke volumes to a psychology of tribal affiliation among Black women, which is noteworthy in light of the democratic ideology she espoused as a presidential candidate. It is worth noting that we have a long history of US presidents and presidential candidates who have had affiliations with fraternities, Masonic organizations, and secret societies. However, these affiliations were often kept private and not used as currency to garner public support. The point here is that politicians tend to keep their memberships in such organizations repressed in order to gain the widest number of supporters or to prevent the alienation of potential allies and voters. In taking the opposite route, Kamala Harris placed a light on the tribal dimension of Black womanhood in the United States.[20] Black American women who were members of these woman-led Greek organizations responded to Harris' cultural and organizational affiliations in a powerful way. As a potential Vice President, Kamala Harris, who identified as a Black woman with membership in a Black sorority, was enough to secure the support of Black women similarly situated. In her candidacy as Vice President, her political ideology and career in politics were secondary considerations in relation to her fitness for public office. This was very telling in light of the fact that Kamala Harris achieved a political record as a prosecutor and District Attorney in San Francisco and as the Attorney General for the State of California, which was the object of intense evaluation and criticism among many social and political critics (I, the author of this book, was very critical of her political record).[21] Despite her questionable political career, her tribal affiliations won her favor with Black American women. Overall, her membership in a tribe trumped the questionable content of her political ideology and professional career. To be clear, tribal affiliations are not new nor are they exclusive to Black women or any group in the United States. However, the unapologetic tribalism of Kamala Harris and Black American women is integral to the bifurcation of Black America and the preservation of the dominant White ruling class in America. This tribalism, bolstered by decades of gender ideology, is nonsensical without attending to the many changes which have occurred institutionally and politically since the 1970s.

As I have indicated above, tribalism is analogous to denominationalism.[22] In the 2020s, Black American women are now a denomination of women. Here, I am speaking of denominationalism in the Protestant sense of the term. In this sense, a denomination is understood as a dissenting group, an entity that sets itself apart from an inherited or received tradition. Historically, such dissenting groups include Baptists, Methodists, Lutherans, Anglicans, Episcopalians, and Pentecostals. These denominations possess their own creed, liturgy, and institutions. Some denominations entertain ecumenism or openness, others pride themselves in their purity or separation from other groups. The denominationalism that characterizes Black women as a group has built itself up gradually since the 1970s. Since 2010, the denominationalism/tribalism of Black American women has been amplified and propagated by White ruling-class White interests. This tribalistic and denominational force and the manner in which it expresses itself in the present has no precedent in the past and cannot exist as it does without the support of the White American ruling class. As I write this chapter, tribal and denominational affiliations among Black American women are an unrelenting force which sanitizes and whitewashes the deep wells of anti-Blackness in the United States. It supports and legitimates ruling-class White interests in America.

In the 2020s, there is no healthy critique of tribalistic womanhood and its relationship with White ruling-class interests. Tribalistic Black womanhood, underwritten by White ruling-class interests, is assumed to be the final solution to the anti-Black conundrums of Black Americans. As such, tribalistic Black womanhood is protected from all forms of scrutiny and interrogation. Because sexism and racism are real facts in American life, to critique such tribalism invites accusations of racism and sexism among Black women who possess a tribal identity. More significantly, the manner in which tribalistic Black womanhood is protected from evaluation and critique is heightened by the general status of women in the United States, which is tinged by sexism. Criticism of any group of women is perceived as an attack on all women. It is regarded as an act of misogyny and sexism whose primary victims are women.[23] In light of the concerns of this chapter and that of this book, such protectionism is abhorrent, antijustice, and politically illiberal. What is more, when it comes to the present status of Black Americans and the centuries-long tradition of struggle against anti-Blackness, it is a complete betrayal of a legacy of protest and dissent undertaken by Black women and Black men historically. Tribalistic Black womanhood assumes that the political and economic interests of Black women, especially women in the professional classes, benefits and speaks to the interest of all Black Americans, particularly those Black Americans outside of the professional classes, the Black majority. This presumption flies in the face of a tradition of linked fates that was once represented by Black women, political actors who struggled against anti-Blackness prior to the 1970s. Late twentieth-century figures such as Fannie Lou Hamer and Ella Baker and twentieth-century figures such as Ida B. Wells are among those actors, driven by linked fate actors who personified this tradition. One can go further to the legacy of the abolitionist Harriet Tubman, whose activism under conditions of slavery was not relegated to or reduced to one side of the enslaved Black population, Black women. In the 2020s, this tradition has been lost. Not only has this tradition of linked fates been lost, tribalistic Black womanhood has produced extreme elements among its ranks which legitimate the bifurcation of Black America. These extreme voices, which can be found in academia, politics, media, and entertainment writ large, which have been elevated by ruling-class White interests, diminish the deep wells of anti-Blackness in the United States and, in doing so, reinforce ruling-class White interests. These extreme voices, which include women studies professors Beth Richie, Tricia Rose, and Brittany Cooper, journalist Jamilah Lemuiex, media personality Tiffany Cross, actress Amanda Seales, political consultant Symone Sanders, and Black Lives Matter founder Aliza Garza, to name several, reinforce ruling-class interests with an aggressive anti-Black male ideology (misandry) which propagates anti-Black myths and stereotypes of Black men as a group.[24] This misandry, which perpetuates American fears of Black men, echoes in a loud fashion the antebellum era and the early twentieth century, where Black men were designated as savages and criminals. Throughout this book, I have framed this orientation as *the demonic imaginary*. Extremists among tribalistic Black women revel in this *demonic imaginary* in relation to Black men as a group. At the core of such extremism is the influence and imprint of radical White feminism.

THE DEFAMATION OF BLACK MEN: THE EXTREMES OF TRIBALISTIC BLACK WOMANHOOD

Tribalistic extremists delegitimize and discredit Black men with respect to the household, their status in Black communities, and Black organizations. Such extremists militate against all forms of critique and dissent, including Black women who do not share this extreme orientation. Black women who are not extremists exist in a condition of censure and silence.[25] Fear of going against the consensus and the perspective of loud extremists keeps their mouths shut. I regard the extremists among Black women as similar to religious fundamentalists of all stripes whose religious orientations are fixed and hostile to criticism. These extremists operate as spokespersons and authorities of Black American women as a group. They also operate as authorities and experts on the Black American condition in the United States. During *The Decade of Death (2012–2022)*, the queer feminist women who led the Black Lives Matter movement perpetuated extremism within the tribalistic sisterhood. During *The Decade of Death (2012–2022)*, they propagated a Black feminist queer ideology, under the guise of anti-racist politics, that was hostile to Black men, heterosexual Black men in particular. This ideology was given expression on the official website of Black Lives Matter where a mission statement and guiding principles and beliefs were displayed for the public. On the official website of the Black Lives Matter Global Network, in a section, What We Believe (which has been scrubbed from the Internet as of this writing), the queer Black feminist posture toward heterosexual Black men is made plain.

> We are self-reflexive and do the work required to dismantle cisgender privilege and uplift Black trans folk, especially Black trans women who continue to be disproportionately impacted by trans-antagonistic violence. We build a space that affirms Black women and is free from sexism, misogyny, and environments

in which men are centered. We practice empathy. We engage comrades with the intent to learn about and connect with their contexts. We make our spaces family- friendly and enable parents to fully participate with their children. We dismantle the patriarchal practice that requires mothers to work "double shifts" so that they can mother in private even as they participate in public justice work. We disrupt Western- prescribed nuclear family structure requirement by supporting each other as extended families and "villages" that collectively care for one another, especially our children, to the degree that mothers, parents, and children are comfortable. We foster a queer-affirming network. When we gather, we do so with the intention of freeing ourselves from the tight grip of heteronormative thinking, or rather, the belief that all in the world are heterosexual (unless s/she or they disclose otherwise).[26]

The above statement is representative and symbolic of tribalism and extremism. The *demonic imaginary* with respect to heterosexual Black men colors every word. The framers of this statement propagated it as an inclusive and expansive position on social justice with respect to Black Americans. I regard it as reductive and fixed in relation to all Black Americans, especially those who exist outside of the mainstream of White American capitalist society, those Black Americans who are unincorporated, including heterosexual Black men. Again, I regard those Black women who promote such tribalism and extremism as no different from second- wave White radical feminists. White radical feminists such as the late Andrea Dworkin and the late Mary Daly and the legal scholar Catherine MacKinnon are the feminist extremists who I have in mind. They take a completely oppositional stance toward men, heterosexual men in particular, regarding them as villains, morally abject, and evil. They frame all women's relationships with such men as fraught with abuse, danger, and oppression. Indistinguishable from their radical White feminist counterparts, these voices which revel in misandry apply White-oriented anti-Black logic to Black American culture. These extremists make no distinctions between the dominant White men who control the United States and Black men who are subordinate to them. The claims they make regarding male domination, particularly the perceived hegemony of Black men, and its effects on women, especially Black women, are undifferentiated. More importantly, it thrives without serious intellectual interrogation and critique. The political end of this extreme element among Black women is a virtual *No Man's Land*, a world without Black men, heterosexual Black men in particular. During *The Decade of Death (2012–2022)* the queer Black feminists of Black Lives Matter gave credence and validity to this *No Man's Land,* through protest rhetoric and ideology, with respect to heterosexual Black men. Such promotion was bizarre in light of the ground upon which the Black Lives Matter movement sprung, the murders of Black men, and boys at the hands of private citizens and law enforcement agents.

Although the murders of Black men and boys at the hands of private citizens and law enforcement were the main instigators of social protest, the founders of Black Lives Matter were intentional in producing a narrative of politics and social engagement whose primary focus was Black women and Black LGBTQ+ people. Despite the social facts which produced Black Lives Matter, the primacy given to women and LGBTQ+ people was ideological and deliberate. Driven by a neoliberal obsession with identarian representation (symbolism) and by anxieties regarding the gender arrangements (stereotypically chauvinistic and sexist male-driven leadership) that characterized the Civil Rights and Black Power movements, and by an imperative to stake claims (as the new Black and female faces of social justice) on a new era of social justice activity, this narrative as uttered by Black women was articulated as Herstory, Black women as *the* leaders of a new era of social justice in the United States. It should be noted that during *The Decade of Death (2012–2022)*, which gave rise to Black Lives Matter, White liberals, leftists, and feminists endorsed this orientation whose support for their efforts was characterized by an exclusive concern with Black women as agents of justice and social change. Bolstered by the support of White liberals, leftists, and feminists, with an exclusive focus on Black women as activists and political voices, Black Lives Matter was treated, interpreted, and understood exclusively as a Black woman's enterprise. Although the gravity and force of Black Lives Matter were motivated and driven by the murders of Black men and boys at the hands of private citizens and law enforcement, its appropriation and support on behalf of ruling-class White interests was restricted to Black female gender politics or the concerns of Black women, particularly Black women who identify as queer. It was primarily through a queer feminist orientation that Black Lives Matter registered and was legible to White ruling-class elites. Without such legibility, it is highly doubtful that White ruling-class interests would have endeared itself to such activism. It is highly doubtful that Black Lives Matter, under the leadership of Black men, heterosexual Black men in particular, would have moved, in a positive way, White ruling-class interests. With White ruling-class interests and its decades-long incorporation of Black women in its limited calculus of racial justice, the precarious condition of Black men and boys in the United States was rendered null and void. At best, the murders of Black men and boys were useful to the extent that such murders gave currency to the existential condition of Black women and girls, hence granting this condition a significant concern and priority in relation to ruling-class White interests. In a word, in the ruling-class White imaginary, the total thrust of Black Lives Matters was about Black women, not Black men. During and after *The Decade of Death (2012–2022)*, Black Lives Matter was more beneficial to Black women and girls, institutionally and monetarily, than it was to Black men and boys. This was borne out in the manner in which White ruling-class interests responded, through corporations, philanthropic organizations, and independent wealthy White financial supports, to Black Lives Matter.

THE PROTEST AGAINST PATRIARCHY AND THE EXTREMIST ENDS OF AN ERA

The dominant theme that characterizes the tribalistic extremism that is in question is patriarchy, unrelenting male tyranny and domination. The tribalistic extremists see themselves as warriors against patriarchy. This war is essentially an endless protest which seeks to eliminate patriarchy from America in general and Black America in particular. This protest against patriarchy is integral to the decades long dissent against sexism and misogyny which emerged at the end of the twentieth century with rise of second-wave feminism. That the United States, a nation shaped by White settler colonialism whose core trait is a White male patriarchal ethos, is an unremarkable fact and truth that is controversial to a few. However, that the force of such patriarchy has an analog with Black American culture has been subject to endless debate. In fact, contrary to the propagations of tribalist extremists, it remains an unsettled proposition and assertion. As I have stated elsewhere, the tribalism of Black women and its support by ruling-class White interests and the present bifurcation of Black America along the lines of gender renders this thesis suspect and worthy of interrogation and debate. In fact, it is a highly refutable perspective. In light of the concerns of this chapter, the protest against patriarchy over the last half-century misrepresents the condition of Black America writ large and has obscured the rise of an elite class of professional Black women in the United States. As I indicated earlier in this chapter, this professional class has no comparable analog among Black men as a group.[27] What Black men and boys represent in the American imaginary is nowhere near what Black women and girls represent in this same imaginary. The protest against patriarchy and the ideology of patriarchal victimization has hidden wide gaps in terms of economic and social mobility and visibility between this elite population of Black American women and the majority of Black men in the United States. It is worth noting that over the last forty years, the presence of a handful of elite Black men in the professions, occupying positions of influence in White America, has been useful in glossing over the now highly visible class of professional Black American women who are in close proximity to White power in America.[28] At present, the proximity of professional Black women in relation to White power in America outstrips, numerically, the proximity of a handful of Black men, in the professions, to White power. In very powerful ways, the protest against patriarchy works in an insidious way to downplay the incorporation of Black American women (and its significance) into the mainstream of White capitalist America. More significantly, the protest against patriarchy is a distraction from an unprecedented divide in Black America tinged by race, class, and gender. As I have said earlier, this divide is a uniquely American phenomenon, where the White ruling-class manages the Black American population along the lines of male and female. This managerial apparatus authorizes a separate sphere for controlling the participation of Black men and boys in America society and a distinct sphere for administering the participation of Black women and girls in American society. In the managerial sphere designated for the Black men and boys, Black men and boys, collectively, are socially, economically, and politically distant from the mechanism of incorporation of the White ruling class. In the managerial sphere designated for Black women and girls, Black women and girls, as a group, are socially, economically, and politically close to the mechanisms of incorporation of the White ruling class. In the 2020s, there is no dearth of sociological and economic data and research which confirms what is now a two-tier condition in relation to the Black American population in the United States. What is more, this condition is observable and evident in the state-driven and supported and the corporate-motivated strategies which contribute to radically different life outcomes for each gender. The protest against patriarchal victimization in relation to Black women as a group has no way to account for this unprecedented state of affairs. After four centuries of struggle in the United States, Black Americans have been reduced, by the White ruling-class interests, to male and female. In relation to ruling-class White America, Black men and boys, collectively, are outsiders in America and Black women and girls, collectively, are insiders. This condition is so profound that it is difficult to discern and locate similar bifurcation in other non-White groups (Latino/as, Asians, Continental Africans, Caribbeans, Middle Easterners, etc.) in America and beyond. To be dramatic, one is compelled to ask the question: Where else in America and across the globe does such a divide among men and women exist? Overall, the incessant preoccupation with patriarchal victimization with respect to professional Black American women needs to be thoroughly reassessed. It stands in stark contrast to observation and empirically measured conditions. On one level, it over-exaggerates the disadvantages suffered by Black women and girls. At another lever, it overinflates and exaggerates the advantages the Black men and boys are *perceived* to have over Black women and girls.

In the protest against patriarchy, mainstream Black feminists and womanists have been largely disingenuous regarding the extent to which Black women, especially the professional class, are an integral part of the mainstream of American society. As a group, elite and professional Black women are useful to the propagation and maintenance of ruling-class White interests in the United States. The mechanism of ruling-class White power is mainly responsible for the bifurcation of Black America. Based on this state of affairs, one can only conclude that Black women as a group strike no fear in the hearts and minds of White America, especially not in the manner that Black men as a group of men do. To be sure, Black women are not White Americans and do not have the same status as White American women who abide in the middle to the upper class. However, their tribalistic perspectives and outlooks, especially their views on politics and justice in the United States are recognized and influential. It is a telling fact that one of the most popular theories on justice in the United States (and across White Western nations), intersectionality, produced under tribalistic Black womanhood, was crafted by a Black woman, a professor of law, Kimberle Crenshaw.[29] She is one influential figure among many Black women (academic elites) including Angela Davis, Patricia Hill-Collins, Barbara Ransby, Cathy Cohen, and Brittney Cooper, whose perspectives are taken seriously, bought and sold by large White audiences. The professional work and reputations of these women and their views are concurrent with colleges and universities in America and across the world and with national media organs such as *Time Magazine*, *Nation Magazine*, *Vanity Fair*, *Elle Magazine, Ms. Magazine*, and the *Atlantic Monthly*. In those places where they are known, where their views are given a platform, they are regarded as normative and authoritative. The status of these middle to upper-middle-class Black women is amplified by the presence and influence of Black women in Congress, Black women who are mayors of cities, Black women in the courts (as judges and prosecutors) and Black women in corporate media and education. To say that these women are marginal or represent a fringe group or that they possess the same status as lower-class or working-class Black Americans, is deceptive. Those who are concerned about the deep wells of anti-Blackness in the United States must be honest about this state of affairs. We must be honest about how this happened and why the bifurcation of Black America through ruling White interests is the reason this is the case. It is a gross abomination that the dominant way in which the condition of more than forty million Black Americans and the connection of these Black Americans to a long history of struggle, four centuries in length, has been reduced to the condition and circumstances related to half of the Black American population. More significantly, the standards by which we understand Black America in the 2020s have been reduced to the last fifty years of American history. The history and struggles of Black Americans did not begin in the 1970s with second-wave feminism and the women's movement. As long as it is presumed that this is the case, comprehensive assessments and calculations of the condition of forty million Black Americans will be thwarted.

CONCLUSION

As I indicated at the outset of this chapter, the bifurcation of Black America and the creation of tribalistic class of Black women, led by professionals, is fundamentally the creation of White ruling-class interests. The creation and propagation of gender ideology which focuses primarily upon women as exclusive victims of prejudice, discrimination, and victimization is largely responsible for this state of affairs. The conformity of all institutions in the United States to this gender ideology has contributed to the existence of a two-tier reality, along the lines of gender and ideology which insures separate tracks for Black women and girls and Black men and boys. At the time of this writing, the quality of life and outcomes, socially and economically, for both genders are radically different. These differences are often attributed to success and failure in America society. If there is a significant class of Black American women who have been fully incorporated into the mainstream of White capitalist America, then the upward mobility of this class is attributed to their success at effectively navigating White capitalist America. If there is a significant population of Black men who have *not* been incorporated into the mainstream of White capitalist America, their lack of incorporation is attributed to failure, their inability to enter this mainstream after the doors of this mainstream were opened after the political movements of the 1950s and 1960s. In other words, the barriers that existed in relation to Black American advancement prior to the movements were effectively removed or erased after these movements declined. The conviction that the United States corrected its anti-Black racial problems of the past, opening new possibilities for Black Americans, based upon merit and exceptionalism, is what drives this point of view. In this view, White Americans, particularly those among the ruling class, are absolved from any responsibility for dictating racial relations or racial affairs in the United States. In other words, ruling-class Whites as architects and engineers of how all institutions operate in the United States, who function as managers of who participates in its infrastructure, are lessened or completely dismissed as gatekeepers of American institutions. From the standpoint of this chapter, this assumption is false. The argument here is that the incorporation of Black Americans into the mainstream of White capitalism in the United States has been highly selective in nature. Since the 1980s, such selectivity has been shaped and molded by gender ideology and how institutional practices among the White ruling class has been informed by such ideology. As I have stated in the earlier parts of this chapter, the unprecedented incorporation of all women into the mainstream of White capitalist America did not occur in a vacuum. It was the result of not only historical and political forces but also of deliberate social engineering. Hence, the belief that merit and merit alone is solely responsible for the advancement of women in the United States, is disingenuous, deceptive, and dangerous. This myth fuels prejudice and discrimination as well as fear and hatred directed at Black men and boys in the United States. Black men and boys are casted as problems in and of themselves whose condition in America is largely self-inflicted. Unlike Black American women and many non-White groups (non-White immigrants in particular), they have failed to become model minorities. The idea that Black men as a group are not model minorities is pervasive. For this reason, at the level of politics, Black men as a group are regarded as criminal, law-breaking deviants in the making or actual violators of law. Hence, criminal punishment not affirmative action is symbolic of how Black men are imagined and treated as a group.

Overall, the relationship that the White American ruling class has with respect to Black American women is colonial in nature. The manner in which ruling-class White Americans selectively incorporate Black Americans as a group leans primarily toward Black American women. From the standpoint of this chapter and book, this is a function of management and social control with respect to the overall Black population. The selective incorporation of a class of Black Americans over the last fifty years is similar to the creation of elites and model minorities among populations of people who were conquered and dominated by European imperial powers. Hence, the creation of colonized elites by the British in British-ruled colonies, the creation of such elites in colonies ruled by the French, the Dutch, and the Portuguese has an analog in the United States, particularly twenty-first-century America. Under this colonial condition, clear and distinct lines of demarcation are made between the colonized elites and the rest of the colonized population. The colonized elite is marked by its close proximity to the colonizing population. This proximity includes the adherence to and propagation of the interests of the colonizing dominant group. The colonized elite shares its values, norms, and worldviews. What I see as a colonial condition, as it is articulated here, among Black Americans, has received little to no attention. The view that liberal democracy, not coloniality, is the core feature of American reality in the United States is the norm. To say that coloniality, not democracy is the norm that governs the United States is foreign to many. From the perspective of this book and chapter, coloniality is the norm, and this norm confounds and contradicts the conviction that the United States is essentially a liberal democracy.

Essentially, the argument presented in this chapter is that the White American ruling class is fundamentally afraid of Black men as a group. This fear of Black men, as a group, lives in the psyches of the White American population and it lives in the minds of those populations who are not White who identify with the interests and imperatives of the White ruling class. This means that phenotypical Whiteness is not the sole marker of White ruling class interests. The affirmation and promotion of White ruling interests and its fear of Black men as a group have no boundaries. The fear of Black men as a group is largely responsible for the condition of Black men in the United States. This fear is what produced *The Decade of Death (2012–2022)* and the movement that came out of it, Black Lives Matter. The fear of Black men is largely responsible for the high levels of surveillance by law enforcement, institutions, and private citizens, to which Black men are subject, which often has lethal consequences. The fear of Black men fuels aggressive programs of censorship, in the past and in the present, when Black men have attempted to articulate their grievances, in a political fashion, in the United States.[30] This includes *The Decade of Death (2012–2022)* where efforts were made to censor the voices of Black men as they engaged in street protests and used social media to speak to a phenomenon of Black male death. The extent to which the fear of Black men as a group is maintained, especially as it is tinged by White ruling-class interests, justice for all Black Americans (over forty million people), not just Black women as a group, will remain elusive.

NOTES

1. Arundhati Roy, *Capitalism: A Ghost Story* (Chicago: Haymarket Books, 2014).

2. Eugene Robinson, *Disintegration: The Splintering of Black America* (New York: Anchor Books, 2010).

3. Michelle Obama, *Becoming Michelle Obama* (New York: Crown Books, 2018). Also see Sophia A. Nelson, *Black Women Redefined: Dispelling Myths and Discovering Fulfillment in the Age of Michelle Obama* (Dallas: Benbella Books, 2011) and Ta-Nehisi Coates, American Girl, in *We Were Eight Years in Power* (New York: One World, 2017), pp. 45–57.

4. See Hannah Rosin, *The End of Men: And the Rise of Women* (New York: Riverhead Books, 2012).

5. See Patricia Hill Collins, *Black Feminist Thought: Knowledge, Consciousness, and the Politics of Empowerment*, 2nd Edition (New York: Routledge, 2000).

6. Keri Day, *Religious Resistance to Neoliberalism: Womanist and Feminist Perspectives* (New York: Palgrave Macmillan, 2016).

7. Ibid.

8. See Gloria Steinem, After Black Power, Women's Liberation, *New York Magazine*, 1967.

9. The bifurcation that I am referring to can be found in the writings of select Black feminists. In 1988, the Black feminist sociologist Deborah K. King acknowledged class differentiation along the lines of men and women as an important component in making assessments about the socioeconomic condition of Black Americans. See Deborah K. King, Multiple Jeopardy, Multiple Consciousness: The Context of Black Feminist Ideology, *Signs*, Vol. 14, No. 1 (Autumn 1988), pp. 42–72, The

University of Chicago Press Journals, JSTOR (https://www.jstor.org/stable/3174661). Also see Angela Y. Davis, *Women, Race & Class* (New York: Vintage Books, 1983).

10. Daniel Patrick Moynihan, *The Negro Family: The Case for National Action*. Office of Policy Planning and Research, United States Department of Labor, March 1965.

11. See James T. Patterson, *Freedom Is Not Enough: The Moynihan Report and America's Struggle Over Family Life from LBJ to Obama* (New York: Basic Books, 2010).

12. See Dianne M. Stewart, *Black Women, Black Love: America's War on African American Marriage* (New York: Seal Press, 2020).

13. W.E.B. Dubois, *The Gift of Black Folk: The Negroes in the Making of America* (Garden City Park: Square One Publishers, 2009).

14. See Hortense J. Spillers, Mama's Baby, Papa's Maybe: An American Grammar Book, *Diacritics*, Vol. 17, No. 2, Culture and Countermemory: The "American" Connection (Summer, 1987), pp. 64–81.

15. The work of the late critical race theorist, Derrick Bell, is noteworthy here. Bell postulated a theory of interest convergence to explain the interventions of the White capitalist ruling class during moments of intense racial conflict in United States. This interest convergence theory is relevant to the argument that I am making. White capitalist interventions are driven by White interests. In *Silent Covenants: Brown v. Board of Education and the Unfulfilled Hopes for Racial Reform,* Bell says the following regarding interest convergence: "Given their history of racial subordination, how have Black people gained any protection against the multifaced forms of discrimination that threaten their well-being and undermine their rights? The answer can be stated simply: Black rights are recognized and protected when and only so long as policymakers perceive that such advances will further interests that are their primary concern . . . Throughout the history of civil rights policies, even the most serious injustices suffered by Blacks, including slavery, segregation, and patterns of murderous violence, have been insufficient, standing alone, to gain real relief from any branch of government. Rather, relief from discrimination has only come when policymakers recognize that such relief will provide clear benefit for the nation or portions of the populace." See *Silent Covenants: Brown v. Board of Education and the Unfulfilled Hopes for Racial Reform* (New York: Oxford University Press, 2004), pp. 49.

16. Before and during *The Decade of Death (2012–2022)* Liberal feminist writers such as Hannah Rosin and Rebecca Traister gave voice to the consequences of feminist ideology and politics on American institutions. Rosin has written about the world of work, corporate America in particular, and the changes which have taken place in this arena. Traister has written about the political significance of unmarried professional women and their importance to US elections. See Hannah Rosin's, *The End of Men/And the Rise of Women* (New York: Riverhead Books, 2013). Also see Rebecca Traister, *All the Single Ladies: Unmarried Women and the Rise of an Independent Nation* (New York: Simon & Schuster Paperbacks, 2016).

17. What I am calling Tribalistic Black Womanhood is found in works by Black women scholars. Daina Ramey Berry and Kali Nicole Gross's, *A Black Women's*

History of the United States (Boston: Beacon Press, 2020) and Brittney Cooper's, *Eloquent Rage: A Black Feminist Discovers Her Superpower* (New York: St. Martin's Press, 2018). Also see Feminista Jones, *Reclaiming Our Space: How Black Feminists Are Changing the World from the Tweets to the Streets* (Boston: Beacon Press, 2019).

18. See Melanie Mason, *A Place in History in Los Angeles Times: Special Edition: Vice President Kamala Harris* (New York: Meredith Premium Publishing, 2021), pp. 4–7.

19. See Evan Halper, Political Education in *The Los Angeles Times*: Special Education: Vice President Kamala Harris, New York, 2021, pp. 14–17. Also see Knowledge Is Power in American Legends, Special Issue: Kamala Harris, New York: Centennial Media LLC, 2021, pp. 26–29.

20. See I Accept Your Nomination in *Los Angeles Times*, Special Edition: Kamala Harris, New York: Meredith Premium Publishing, 2021, pp. 51–55.

21. For an account of Harris' record as a public official and the political scrutiny that plagued her presidential candidacy see Molly Ball, Finding Kamala Harris in *Time Magazine*, October 19, 2019, pp. 32–37. Also see Melania Mason and Michael Finnegan, A Mixed Record on Police Reform in *Los Angeles Times*, Special Edition: Kamala Harris, New York: Meredith Publishing Group, pp. 32–37.

22. For a historic definition and account of denominationalism see the classic work of H. Richard Niebuhr, *The Social Sources of Denominationalism* (Gloucester: Peter Smith, 1987).

23. For an academic account of how male criticism of feminism is classified as misogyny, see Kristin J. Anderson, *Modern Misogyny: Anti-Feminism in a Post-Feminist Era* (Oxford and New York: Oxford University Press, 2015).

24. The emergence and expansion of Women, Gender, and Sexuality Studies across American colleges and universities since the 1970s has been integral to the propagation of extreme voices which are critical of men and masculinity. Where Black men and Black masculinity are concerned these voices are exceptionally harsh and criminogenic in nature. Radical expressions of feminism have characterized this approach to Black men and masculinity. White radical feminists such as the late Mary Daly and the late Andrea Dworkin and the legal scholar Catherine MacKinnon have informed this extremism. Black American women such as the late Audrey Lorde, Alice Walker, Cheryl Clarke, and Brittney Cooper have contributed to this perspective in relation to Black American men. See Emily Jackson, Catharine MacKinnon and Feminist Juris Prudence: A Critical Appraisal, *Journal of Law and Society*, Vol. 19, No. 2 (Summer, 1992), pp. 195–213. Also see Barbara Smith, Ed. *Home Girls: A Black Feminist Anthology* (New Brunswick, New Jersey, and London: Rutgers University Press, 2000) and Cooper, *Eloquent Rage*.

25. The work of Clenora Hudson-Weems is noteworthy in this regard. Hudson-Weems is the pioneer and propagator of African Womanism. She is one academic and intellectual voice among Black women who expressed, as feminist-driven gender ideology proliferated from the 1980s to the 2000s, deep reservations and concerns regarding feminist ideology as an adequate framework in matters pertaining to Black liberation. Her perspective has been ignored and suppressed in the cannon of Black

feminist thought. See Clenora Hudson-Weems, *Africana Womanism: Reclaiming Ourselves*, 5th Edition (London and New York: Routledge, 2020).

26. The Black Lives Matter Global Network issued an official mission statement on its website (https://www.blacklivesmatter.com) which was later removed when it became the subject of intense criticism by White right-wing activists during the summer protests of 2020. This statement elevated the concerns of Black women and LGBTQ+ people while simultaneously condemning the heterosexual nuclear family. Among the critics of this statement were Black American men (including myself) who regarded it as a hostile rebuke of heterosexuality, particularly heterosexual Black masculinity. See Brittany Bernstein, Black Lives Matters Removes Language About the Heterosexual Nuclear Family From Website, https://www.news.yahoo.com/black-lives-matter-removes-language-185621063.html?fr=sycrp-catchall.

27. See Raj Chetty, Nathaniel Hendren, Maggie R. Jones, and Sonya R. Porter, *Race and Economic Opportunity in the United States: An Intergenerational Perspective* (Washington, DC: The Brookings Institute, March 2018).

28. See the chapter on Blacks in the Power Elite in Richard L. Zweigenhaft and G. William Domhoff, *Diversity in the Power Elite*, 3rd Edition (Landham, Boulder, New York, and London: Rowman and Littlefield, 2018).

29. See Tom Bartlett, When a Theory Goes Viral: Intersectionality Is Now Everywhere. Is It a Good Thing? *The Chronicle of Higher Education*, May 21, 2017.

30. See Tommy J. Curry, *The Man-Not: Race, Class, Genre, and the Dilemmas of Black Manhood* (Philadelphia: Temple University Press, 2017).

Chapter 6

Legal Misandry

The Prosecutor Who Is Afraid of Black Men

In the 2019 book *Rap on Trial: Race, Lyrics, and Guilt in America*, Erik Nielson and Andrea L. Dennis take on the troubling problem of rap artists being policed, arrested, prosecuted, and convicted of crimes based exclusively on crime fiction, lyrics in music.[1] *Rap on Trial* deals primarily with First Amendment issues and the larger problem of constitutional violations which have plagued hip-hop artists, primarily Black men, since the 1980s. Seen by many as a dangerous artform harmful to the public and connected to Black masculinity, the prosecution of rappers and rap music is fodder for the concerns of this chapter. As I have indicated in earlier chapters, Black masculinity is regarded as a threat to the interests of others. This imagined threat to others is what I have called throughout this book, the *demonic imaginary*. The *demonic imaginary* is the projection of fear toward Black men and boys, on the part of others, such as White men, White Women, women of all stripes, non-Black model minorities, and LGBTQ+ populations. The fear of Black masculinity, especially in its heterosexual expression, is displayed through heightened levels of surveillance and policing and such surveillance and policing are pervasive in nature. Connected to this entrenched fear of Black masculinity is bias, stigma, prejudice, and discrimination. This fear of Black masculinity legitimates all forms of exclusion (social, political, economic, and legal) and societal removal. The prison industrial complex and the overall criminal justice system in the United States, represent a public manifestation of the fear of Black masculinity. In the pages that follow, I point to the prison industrial complex (PIC) and the criminal justice system as mirrors of American society, its institutions, and its relationship to Black men and boys. It was during *The Decade of Death (2012–2022)* that the relationship between the PIC, the criminal justice system, and Black masculinity was exposed. *The Decade of Death (2012–2022)* also brought unusual levels of attention to once underground movements which are presently known as prison abolition and criminal justice reform. The movement to abolish prisons in the United States and the movement to reform the criminal justice system seek to undo decades of misconduct, legal practices, and bad ideas in relation to mass incarceration. However, their noble efforts and goals are faced with a conundrum which is essentially the institutionalized fear of Black men and boys. The fear of Black men and boys is inextricably linked to the flourishing of the PIC. The movement to abolish prisons and the movement to reform the criminal justice system are incomplete without attending to this reality and the unrelenting impact of the *demonic imaginary*.

In present-day movements which seek to reform the criminal justice system and to abolish prisons, the work and role of prosecutors loom large as actors and decision-makers who are in part responsible for the problem of hyper-incarceration in the United States.[2] In maintaining law and order, protecting the public good, their role is to bring forth criminal indictments and induce guilty pleas and verdicts of guilt in relation to criminal defendants. As I write, the role of prosecutors in contributing to the build-up of prisons and jails across America is under public interrogation. Cases of prosecutorial misconduct, spanning decades, resulting in death sentences and wrongful convictions, have brought critical scrutiny to these perceived agents of justice in relation to law and order. Up until recent times, prosecutors have enjoyed a free reign of criminal prosecutions with virtually no checks and balances. Public trust, which grants prosecutors godlike powers and authority, grants these authority figures a license to get away with much public harm.[3] Where the lives of Black American men are concerned, such harms have been lethal. The current critique of prosecutors is largely concerned with the practice of law in criminal courts. In this chapter, I want to build upon and extend this critique to legal experts in American law schools—the very class of professionals responsible for the training and/or education of future prosecutors, agents of law and order. The American law school and those who teach law are equally culpable for the scourge of prosecutorial overreach that plagues the criminal justice system. What happens in American law schools, what legal scholars publish and teach in those schools, is just as important, if not more important, than how criminal law is practiced. Where Black men are concerned, the criminal prosecutor, the American law school, and legal scholars (law professors) are metaphors for this punitive regime, negatively affecting the lives of Black men, that exists all over the United States. In other words, the relationship between Black men and the United States is an extension of the relationship between Black men and the criminal justice system, especially that side of the system whose task it is to prosecute criminal defendants. The analysis that follows is concerned with the realm of criminal law, especially legal scholarship and teaching. However, this analysis is relevant to other arenas in the realm of higher education where it is applicable.

The above concerns about prosecutors are crystallized in the recent work of a legal scholar and former federal prosecutor, Paul Butler. In his 2017 book *Chokehold (The Policing of Black Men): A Renegade Prosecutor's Thoughts on How to Disrupt the System*, Butler writes and positions himself as a male feminist and progressive legal scholar, someone who purports to be sensitive to the extra-punitive nature of the criminal justice system as it relates to Black men.[4] *Chokehold* is an effort which engages various dimensions of criminal justice and its treatment of Black men. It is a sobering account of the challenges that Black men confront when entangled by this extra-punitive system. In *Chokehold*, Butler posits a viewpoint that sees no future for reform or transformation of the criminal justice system. Butler treats the American criminal justice system as an immutable and infallible enterprise which defies all expressions of critique and resistance. In his view, social justice advocates who seek to reform or abolish the criminal justice system are understood as short-sighted and naïve. *Chokehold* is a book that is written with good intentions. However, its conclusions about the American criminal justice system and the legal status of Black American men are less than emancipating. More significantly, *Chokehold* is a book which, from beginning to end, is plagued with the historic fears and perceptions that haunt Black men. A book written by a Black man on Black men, *Chokehold* is tainted with a *demonic imaginary*, a socially constructed view of evil, projected upon Black men. His legal perspective as a Black male feminist, or more pointedly, a carceral feminist, bolsters a thoroughly demonic outlook on Black men's relationship to the criminal justice system and, by extension, American society. Butler's feminist perspective on Black men, which collaborates with the carceral state, gives greater rationalization and justification for the endless surveillance, policing, and mass incarceration of Black men and boys.[5] As I will demonstrate in the remaining pages of this chapter, Paul Butler, a former federal prosecutor and law professor, is no *Renegade*. He is not a progressive ally of criminalized Black men.

COLONIALISM AND CRIMINAL JUSTICE

In 2010, it was the legal scholar and lawyer Michelle Alexander who introduced the idea of caste and the caste system as a way of addressing matters of criminal justice in the United States.[6] In doing so, she offered clear markers for determining which parts of the American population are most vulnerable to this racial caste system. Her initial efforts focused on young Black men, mired in poverty who were casualties of the War on Drugs. In *The New Jim*

Crow: Mass Incarceration in an Age of Colorblindness, Alexander made a clear distinction between those whom the criminal justice harms and those who benefit from its existence (and reason for being). In this vein, what is clear is the difference and distance between those who run and administer the criminal justice system and those who are managed by it. Those who manage and administer the imperatives of the criminal justice system, which includes African American law enforcement officials, are among a different class and even a different caste from Black Americans who are subject to the punitive machinations of the system. These administrators work in the best interest of this system, invested in its maintenance, and are rewarded for upholding its values. The fact that Black Americans are among the criminal justice administrators is inconsequential to the problem of mass incarceration in America. In fact, recent legal scholarship has demonstrated, especially that of Pulitzer Prize-winning legal scholar James Forman, that Black Americans who work as criminal justice administrators do not administer justice in ways that significantly distinguish them from their White counterparts.[7] In fact, at some levels, such administrators are more punitive than their White peers. In other words, Black American judges, prosecutors, correctional officers, and police officers are not qualitatively more fair and just than White Americans tasked with the same jobs. The celebrated journalism and autobiographical writings of Ta-Nehisi Coates, which gives an account of criminal justice in predominately Black American Baltimore, Maryland and Washington, DC, also attests to this state of affairs.[8] Where Baltimore, Maryland, is concerned, there is an entire genre of journalism as well as fictive writings and made-for-cable television accounts, particularly those dramatic series produced by Home Box Office (The Corner, The Wire, and We Own This City) which affirm this narrative. In relation to Michelle Alexander's racial caste interpretations, what we essentially have is a system of criminal justice whose administrators do not represent a vulnerable racial caste group. Rather, we have a system of criminal justice whose managers are members of a racial caste hierarchy. In contrast to lower caste and outer caste groups who are swept away by the punitive arm of the criminal justice system, we have higher and upper-caste groups whose work is to oil the machinery of the criminal justice system and are rewarded in the process. Judges and prosecutors are the chief symbols of this upper-caste group. The manner in which these managers administer justice reflects the interests of this group as it preserves the criminal justice system as it is. Michelle Alexander's provocative thesis on racial caste was not extended to the criminal justice administrators in question. However, for the purposes of this book and chapter, it is necessary to illuminate the work, role, and imperative of criminal justice administrators along racial caste lines. The vast body of thinking on colonialism and anti-colonialism, produced over the last several decades is useful for this enterprise.[9] Such colonial/racial caste thinking, more than traditions of Anglocentric American democratic thought and philosophy, is more beneficial. Anglocentric American democratic thought has demonstrated, historically and consistently, an aversion to colonial and more significantly, racial caste analysis. The Anglocentric American Democratic tradition, with its pretensions to exceptionalism and social mobility, despite the contradicting force of anti-Blackness, has refused to admit that a phenomenon of racial caste exists in the United States. What is more, the Black American version of this tradition has been equally reluctant to identify the differences in social and economic status, within the Black American population, along these lines. One of the contributions of Michelle Alexander's work is that the force of mass incarceration exposes real differences between the most criminalized Black Americans, those penalized the most, and those Black Americans who are barely touched by the criminal justice system. Decades after the legislative achievements of the Civil Rights and Black Power eras, the internal status differences (education, income, and close proximity to the White ruling class) among Black Americans are hard to ignore.[10] For this reason, a Black American who is an administrator in the criminal justice system, a prosecutor or a judge, must be viewed in this light. Such figures are colonial elites, authority figures, who occupy an exceptional space in America's racial caste system. The law professor and former federal prosecutor, Paul Butler, is a member of this late twentieth century and early twenty-first century colonized elite. This elite class of Black Americans who are formally educated professionals are analogous to those Brahmin elites on the subcontinent of India during the period of British imperialism. Such elites occupied special positions and possessed exceptional status during India's subjection to the colonial imperatives of the British Empire.

Before and leading up to the twentieth-century political movements which resulted in India's independence from the British Empire, a significant element from this class was not in opposition to Great Britain's dominance and control over India's resources. In contrast, they served as useful managers and guardians of British interests in India. Their positions as administrators of British colonial interests were heightened and exacerbated by their position within the Hindu Caste System. Their obeisance to the British Empire was not distant from their loyalty to the Hindu Caste System.[11] In his book, *Chokehold*, Paul Butler ruminated on the relationship between Black men and the criminal justice system in the United States. In doing so, he was deferential to the American criminal justice system in such a way that echoed the deference of Brahmin elites under British rule in India as well as their submission to the Hindu Caste System. Butler wrote as a legal scholar and former federal prosecutor who cautioned Black men against contesting the criminal justice system in the United States, including all of its racist justifications for the policing, incarceration, and extermination of Black men in the United States.

What is more, Butler articulated an uncritical deference to feminist ideology as a way of policing the efforts of Black men as they sought to overcome a caste-like condition in the United States.[12] His feminist and legal perspective echoed the manner in which upper-caste Brahmin elites policed the activities of lower-caste and outer-caste groups in India. His deference to and promotion of feminist ideology as an arbiter and referee of the condition of Black men harkened back to and replicated a nineteenth-century colonial imagination which sought absolute dominance and control over the lives and political interests of Black men. In *Chokehold*, Butler is neglectful of the history of ideas in America and the West writ large that connects US feminism with British colonialism and other forms of European imperialism.[13] Such connections represent the basic flaw in his work. Such connections tainted his purported concerns for Black men and their relation to the criminal justice system in the United States.

Interestingly, there is a great irony to the imperial and colonial impulse that guides Paul Butler's treatment of Black men and the criminal justice system. His submission to colonial and imperial imperatives stands in stark contrast with his own life experience as an adult Black man, which includes personal run-ins with criminal justice system, not as a prosecutor within the system but as a criminal defendant in it. In *Chokehold* and other outlets, Butler recounts and has reported a criminalizing experience during his tenure as federal prosecutor where he was once falsely accused of a crime. The nature and gravity of this accusation compelled him to stand as his own defense attorney during a criminal proceeding, including a criminal trial. Butler was successful in beating this criminal case.[14] However, his experience speaks volumes to the extent to which Black men are policed and prosecuted in the United States. It also speaks to the hard fact that no Black man, including a member of the Brahmin elite, is immune to the process of criminally prosecuting Black men. Tragically, Butler's personal experience as a criminal defendant for a crime he did not commit has not led him to an outright condemnation of the criminal justice system and the ideological and cultural systems in place which justify it. Rather, his work as a prosecutor who happens to be a Black American man compelled him to admonish Black men to accept and submit to the punitive authority and machinations of the criminal justice system.

DEMONIC THREATS TO BLACK WOMEN: BLACK MEN AND FEMINIST POLICING

Throughout this book, I have echoed the socially constructed phenomenon of evil which I call the *demonic imaginary* as it relates to Black men. This imaginary permeates the thinking of Paul Butler. Again, Butler's perspective is that of a former federal prosecutor and a Georgetown law professor. He is also a Black male feminist. In what is supposed to be an intervention in relation to Black men and the criminal justice system, Butler gives ideological fodder, justification for the very system which punishes Black men. Butler promotes intersectional feminism which places a high premium on limiting state and private-sponsored interventions that bring attention to the predicament of Black men. As I will demonstrate shortly, Butler's feminist perspective on Black men is similar to the perspectives of White Americans, in the past and in the present, who have opposed civil rights protections for Black Americans. It is also similar to the perspectives of those Americans, from varying backgrounds, who are hostile to affirmative action policies as they are applied to Black Americans. In a word, Paul Butler articulates a viewpoint on Black men that is illiberal and highly restrictive. In Butler's worldview, Black men must always be policed and efforts to ameliorate their criminalized condition must be held under intense surveillance. Feminist ideas about men in general and Black men in particular drive Butler's limited and reductive view of Black men. For Butler, Black men must be subject to feminist policing, for such men stand as constant threats to women, Black women in particular. Due to the perceived threatening status of Black men and those efforts to overcome their criminalized condition, too much attention has been devoted to the plight of Black men at the expense of interventions needed for Black women. In contrast to Black women, Butler regards the plight and victimization of Black men as an overwhelming source of political currency which has the potential to eclipse the plight and victimization of Black American women. Butler's intersectional feminist reasoning is tied to a dominant strand of thinking among feminists and gender theorists who are largely indifferent and hostile to the problems of men, especially Black men, as it is perceived to impede the empowerment of Black American women.[15] For intersectional feminists and gender theorists, the problems of women, Black women in particular, are more significant and more profound than those of Black men. In other words, Black women's victimization is profound and exceptional. Hence, any undue attention to the problems of men, Black men in particular, is harmful to Black women.[16] In *Chokehold*, through an espousal of intersectional feminism in relation to past, present, and future interventions that seek to positively impact Black men and boys, Butler warns against any interventions in relation to Black men which he regards as dangerous to Black women and girls. In doing so, he criticizes interventive efforts aimed at Black men which frame Black men as a population in crisis, a group whose existence is under constant threat, including extinction. Along these lines, Butler states the following:

> The rhetoric about black men as an endangered species must be dismissed. Black male intersectionality is a more accurate way of conceptualizing the

issues. It acknowledges that Black men have specific issues, but they are not worse than Black women's and do not require a hierarchy that displaces black women and girls . . . Black male programs should be closely examined to eradicate any hint of anti-female ideology or practice . . . Understanding male privilege means acknowledging that black men's issues have been historically prioritized over black women's issues. Black male interventions should create space for African American women to be racial standard-bearers, a conversation that would position poverty and reproductive freedom as racial issues, in the way that advocates for black men have already done with criminal justice. Attention to women's issues is justified in part because African American men have been complicit in their subordination. Black men are still men. The scholar Michael Eric Dyson notes, "If we have a glorified sense of our own victimization as black and brown men, what we must not miss and what we often to, is to understand that black and brown women themselves are so victimized, not only by white patriarchy but by black male supremacy and by the violence of masculinity that is directed toward them."[17]

Notice what Butler says, "Attention to women's issues is justified in part because African American men have been complicit in their subordination. Black men are still men." For added support he invokes the words of the public intellectual Michael Eric Dyson for whom "black male supremacy" and the "violence of masculinity" is the proper way for engaging the predicament of Black men. Butler holds a view of Black men that is categorial, unqualified, undifferentiated, and wrought with danger. It is tainted by a *demonic imaginary*. Butler's intersectional thinking is troubling. It is deficient, misguided, and uninformed in light of our current twenty-first-century context and the magnitude and plethora of challenges which Black men and boys face on a daily basis in the United States.[18] This condition entails far more than the subordination of women on the part of men and their perceived threats to women. Butler's perspective on Black men is a diminishment of and flies in the face of current social, economic, and political conditions, unrelated to male sexism and misogyny, which contest his ideological assertions and assumptions.[19] This quoted articulation by Butler found in *Chokehold*, located in chapter 5, Do the Brothers Need Keepers? How Some Black Male Programs Perpetuate the Chokehold, is where his intersectional perspective is explicit and pronounced. What is even more troubling about Butler's intersectional perspective is the moment when it appeared, in 2016, during *The Decade of Death (2012–2022)* when *Chokehold* was published. Butler is convinced that Black men as a group occupy positions of male privilege and power. Such privilege and power are assumed to be self-evident with no need for substantiation and elucidation. Based on his conclusions, one is compelled to ask the empirical question, What exactly is Black male privilege and Black male power in relation to *The Decade of Death (2012–2022)*, a period characterized by homicide, the murders of Black men and boys at the hands of private citizens and law enforcement, from Trayvon Martin in 2012 to Michael Brown in 2014 to George Floyd and Amhad Arbery in 2020? When thinking about the horrific and spectacled murder of George Floyd at the hands of a police officer in the summer of 2020, an event which set off protests all over the world, how does one make sense of Butler's intersectional feminist perspective? What type of Black male privilege and power, especially patriarchal power, did George Floyd possess, a man who begged for his life as he was executed by a Minneapolis police officer, a homicide that was caught on camera and uploaded to the Internet for the entire world to see and consume? The spectacled police killing of George Floyd and the long list of Black male deaths at the hands of private citizens and law enforcement officers, over a decade, which produced the movement Black Lives Matter, is too long to list here. In light of *The Decade of Death (2012–2022)*, Butler's intersectional logic with respect to Black men strikes me as ridiculous and absurd! How *The Decade of Death (2012–2022)* has any relationship to and is relevant to concerns regarding male sexism and misogyny and male dominance (the subordination of Black women) is nonsensical to me.

The reader should know that Butler's intersectional perspective outlined in chapter 5 of *Chokehold* was first published as an academic article, under a different title, in 2013 and then later included in this 2016 book. A *demonic imaginary* in relation to Black masculinity colors the entire article.[20] Again, where the *demonic imaginary* is concerned, Butler promotes longstanding myths about Black men, beliefs about the status of Black men that are devoid of any substantive socio-economic and political analysis pertaining to the material conditions that impact the lives of Black men and boys in the United States. Although his work seeks to speak to a twenty-first-century American context, Butler's line of reasoning is eerily reminiscent of the worst thinking about Black men and race in the United States. It echoes perspectives on Black men, popularized after the Civil War which persisted into the early decades of the twentieth century. Black men were targeted for death through terrorism, castrations, and lynchings as a consequence of these perspectives.[21] As I have indicated in other places in this book, this anti-Black mythology has existed for more than a century.[22] It was later reinvented and reignited at the end of the twentieth century, during the Civil Rights and Black Power Era. It took on a unique form after the 1970s, with the rise of second-wave feminism. It has remained a dominant mythology from the 1970s to the present. In this racial mythology, Black men are imagined as aspiring patriarchs who are abject in nature and possess pretensions to despotism. As imagined demonic patriarchs, Black men seek the same power and status as ruling-class White men. In this patriarchal mythology, there are no qualitative distinctions to be made between Black men as a group and ruling class White men, as a group.

In this undifferentiated understanding of race, masculinity, and patriarchy, Black men are accorded power, status, and authority that cannot be substantiated or verified by historical and contemporary empirical data. In promoting this racialized mythological patriarchal perspective on Black men, Butler's arguments are fundamentally *moral* and *ideological*. When Butler uses data, his employment of empirical evidence is slim, narrow, suspect, and selective. In this chapter in *Chokehold*, Butler goes to great lengths to refute the claim that Black men have a unique status as victims in the United States. In many respects, this one chapter in *Chokehold*, on intersectionality, refutes the limited yet interventive aims of his entire book. Overall, his refutation of what he terms *Black Male Exceptionalism* is drenched in fear and female protectionism, the protection of Black women in particular and women writ large.

LONG MEMORY: ADDITIONAL HERMENEUTICAL CONSIDERATIONS WITH RESPECT TO HISTORIC WHITE SUPREMACY AND THE POLICING OF BLACK MEN

In profound respects, the *demonic imaginary* in operation in Butler's application of intersectional feminism to the lives and challenges of Black men reads as a complete erasure of the plight and victimization of Black men. Those who read Butler's intersectional feminist treatment of Black men and take it seriously, especially those among the power elite of the United States, lawmakers and policy makers, are given a license to do nothing to intervene in the plight and victimization of Black men. Because Black men are not different from ruling-class White men in their aspirations and quests for power, their condition is not worthy of massive resources with the aim of addressing their predicament. Butler's *demonic imagination* is baseless and founded upon utter speculation. The imagined patriarchal status of Black men, which has been replicated in and perpetuated by feminist thought, for the last fifty years, is pure mythology.[23] It is ahistorical, overly ideological, and profoundly anti-intellectual. To reiterate an earlier point, Butler's intersectional treatment of Black men is consistent with White nationalist thinking about Black men which emerged after the Civil War. This is a history that is worthy of repeating and remembering (over and over again). It is important for the reader to know that in the United States, we have a history of horror and terror involving angry White men, who ascended all across the southern part of the United States, who sought to punish Black people, Black men, in particular, for the blood fest of the Civil War. These White redeemers are responsible for the creation of Jim Crow, a bifurcated anti-Black society along racial lines. These redeemers created an anti-Black mythology which imagined Black men as threats to White society, especially White women. Animated with a *demonic imaginary,* they created legal and cultural barriers intended to contain this threat. The redeemers often went a step further and exterminated their imagined threats, Black men. From the 1880s to the 1960s, Black Americans in general and Black men in particular were the main objects of terrorism. The most famous depiction of the perceived threat of Black men in relation to this history is D.W. Griffith's 1915 film, *Birth of a Nation.*[24] I am sure that Paul Butler, a Black man, would shudder at the comparisons that are being made here. I am sure that he would say that being a legal scholar and former prosecutor, a Black man, he is working in the service of justice, law, and order. In light of America's anti-Black past, it should be remembered that the early to mid-twentieth century White nationalists that terrorized Black men for close to a century also saw themselves as guardians and protectors of law and order. From my reading of American history and contemporary politics, it appears that the intersectional feminism promoted by Paul Butler and White nationalism look like strange bedfellows. This comparison may sound absurd and even strange to some readers, but both, when analyzed seriously, in relation to Black men, come together in a joint effort to subordinate and keep Black men in their respective places. Both ideologies (White Nationalism and American feminism) have the protection of women in common. Where the *demonic imaginary* is concerned, both White nationalism and intersectional feminism are fundamentally anti-Black male. As I have stated earlier, Butler's appeals to feminism are oblivious to the anti-Black history of feminism in the United States. It does not consider the legacy of racism in feminist thinking and activism that goes back to the suffrage movement of the nineteenth century.[25] It is also ignorant of past and present critiques of feminism, White feminism in particular, on the part of Black women and Brown women (feminists) which indicts the marriage between racism and feminism in America. Among the non-White critics of feminism was the late bell hooks.[26] Her career-long criticisms of White feminism have been followed by younger generations of women who scrutinize feminism as a White women's enterprise that is indifferent to anti-Black racism. As I write this chapter, academic articles and books under the banner of White feminism (as a racist enterprise) are now a staple in feminist literature. This should be kept in mind when considering Butler's employment of the work of Catherine MacKinnon, a profoundly influential legal scholar and radical feminist whose work has influenced more than one generation of legal scholars and practitioners of law. Butler uncritically defers to MacKinnon's radical feminist views on men and masculinity and applies it to Black men. This is tragic in light of the fact that MacKinnon's perspective has been contested by White feminist scholars.[27]

PRIMITIVE AND OBSOLETE: ARCHAIC THINKING ABOUT BLACK MEN

The major flaw at the heart of Paul Butler's thinking regarding Black men and the criminal justice system are the claims he makes about the privileged position of Black men in African American politics. In *Chokehold*, Butler forwards the unquestioned proposition that the collective condition of Black men in the United States has been a major preoccupation of Black American politics and activism. As such, this preoccupation reflects the power and impact of sexism in African American politics and activism. As I stated at the outset of this chapter, Butler's maintains that an excessive focus on the condition of Black men has subordinated the condition and situation of Black American women, that the dilemmas of Black American women have been and are overshadowed by those of Black men. Moreover, any imagined or actual social, legal, and political intervention undertaken on behalf of Black men, will of necessity, marginalize, crush, or erase interventive efforts directed at Black women. In terms of criminal justice, what this means is that Black men who are arrested, prosecuted, and incarcerated in far greater numbers than Black women get far greater attention than Black women who are also targets/subjects of criminal justice reform and prison abolition efforts (although greater numbers do warrant the attention). Accordingly, any and all efforts to address the condition of Black men must be circumscribed by the plight of Black women. As was intimated earlier, Paul Butler's assessments of Black men reflect a dominant flaw in decades of ideological reasoning in how social disparities exist and how such disparities should be addressed in the United States. It is indebted to a dominant impulse (over the last fifty years) within feminist thought and gender ideology writ large which regards all disparities between all men and women in absolute terms. However, this type of thinking, in the 2020s and beyond, does a major disservice to the particularities of the Black American condition in the United States, that such gendered thinking does more harm than good. This type of thinking, which has been protected from rigorous historical and empirical scrutiny, creates tensions and antagonisms where such tensions and antagonisms do not have to exist. What this means in terms of the predicament of Black men and Black women is that it is quite possible to promote robust interventions, separate and distinct, for Black men and Black women simultaneously, without one negating the other. Neither group has to be in competition for substantive redress for their respective social conditions. In order for this to happen, it is necessary to discard, overcome, and render primitive and obsolete this type of unnecessary bifurcated reasoning. A new century such as ours demands a new calculus with respect to how we think about Black men and Black women.

UNCONTESTED DEMONIC NARRATIVES: QUESTIONING THE FEMINIST POLICE

Overall, Butler's claim that Black American politics and activism has preoccupied itself with Black men's interests and conditions at the expense of the situation of Black women belongs to a decades-long Black feminist narrative of Black women's victimization and invisibility. This narrative has been propagated for half a century and is used to impede and obstruct efforts intended to intervene in the predicament of Black men. This Black feminist narrative that Butler promotes has not been held to critical scrutiny and has gone unchallenged as divine truth. This narrative is filled with grandiose assumptions about the historic political priorities of Black Americans in relation to the lives of Black men. It is also fraught with erroneous assumptions about Black American advocacy and politics in relation to Black American women. In short, Black men are painted as privileged class group in Black society and America writ large and such privilege has resulted in levels of recognition and redress that surpasses and eclipses Black women. It also underplays and minimizes the enormous efforts, which have been made over the last five decades, to address the specific conditions that affect Black American women. The Black feminist narrative that informs Butler's treatment of Black men which was crafted during the 1970s and 1980s and was largely a response to the Black political movements of the 1960s.[28] This Black feminist narrative was fraught with problems when it was initially conceived and articulated and remains, decades later, a flawed perspective on the manner in which Black American politics and activism addresses the unique dilemmas of Black men and the particular challenges which face Black women.[29] As far as contemporary times are concerned, I regard the Black feminist narrative that informs Butler's thinking as anti-historical and mythical. It is simply not true that Black Americans, as a group, and Black politics and activism, in particular, have placed a low priority on the lives of Black women. Black American activism and politics have never been exclusively concerned with the empowerment of Black men.

As I have indicated above, the Black feminist narrative of oppression was created during and after the 1970s, by second-wave Black feminists. Such Black feminists were critical of charismatic Black male leadership during the Civil Rights and Black Power Eras. Characterizing such men as chauvinist and committed to male supremacy, they were imagined as men who were committed to censoring the voices and concerns of Black women. Among the second-wave representatives of this position are Beverly Guy Sheftall and Johnetta Cole. Their 2003 book *Gender Talk: The Struggle for Women's Equality in African American Communities* encapsulates this position.[30] More recently, during *The Decade of Death (2012–2022)*, this same perspective was taken up in 2018 by political scientist Barbara Ransby in *Making All Black Lives Matter: Reimagining Freedom in the 21st Century*.[31] Ironically, this Black feminist narrative of oppression is contrasted by a competing narrative of Black women's agency. This narrative of agency is forwarded by women of the same generation as well as women slightly younger than Sheftall and Cole. Black women scholars such as Evelyn Brooks Higginbotham, Marcia Riggs, Rosetta Ross, Emily Townes, Delores S. Williams, and Patricia Hill Collins have, since the 1980s, produced significant works on Black women's activism over the centuries.[32] More recently, new histories of Black women have appeared which refute the idea that Black women have been neglected as victims of American history and anti-Black racism, bereft of agency and devoid of recognition, that Black women's lives and concerns have always been marginal to Black men's concerns.[33] Simply stated, since the days of the abolitionist Harriet Tubman, Black women's interests and concerns as well as their activism on behalf of *all* Black Americans have been an integral part of African American politics and advocacy. From the antebellum period to the twentieth century, with figures such as Ida B. Wells, Helen Nannie Burroughs, Mary Mcleod Bethune, Amy Jacque Garvey, Pauli Murray, and Ella Baker, Black American women have shaped Black American activism and politics. It is logically impossible to survey the long history of Black American women's activism and walk away with the conclusion that Black American women have been neglected by and subordinated within the history of Black American activism. Overall, Paul Butler's narrow and selective reading of Black American politics and activism is shameful.

THE FALLIBLE BLACK MALE FEARS OF A LEGAL EXPERT

In profound ways, Butler's thinking about Black women is myopic and provincial. It is bound to what I regard as a primitive view of Black Americans, that Black Americans still exist in a pre-Civil Rights condition, living on a racial island untouched by the societal changes which have affected the United States since the assassination of Martin Luther King, Jr. It traffics in a view of Black Americans that ignores the unprecedented fragmentation of Black America, over the last forty years, which has produced major gaps in terms of income, education, and social mobility between and among Black Americans. These gaps are reflected in the very life outcomes of Black men and Black women. As I have stated in chapter five, these gaps are indicative of a two-tier condition, radical bifurcation, in relation to Black women and Black men. The gaps have been engineered, deliberately, by the interests of the White ruling class in the United States. There is virtually no substantive analysis of social class and caste analysis in Butler's view of Black men in relation to Black women. There is no acknowledgment of the extent to which Black women as a group have been incorporated into White capitalist America. In a word, Butler's thinking is dishonest, deceptive, and absurd in relation to the twenty-first century moment that we are in. The reader should also note that Butler's book, *Chokehold*, was published during an election year where Hillary Clinton ran as the Democratic nominee for the US presidency. The presidential race of 2016 marked Hillary Clinton's second effort at running as a candidate for the US presidency. Both of her attempts at the Oval Office are not fathomable apart from the changes that have taken place in American society which elevated and expanded the status of women. At the moment that this chapter is being written, a Black woman, Kamala Harris, resides in the Oval Office as the first woman to ever serve as Vice President of the United States. Two decades into the twenty-first century, Butler ignores the current status of women, particularly Black women, in the United States. Butler is negligent of the extent to which Black women are among American women whose status has been elevated and enhanced in unprecedented ways. What Butler omits in his account of Black women and intersectional feminism is the liberalization of the United States over the last half century and the historic incorporation of women into the dominant institutions of United States. The status of Black women in America has been positively impacted by 50 years of liberalization which includes their incorporation into White capitalist America, at all levels of American society. In fact, the very intersectional feminist ideology Butler espouses is also a part of this incorporation. In fact, since it was initially conceived by Kimberle Crenshaw, the legal scholar, over three decades ago, intersectionality has been a useful tool in facilitating the incorporation of Black women into the dominant institutions of the United States. Bolstered by civil rights legislation and the enormous push by American corporations and political elites, the incorporation of women since the 1970s pales in comparison to incorporation of Black men. From K-12 education to colleges and universities to corporations and white-collar professions, there has been no dearth of efforts to bring women and girls in the mainstream of White capitalist America. Such facts are not considered in Butler's thinking about Black men (It is hardly a consideration in any wave of feminist thought in the United States). In his critique of Black men, Butler cites and magnifies former president Barack Obama's men of color initiative, My Brother's Keeper, as a major intervention.[34] My Brother's Keeper was a philanthropic endeavor, experimental in nature, launched during Obama's tenure as President of the United States, which was not tied to tax dollars and the federal government. In Butler's invocation of My Brother's Keeper as an example of the privileged treatment of Black men, he failed to acknowledge The White House Council on Women and Girls, the governmental entity, set up for women and girls, by the Obama Administration, led by a Black woman, Valerie Jarrett.[35] President Obama's My Brother's Keeper initiative was in no way comparable to The White House Counsel on Women and Girls, a federal entity which thrived during Obama's two-term tenure as POTUS. In the 2020s, advocacy for Black men and boys is in no way comparable to over four decades of advocacy for women and girls, including Black women and girls.

Paul Butler's criticism of private and state-related initiatives which seek to address the plight of Black men and boys is disingenuous in relation to policies, programs, and initiatives dedicated to women's empowerment, all women, all over the United States. It is dishonest in relation to a political economy driven by diversity and inclusion with women (including Black women) being the primary targets of diversity and inclusion initiatives. This broader political economy of diversity and inclusion that targets women is of gargantuan proportions in relation to the paucity of initiatives Butler highlights which seek to impact Black men. In a word, the political economy of diversity and inclusion does not target Black men as a group. In fact, there is overwhelming evidence to the contrary, that such an economy is hostile to Black men as a group.[36] In fact, the manner in which the White ruling class, its philanthropy, and corporations responded to the Black women-led Black Lives Matter movement is a decade-long instance of this condition. Overall, at the level of advocacy, Butler's trite comparative treatment of Black men and Black women ignores the enormous irreconcilable differences between the material lives of Black men and Black women in America. At the levels of education and socioeconomic status, Black men as a group have very little in common with all groups of women in the United States, including Black American women.

In the final chapters of *Chokehold*, chapters 6 and 8, Paul Butler articulates much skepticism in relation to the prison abolition movement and grassroots efforts to reform the criminal justice system.[37] He is sensitive to the goals of this work but is unpersuaded that such efforts will have any real impact on the criminal justice system in the United States. For Butler, Black men are stuck with a biased system of criminal justice which is overly punitive to Black men. He implores Black men to avoid this system at all costs and when entangled by its snares to not aggressively contest it, even if legal misconduct has taken place. Butler's perspective on prison abolition and criminal justice reform is not commendable and is worthy of criticism in light of the aims of these efforts and all of the concerns outlined in this chapter. Butler's perspective on the criminal justice system in relation to Black men protects this very system from rigorous scrutiny and interrogation. It guards the entire administrative apparatus including the legal experts connected to it. In contrast to Butler's position, prison abolitionists and activists who seek criminal justice reform treat the criminal justice system as a mutable and fallible enterprise. It treats criminal jurisprudence, those who administer the law, and those who teach it as human actors. It must be stated emphatically that the entire criminal justice system and the administrative machine connected to it is, "man-made." Because judges, prosecutors, and legal experts are not divine agents sanctioned by heavenly authority, calls for a thorough reassessment of the system including the revision and abolition of laws and legal practices are warranted. The prison abolitionist movement and movements to reform the criminal justice system are responsible for the current spotlight that is placed on bad actors, judges and prosecutors, who engage in deliberate legal misconduct. In acknowledging the fallibility of legal experts, it is necessary to place such experts under the same level of scrutiny as those who are targets of its extra punitive aims, particularly Black men. The same level of effort, energy, and investment devoted to the policing and prosecution of Black men should be applied to judges, prosecutors, and other legal actors who administer criminal justice in the United States. If this system of justice were policed and subject to the same checks and balances as Black men as a group, the aims of prison abolitionists and those who seek to reform the criminal justice system would not seem far-fetched. The complete overhaul of the criminal justice system would not seem out of the realm of possibility. More significantly, in the United States, there is a very real history and tradition of jurisprudence where laws and legal practices, once treated as immutable, were changed. The history of revision, related to the US Constitution, is evidence of this very fact. It is necessary to invoke this history when shedding light on the fallible dimensions of jurisprudence in the United States. When this history is taken into consideration in light of the legacy of anti-Blackness in the United States and those historic efforts to change and overturn existing laws, the gravity of policing the criminal justice system is amplified. To this end, it is important to invoke the work of Critical Race Theorists. Among those theorists is the late legal scholar, Derrick Bell. Critical Race Theory exposes the deep fissures of anti-Black racism in the American legal system.[38]

CONCLUSION

As I indicated in the first chapter of the book, there is a dire need to reassess and even overhaul postmodern theories of social justice which came out of the decades of the 1980s and 1990s. These postmodern theories of social justice are highly suspect in terms of their applicability to our contemporary context. Paul Butler is a part of that generation who was formally educated and became a professional, a federal prosecutor, as these theories became popular. Intersectional feminism emerged in this period. These theories are largely responsible for how he views American law and the legal system writ large and how he views the condition of Black men in the United States. Overall, my concerns about the fallibility of criminal prosecutors and legal experts are connected to the postmodern theories of justice which became popular at the end of the twentieth century. The postmodern theory of intersectionality, which was produced by a legal scholar, Kimberle Crenshaw, during this moment and enjoys popularity today, is not an infallible and uncontestable postmodern theory of justice. Like all legal theories and the overall construction of law, it is an all-too-human product of space and time. To neglect, dismiss, and ignore the time-bound nature of such legal thinking and its application to the production and practice of law is to commit the same errors which American prosecutors have been found guilty of over the last decade. More importantly, it ignores those monumental shifts in law and legal thinking which have taken place at various points in the history of the United States. The most profound among these shifts occurred after the Civil War with historic Amendments that were added to the US Constitution and the reversal of the US Supreme Court decision in the landmark case *Plessy v. Ferguson* in the 1954 decision *Brown v. Board of Education*.[39] Dramatic changes in American law were amplified during the 1960s with the historic passage of civil rights legislation, including the Civil Rights Act of 1964 and the Civil Rights Act of 1965.[40] These instances combined point to the fallible nature of law, legal thinking, and the time-bound nature of justice in American society. These facts of history teach us that no institution, legal or otherwise, and no body of legal thought, regardless of how well-intended, stands outside of history.

In the 2020s and beyond, the fallibility of law and that of legal experts is a serious matter in light of *The Decade of Death (2012–2022)*. Over the course of a decade, with the aid of technology, social media, the errors endemic to the law have been exposed. In prior eras, the writing of journalists exposed the problems of the law. Today, camera phones and platforms such as YouTube, Twitter, and Facebook are vehicles for images and information which give public exposure to problems such as prosecutorial misconduct. New technologies have elevated the necessity and veracity of public scrutiny of the American legal system, especially the criminal justice system. Such public scrutiny is worthy of amplification. Public surveillance of our legal system, especially at the criminal justice level, is a necessary mark of citizenship. Such policing has been at the heart of those movements to reform the criminal justice system and abolition of the prison system in the United States. Additionally, those who are most vulnerable to the errors of the legal system are more than warranted in participating in the public critique of this system. What this means is that Paul Butler's admonitions to Black men to not contest the criminal justice system are found wanting. They are tainted by the fear of Black men in America. Such advice, admonitions, and recommendations, rooted in the fear of Black men, should be condemned.

NOTES

1. Erik Nielson and Andrea L. Dennis, *Rap on Trial: Race, Lyrics, and Guilt in America* (New York: The New Press, 2019).
2. See Angela J. Davis, Ed. *Policing the Black Man* (New York: Pantheon Books, 2017). Also, see Ben Crump, *Open Season: The Legal Genocide of Colored People* (New York: Harper Collins Publishers, 2019).
3. The Innocence Project, founded in 1989 by attorneys Barry Scheck and Peter Neufeld, has been a major leader in exposing legal misconduct in the criminal justice system. See *Innocent: The Fight Against Wrongful Convictions, Time Magazine* (Special Edition) (New York: Time Inc. Books, 2017).
4. Paul Butler, *Chokehold (Policing Black Men): A Renegade Prosecutor's Thoughts on How to Disrupt the System* (New York: The New Press, 2016).
5. Readers of Chokehold are introduced to Butler's male feminist perspective in the book's introduction, Broke on Purpose. His male feminist perspective is outlined in length in chapter 5, Do Brothers Need Keepers? How Some Black Male Programs Perpetuate the Chokehold. My argument in this chapter is that Butler's analysis of the Chokehold, a method used by law enforcement to police and control Black men, is applicable to the intersectional feminist perspective that Butler espouses. From this standpoint, intersectional feminism is an expression of carceral feminism which views Black men as threats to women and other populations. As threats to women and other populations, Black men must be contained. Intersectional feminism perpetuates the very Chokehold that concerns Butler's book.
6. Michelle Alexander, *The New Jim Crow: Mass Incarceration in the Age of Colorblindness*, 10th Anniversary Edition (New York and London: The New Press, 2020).
7. James Forman, Jr., *Locking Up Our Own: Crime and Punishment in Black America* (New York: Farrar, Straus, and Giroux, 2017).
8. See Ta-Nehisi Coates, *Between the World and Me* (New York: Spiegal & Graus, 2015); *The Beautiful Struggle: A Memoir* (New York: Spiegal & Grau, 2008); *We Were Eight Years in Power: An American Tragedy* (New York: One World, 2017).
9. For a past and recent instance of anti-colonial and anti-caste thought, see B.R. Ambedkar, *The Annihilation of Caste* (introduction by Arundhati Roy) (London and New York: Verso, 2014).
10. See Eugene Robinson, *Disintegration: The Splintering of Black America* (New York: Anchor Books, 2010).
11. See Ramachandra Guha, Ed. *Makers of Modern India* (Cambridge and London: The Belknap Press of Harvard University Press, 2011). Also see B.R. Ambedkar, Arundhati Roy, and S. Anand, *Annihilation of Caste* (The Annotated Critical Edition) (London and New York: Verso Books, 2016).

12. In Chokehold, Butler's feminist perspective is outlined in the chapter, Do the Brothers Need Keepers? How Some Black Male Programs Perpetuate the Chokehold, pp. 149–70.

13. See Arudhanti Roy, *Capitalism: A Ghost Story* (Chicago: Haymarket Books, 2014); Rafia Zakaria, *Against White Feminism: Notes on Disruption* (New York: W. W. Norton & Company, Inc., 2021); Michelle Louise Newman, *White Women's Rights: The Racial Origins of Feminism in the United States* (New York and Oxford: Oxford University Press, 1999).

14. See Constructing the Thug, chapter one, in Chokehold, pp. 17–46.

15. For decades, the concept of hegemonic masculinity, coined by sociologist R.W. Connell, has been used by feminists and gender theorists to describe the subordination of women. The articulation of women's issues is perceived as under constant threat in relation to this species of masculinity. See R.W. Connell, *Masculinities*, 2nd Edition (Berkely and Los Angeles: University of California Press, 2005).

16. See Kimberly Crenshaw's 1989 legal article, Mapping the Margins: Intersectionality, Identity Politics, and Violence Against Women of Color, *Stanford Law Review*, Vol. 43, No. 6 (July, 1991), pp. 1241–99, https://ww.jstor.org/stable/1229039. This article introduced the concept of intersectionality to legal studies, the humanities, and the social sciences.

17. Butler, *Chokehold*, pp. 168–69.

18. Black American philosopher and Black Male Studies scholar, Tommy J. Curry, is very critical of the intersectional feminism of Paul Butler and that of its founder, Kimberley Crenshaw. His 2017 book, *The Man-Not: Race, Class, Genre, and the Dilemmas of Manhood* (Philadelphia: Temple University Press, 2017), presents new data and an alternative framework to feminist approaches to masculinity. For a detailed discussion of the limitations of intersectionality with respect to Black men, see Not MAN but Some Nothing: Affirming Who I Cannot Be through a Genre Study of Black Male Death and Dying, The Man- Not, pp. 197–228.

19. For a recent account of the socioeconomic condition of Boys and Men in the United States, see Richard V. Reeves, *Of Boys and Men: Why the Modern Male Is Struggling, Why It Matters, and What to Do About It* (Washington, DC: Brookings Institution Press, 2022). Similar to Tommy J. Curry, Reeves presents new data and proposes an alternative framework for engaging the challenges facing men and boys in the twenty-first century. Overcoming longstanding beliefs and assumptions about gender and masculinity is at the heart of this endeavor.

20. Paul Butler, Black Male Exceptionalism? The Problem and Potential of Black Male-Focused Interventions, *Du Bois Review*, Vol. 10, No. 2 (2013), pp. 485–511.

21. For a recent account of this history see historian Jane Dailey's *White Fright: The Sexual Panic at the Heart of America's Racist History* (New York: Hatchet Book Group, Inc., 2020).

22. For an account of anti-Black male mythology from the Civil War to the present, see Riche Richardson, *Black Masculinity and the U.S. South: From Uncle Tom to Gangsta* (Athens and London: University of Georgia Press, 2007).

23. See Tommy Curry.

24. D.W. Griffith, *The Birth of a Nation* (Epoch Producing Corporation, 1915).

25. See Newman, *White Women's Rights*.

26. See bell hooks, *Ain't I A Woman: Black Women and Feminism* (Boston: South End Press, 1981).

27. See Emily Jackson, Catherine MacKinnon and Feminist Jurisprudence: A Critical Appraisal, *Journal of Law and Society*, Vol. 19, No. 2 (Summer, 1992), pp. 195–213, htttps://www.jstor.org/stable/1410220.

28. See Michele Wallace, *Black Macho and the Myth of the Superwoman* (London and New York: Verso Books, 1999).

29. Ibid., The Way I Saw It Then and the Way I See It Now.

30. Johnnetta Betsch Cole and Beverly Guy-Sheftall, *Gender Talk: The Struggle for Women's Equality in African American Communities* (New York and Toronto: One World Books, 2003).

31. Barbara Ransby, *Making All Lives Matter: Reimagining Freedom in the 21st Century* (Oakland: University of California Press, 2018).

32. See Beverly Guy-Sheftall's edited volume, *Words of Fire: An Anthology of African American Feminist Thought* (New York: The New Press, 1995). Also, see Patricia Hills Collins, *Black Feminist Thought: Knowledge, Consciousness, and the Politics of Empowerment*, 2nd Edition (New York: Routledge, 2000).

33. See Daina Ramey Berry and Kali Nicole Gross, *A Black Women's History of the United States* (Boston: Beacon Press, 2020). Also, see Keisha N. Blain, *Until I am Free: Fannie Lou Hamer's Enduring Message to America* (Boston: Beacon Press, 2021).

34. Butler's perspective on President Obama's My Brother's Keeper initiative is couched in his critique of what he calls Black Male Exceptionalism, which I discussed in earlier sections of this chapter.

35. See https://obamawhitehouse.archives.gov/administration/eop/cwp. Also, see https://obamawhitehouse.archives.gov/administration/senior-leadership/valerie-jarrett.

36. See Richard L. Zweigenhaft and G. William Domhoff, *Diversity in the Power Elite: Ironies and Unfulfilled Promises*, 3rd Edition (Lanham: Rowman & Littlefield, 2018).

37. See Butler, *Chokehold*. Chapter 6: Nothing Works: Why the Chokehold Can't Be Reformed, pp. 171–201 and Chapter 8: Woke: Unlocking the Chokehold, pp. 227–50.

38. See Derrick Bell, *Silent Covenants: Brown v. Board of Education and the Unfulfilled Hopes for Racial Reform* (Oxford: Oxford University Press, 2004), *And We Are Not Saved: The Elusive Quest for Racial Justice* (New York: Basic Books, Inc., 1987) and *Faces at the Bottom of the Well: The Permanence of Racism* (New York: Basic Books, Inc., 1992).

39. Ibid., *Plessy's* Long Shadow, pp. 11–13 and *Brown's* Half Light, pp. 14–19.

40. See Randall B. Woods, *Prisoner of Hope: Lyndon B. Johnson and the Limits of Liberalism* (New York: Basic Books, 2016).

Chapter 7

Detox

Purging the Demonic

More than a half-century has passed since the publication of Martin Luther King's classic 1967 book *Where Do We Go From Here: Chaos or Community*.[1] More than five decades after its publication, *Where Do We Go From Here* is not only a classic work in late twentieth-century political thought, it is a testament to a culture of duty and linked fates, which up to that point characterized Black American freedom struggles in the United States. This tradition of linked fates is essentially a cultural, moral, political, and theological sensibility, shared across Black America, that sees Black Americans as a nation within a nation that is tied to an inescapable fate. During the 1990s, Christian ethicist and theologian, Victor Anderson, classified this shared sensibility and destiny as *Ontological Blackness*.[2] The tradition of linked fates suffered a major blow after the assassination of Martin Luther King Jr. The effort to desegregate the United States after the assassination of Martin Luther King Jr., and the subsequent incorporation of a segment of the Black population into mainstream White society led to the gradual disruption of this tradition. In the early 2000s, the dismantling of this tradition was outlined by the late historian and political theorist, Manning Marable, in *The Great Wells of Democracy: The Meaning of Race in American Life*.[3] During the Obama era, the death of this tradition and its impact on Black Americans was documented and articulated by Eugene Robinson of the Washington Post in *Disintegration: The Splintering of Black America*.[4] In more recent years, the Christian philosopher and public intellectual, Cornel West, has sought to restore and rehabilitate this tradition in *Black Prophetic Fire*.[5] In the 2020s, the thesis of death, disruption, and disintegration is observable and measurable in its overarching consequences for Black America. The ten-year period, which I call *The Decade of Death (2012–2022)*, has done more than anything to disclose the face and effects of disintegration and the paucity of linked fates among Black Americans. In relation to *The Decade of Death (2012–2022)* the national Black Lives Matters Movement whose founding was and is attributed to queer Black women, was and is an enterprise that is radically distant from the Black American tradition of linked fates. The Black Lives Matters movement was driven primarily by late twentieth century and early twenty-first–century postmodern concerns, specifically queer feminist interests and queer feminist ideology, the concerns of a small subset of Black Americans caught up and entangled in the fragmentation and disintegration of Black America. Over a ten-year period the queer- driven Black Lives Matter Movement merely reflected the death of the linked fate tradition and a precarious condition among Black Americans. The Black Lives Matter movement emerged with good political intentions. It sought to address problems which predated the late twentieth-century popularization of postmodernism and its concerns, particularly queer feminist ideology. However, the queer feminist politics of Black Lives, which was exclusively concerned with queer feminist interests, was a deliberate repudiation of the tradition of linked fates whose most famous representative was Martin Luther King Jr. After ten years of activism, the Black Lives Matter movement did not eclipse the political achievements of the Black American-linked fate tradition. It must be repeated, the death of the linked fate tradition among Black Americans is tied to a decades-long process of fragmentation, disruption, and disintegration. In pointed terms, the cultural and social formations among Black Americans in the twenty-first century, particularly the 2020s, are nowhere near those of past generations. Cultural and social ties among Black Americans today are nowhere near the ties that existed, culturally and socially, prior to the assassination of Martin Luther King Jr. The present formations among Black Americans are not just the effect of inevitable historical and cultural change. The Black America that exists today is in large part the consequence of decades of deliberate social engineering. The architects of such engineering, which have been mainly White, have seen themselves as well-intended do-gooders with altruistic and benevolent intentions. Notwithstanding the alleged good intentions of White social engineers, the unintended consequences of their schemes have led to irreversible harm and damage to the Black American population. The harm and damage that I am speaking of was not among the expectations of those now-deceased Black American generations who produced and led the Black liberation movements of the 1950s and 1960s. In fact, the African American architects of the Civil Rights and Black Power movements did not foresee the disintegration of Black America which now exists decades after the legal and social achievements of the 1950s and 1960s. They did not anticipate the effects of desegregation on the Black American population. They undertook their mission with the assumption that all Black Americans were tied to each other at one level or another, despite the internal differences that existed among them. They were unable to see into the future and fathom the segmentation of Black America into women and girls, men and boys, the middle class and the poor, and straight and gay, which currently colors Black life in the United States. Such high levels of fragmentation among Black Americans have produced an unprecedented state of affairs wherein the assumption of linked fates has eroded. The groups where this condition is most pronounced are the middle- to upper-class sectors of Black America. Sixty years ago, middle- to upper-class Black Americans could in no way sever their ties to the Black American majority. However, desegregation, which granted them greater proximity to White society created opportunities outside of Black America which produced historic levels of separation from the majority of African Americans.[6] Attending predominately White institutions of secondary and higher education, living in predominately White neighborhoods, and socially interacting with White Americans at a variety of levels, has cut away their links to the majority of Black people in the United States.[7] Middle- to upper-class activists and intellectuals are among this class of elite Black Americans whose connections to the majority of Black Americans is tenuous and suspect.

What I have outlined above are preliminary considerations necessary for engaging the Black American condition today. It is important when considering those modes of African American scholarship and intellectual work that take for granted the disintegration of Black America and the death of the Black American tradition of linked fates. African American scholars who take for granted the death of linked fates assume that a robust social and spiritual contract thrives among Black Americans in the twenty-first century. More significantly, such African American scholars fail to take on the root causes of such fragmentation and the further erosion of ties between and among Black Americans. In terms of this chapter and the overall concerns of this book, anti-Blackness, in all of its depths, is at the heart of the disintegration of Black America and the death of the Black American linked fate tradition. In addition, there is the lurking problem of socially constructed evil, the *demonic imaginary,* which contributes to fragmentation and severed ties, the death of linked fates, among Black Americans. A necessary task in overcoming this condition is to excise or purge the *demonic imaginary,* which harms and damages Black Americans.

In illuminating the concerns of this chapter, it is helpful to point to the recent work of religion scholar Dianne Stewart, whose groundbreaking book *Black Women, Black Love: America's War on African American Marriage,* speaks to the splintering of Black America and its tradition of linked fates and its present status among Black Americans.[8] This book is significant because it was published on the heels of decades of internal fragmentation within the Black American population. One arena where this has been most visible is the family formations among Black Americans, where the disintegration of family structures over the last sixty years have been profoundly altered Black American life and is seemingly irreversible. The disintegration of family structures over the last sixty years has not been a priority among the most elite figures and voices in Black America. Nor has it been a major concern of White ruling-class social engineers. That the disintegration of family structures among Black Americans over the last sixty years is a factor in the present condition of Black Americans in the United States has been lost, in a manner that is abominable, on the Black American elite and the White elite. Dianne Stewart's book is a rare piece of interdisciplinary scholarship which touches upon these matters. In addressing this condition, it is primarily concerned with the marital and familial state of Black America and advocates heterosexual marriage as a social, moral, and economic good among Black Americans. More significantly, it regards the acquisition and sustainability of marriage and family among Black Americans as a justice issue, that marriage and family are political goods that impact the quality of life among Black Americans. *Black Women, Black Love* is largely a lamentation on the dearth of marriages among Black Americans. Aimed primarily at Black American women, it is a work that is vexed by the high numbers of heterosexual Black women who are unmarried. Through a study of history, law, religion, and politics, *Black Women, Black Love* explains the unmarried predicament of heterosexual Black women. *Black Women, Black Love* is significant because it was published at the end of *The Decade of Death (2012–2022)*. The aims of Stewart's work stand in great tension with the fragmentation and the death of linked fates which *The Decade of Death (2012–2022)* revealed. Stewart's book is a springboard for confronting and purging anti-Blackness and what I have termed the *demonic imaginary*. A book like Dianne Stewart's *Black Women, Black Love* can only be understood in this light. Her lamentations about love and marriage exist in the aftermath of death, the death of the linked fate tradition that once connected all Black Americans. To understand what has happened, one must take into account the effects of ideologies of desegregation, bolstered by liberalism, feminism, political conservatism, and the disruptive nature of capitalism on the Black American population.

Dianne Stewart's book is the most recent effort to speak to a once-existent cultural and social contract, prior to the 1970s, between heterosexual Black men and women. It is an exceptional work in light of the dominant trend among Black scholars of religion, particularly women, whose work has focused almost exclusively on sexism and homophobia within Black communities. As I have indicated in chapter 4 of this book, the ideas and concerns of LGBTQ+ Black Americans have stood at the heart of these efforts since the 1990s. Heterosexuality as a pathological and demonic enterprise is a dominant trait of this work.[9] The heterosexism of heterosexual Black men has been the focal point of these matters. Stewart's *Black Women, Black Love* is the first work by a Black woman scholar, particularly in the field of religion, which positively affirms heterosexual relationships, marriage in particular, among Black men and Black women. Overall, her book emerged and was produced on the heels of over four decades of liberal and conservative social policies and ideology on the part of feminists and womanists which have cast such relations in demonic terms. The last of such efforts was produced during the early 1980s by Nathan and Julia Hare, a married scholarly couple, who wrote about the crisis of Black marriages and families in *The Endangered Black Family: Coping with the Unisexualization and Coming Extinction of the Black Race*.[10] This Reagan-Era book, published during the early 1980s, was concerned with the sweeping trend of liberal family policies and feminist ideology in the United States and the rest of the Western world which sought to realign definitions of marriage, family, human sexuality, and gender across the world. Between the time since the publication of *The Endangered Black Family* in 1984 and the publication of Dianne Stewart's *Black Women, Black Love* in 2020, an entire enterprise of academic publications, media productions (film, television, theatrical presentations, and music) and political actions have flourished which have imagined heterosexual Black men as horrible fathers, husbands, and domestic partners with respect to heterosexual Black women. Heterosexual Black women were cast as victims of heterosexual Black men in need of salvation and/or redemption from heterosexual Black men through the political, economic, and social machinery of ruling-class White society. Dianne Stewart's *Black Women, Black Love* is best read through this backdrop. Through a critical engagement with history, from slavery to the present, public policy, and popular culture, Stewart grapples with the decimation of heterosexual relationships between Black women and Black men. From the standpoint of this chapter, it interrogates and seeks to repair a broken contract between heterosexual Black women and Black men. In the remaining pages, I illuminate this broken contract and its consequences for future engagements of Black people in the United States. I regard this broken contract as an abysmal state of affairs which is married to the disintegration of Black Americans and the possible erasure and annihilation of what is known as Black America. As I write, the dominant political economy of the United States, in the second decade of the twenty-first century, has moved in this direction. The dominant mode of liberal and feminist politics today which represents Black America in the dominant American public is fundamentally hostile to any and all efforts to rehabilitate heterosexual relationships between Black men and women. I regard such politics as anti-heterosexual and anti-Black male. It is contrary to a politics of life and amplifies a condition of death and jail which haunts Black America. Hence, a full account is needed of the adverse political and ideological forces which are counter to any contract between heterosexual Black men and Black women. Dianne Stewart's account is written in light of four decades of liberal gender ideology which is critical of patriarchal modes of existence. However, it is limited with respect to the excesses of such ideology in relation to heterosexual Black men and Black women. Liberal gender ideology which projects patriarchal norms and power to all groups, particularly all men, is misapplied to Black America, specifically Black men. Such misapplications of liberal gender ideology are exceedingly hostile and inapplicable to heterosexual Black men.

In this contemporary moment, liberal gender ideology promotes and traffics demonic accounts of heterosexual Black men. Such demonization is stridently promoted in service of LGBTQ+ interests, political goals, and aims with the interest of liberal feminists. An alliance between these two sets of interests has displaced the historic alliance between and among Black Americans, particularly heterosexual Black men and Black women. This alliance, which has many Black representatives, particularly among the professional class of Black American women, has dominated the American landscape since the late twentieth century. The Black intellectual and political elite have been major instigators of this politics. In particular, the Black intellectual elite has confined this advocacy for Black America to this domain. By conflating the centuries-long struggle of Black people in the United States with that of LGBTQ+ struggles and liberal White feminist struggles, it has contributed to the political and social decimation of Black Americans in the United States. Concerns about LGBTQ+ populations and concerns about women have nullified and eclipsed concerns about the concrete effects of anti-Blackness in the United States. Hence, concrete conditions that are fundamental to the stabilization of the lives of Black Americans, which include productive family formation, marriage, overall reproduction, and material well-being, are given a backseat to heterosexism, sexism, and an overall politics of recognition. While the dominant White ruling class has not been decimated in its heterosexual formations and continues to enjoy material well-being and power, the converse is true for heterosexual Black women and Black men. As LGBTQ+ populations have witnessed, over the last quarter century, great achievements in terms of rights pertaining to marriage, historic legal protections against discrimination, and significant social advancement and public recognition, Black heterosexuals are dismissed and rendered politically and socially inept. While homosexuality is affirmed, Black heterosexuality is condemned. LGBTQ+ interests are imagined as necessary and universal for all, while Black heterosexuality is rendered unnecessary and even dangerous. Again, Black heterosexuality is imagined as demonic, particularly in its Black and male expression. Though homosexuality cannot exist without heterosexuality, homosexuality has been elevated as a new standard, a calculus, and measure for all. This standard, propagated by liberals, feminists, and LGBTQ+ populations, is in no way accountable to the centuries-long struggle of Black Americans. After decades of liberalization in the United States, which has advanced not only LGBTQ+ interests and feminist interests, with limited to no attention to the historic struggles of Black Americans, the moment has arrived to attend to the heterosexual consequences of anti-Blackness in the United States.

Over the last three decades, the condemnation of Black heterosexuality has revealed a major fallacy. This fallacy is the grand assumption regarding the stability and power of Black heterosexuality, that such heterosexuality has undergone no disruptions historically, rendering such heterosexuality the same and equivalent to White heterosexuality. It has presumed that the historic restrictions placed on homosexuality were enacted and enforced in part by Black heterosexuals, particularly heterosexual Black men. Informed by a liberal feminist imaginary, the prohibitions against homosexuality were regarded as no different from the prohibitions placed on the existence of White women. In the liberal feminist imagination, heterosexual Black men are co-conspirators with ruling-class White men in the subjugation of women, White women in particular. The denial of suffrage rights for White women, the creation of miscegenation laws, and the creation of anti-sodomy laws are attributed in part to Black men. This *demonic imaginary,* which was born in the antebellum era, locked heterosexual Black men into a matrix of victimizing patriarchal authority, a calculus which endures to the present. This is the dominant fallacy associated with heterosexual Black men. This fallacy was given new life and granted renewed political legitimation after the 1960s with the rise of second-wave feminism and the movement for gay liberation. From the 1970s onward, this fallacy has informed the dominant modes of gender ideology in the United States. It is the basis for social policy with respect to heterosexual Black men and Black women. It drove the restructuring of heterosexual relationships between Black men and Black women. This restricting force involved the family court system, the welfare state, criminal justice policies, and affirmative action policies. Its most visible impact is seen in marital and family relations between heterosexual Black men and Black women. The most arduous effects of this fallacy are seen in the life chances and prospects of the children born of heterosexual Black men and Black women. The proliferation of single-parent households, run exclusively by women, is the legacy of this fallacious imaginary with respect to heterosexual Black men and Black women. Generations of Black children, with less-than-optimal outcomes, is the current fruit of such fallacious thinking. This fallacy is one among many which accounts for the broken contract between heterosexual Black men and Black women, a contract Dianne Stewart seeks to repair.

What I have identified as a fallacy with respect to heterosexual Black men and women is not accounted for in the work of Dianne Stewart. Stewart's work, which is informed by a deep reading of history and social policy in the United States, takes for granted the last four decades of gender ideology, its antecedents in the antebellum era, and its current impact on the relations between heterosexual Black men and Black women. It does not take seriously the errors and underside of gender ideology on the relations of heterosexual Black men and Black women. On the contrary, gender ideology is assumed to be progressive, despite the current quagmire between heterosexual Black men and women, a state of affairs which she laments and is the basis of her work. That there is a major gulf between heterosexual Black men and Black women, which drives her concerns, is in no way attributed to the demonic heterosexual imaginary, informed by decades of gender ideology and its public policies. No links are made between first-wave feminism, second-wave feminism, liberalism, and LGBTQ+ politics and the broken contract between Black men and Black women. The feminist assault on patriarchy, which made no distinctions between ruling-class White men and heterosexual Black men, is a key factor in the broken contract between heterosexual Black men and Black women. The decimation of heterosexual relations between Black men and Black women is implausible and unfathomable apart from this fact.

In a word, the broken contract between heterosexual Black men and Black women is the consequence of such a fallacy. This fallacy imposes and projects a myth of patriarchal power on heterosexual Black men that is hard to substantiate. Stewart's reading of heterosexual Black relations across history and the current moment is informed by anti-patriarchal sentiments. However, her analysis and conclusions regarding the historic and contemporary relations between heterosexual Black men and women are found wanting in demonstrating persistent patriarchal relations, across history, between heterosexual Black men and women. From slavery to the period of Jim Crow to the era of hyper-incarceration, heterosexual Black men are shown to be prohibited from any achievement and approximation of patriarchal norms and ideals, especially in a fashion that has persisted among White men, historically, in the United States.[11] No stable patriarchy persisted among Black men and Black women under slavery, nor did it exist under Jim Crow. After the movements of 1960s, a new generation of public policies and social practices, influenced by liberalism and feminism, set in motion a set of social arrangements which amplified the patriarchal restrictions of the past.[12] With social policies and ideas designed to create cleavage and conflict between heterosexual Black men and Black women, there was no way a stable and pervasive patriarchy could flourish among Black Americans. Coupled with female-headed households, which dominate Black America, the bleak state of marriage which animates Stewart's work attests to the absence of patriarchy in the relations between heterosexual Black men and Black women. Stewart, who writes with candor about a large population of unmarried Black women, marriage being a keystone of patriarchy, is oblivious to what her own conclusions demonstrate in terms of the dearth of patriarchy among Black Americans. In other words, her critique of patriarchy is contradicted by the absence of patriarchy evident in her findings. In profound ways, her lamentations about heterosexual relations among Black men and Black women, specifically marriage, is a grievance about the inability of heterosexual Black men as a group to approximate patriarchal norms. In other words, it is the absence of patriarchy among Black Americans as a group (across space and time) not its presence, which leaves large numbers of heterosexual Black women unmarried.

UTOPIAN PERFECTIONISM

The feminist assault on patriarchy in the United States over the last forty years cannot be overstated. In chapters 1 and 5 of this book, this ideology has been cited as an undeniable influence in American life. In 2021, bell hooks, whose work I discussed in chapter 1, one of the most vocal and prolific critics of patriarchal authority and oppression in the United States, passed away (at the age of sixty-seven). A product of the achievements and successes of the Civil Rights Movement and Second-Wave Feminism, bell hooks was a fervent critic of racism and sexism in America. Her participation in the feminist movement is worth restating. As a celebrated academic and public figure, bell hooks influenced and promoted a feminist vision in a shifted landscape of social justice which mushroomed after the 1980s. A heterosexual Black American woman, hooks lived and died as an unmarried and childless person. Though unmarried and childless, she exerted a great deal of energy and imagination, thinking and writing about heterosexual relationships between Black men and women. Black American heterosexual relations in household formations were a staple of her work.[13] Her focus on domestic relations between heterosexual Black men and Black women were part and parcel of an enterprise of feminist criticism of patriarchal oppression in the United States. As it has been indicated in this book, this critique has been profound and deep. Notwithstanding the power and legitimacy of this critique, it is worth repeating, this critique has not been immune to criticism. At the height of her popularity during the 1990s and the proliferation of feminist thought across the United States and the Western World, especially in colleges and universities, questions about the nature and reach of patriarchal oppression, particularly among Black Americans were voiced by academic and intellectual critics. Such critique came with the increased visibility and incorporation of segments of Black Americans into the American middle class, particularly the incorporation of Black American women into the professional ranks of White capitalist America. This incorporation included bell hooks who became a celebrity, a rarified public intellectual. During the late 1990s, the most prominent observer and critic of feminist assessments of patriarchal oppression with respect to Black Americans was the Harvard sociologist of Caribbean origin, Orlando Patterson. A scholar of slavery and family structures among descendants of slaves, Patterson raised historical and sociological questions regarding the conclusions made by feminist critics such as bell hooks about the extent to which patriarchal norms and practices among Black Americans are determining forces in the lives of Black Americans, particularly Black American women. When Patterson raised these questions, Black American women in the professional ranks of the United States were outpacing Black American men. In the late 1990s, when these questions were raised, the United States was at the height of a then new economy of prisons and hyper-incarceration. American cities were plagued by a scourge of guns and drugs which produced high levels of incarceration of young Black men. Moreover, unemployment among Black men as a group had reached an all- time high for that time.[14] The American welfare state had ballooned, taking in the ranks of lower-class Black Americans, particularly Black women, and family courts expanded through an intense program of policing and the extraction of resources from men designated as deadbeat dads. During this era, Black men as a group were designated as absent fathers, men who abandoned their children. These social and political facts of the 1990s drove Patterson's criticism and evaluations of feminist protests against patriarchal oppression, especially as it pertained to heterosexual Black men and women. Feminist views of patriarchal domination and oppression assume that heterosexual Black men have advantages and power over heterosexual Black women and that such privileges negatively affect the outcomes of Black women as a group and population. If such is the case and is true, then what accounted for the existence of a Black middle class, a socially mobile group whose members consisted mainly but not exclusively of women? How can the fates of Black American women as a group be negatively impacted by Black men if such Black women, especially those among the professional class, are outpacing Black men at every index of social well-being? Through an assessment of economic data, collected from the late 1980s to the time of his critique, a different picture was presented of gender and family relations among Black Americans. This portrait was inconsistent with feminist assessments and protests against patriarchal oppression and victimization with respect to heterosexual Black men and women. If patriarchal oppression and victimization possessed godlike power as feminist perspectives maintained, the reverse would be the case. Black men, as a group, not Black women, would possess and display the greatest social and economic advantages. Patterson's

1998 publication, *Rituals of Blood: The Consequences of Slavery in Two American Centuries* is the work where these questions were raised.[15] Unsurprisingly, this book drew the ire of feminist critics, particularly bell hooks. Again, Patterson was not alone in raising questions about the protest against patriarchal oppression and victimization by American feminists, especially Black feminists. However, as a historical sociologist in late twentieth-century America, his work offered assessments and questions which remain relevant in twenty-first-century America. A quarter century after *Rituals of Blood* was published, very little has changed, which, interestingly, is substantiated by Dianne Stewart's *Black Women, Black Love*. At the level of theory and empirical data, an enormous gap exists between the feminist protest against patriarchal oppression and victimization with respect to heterosexual Black men and women and the actual gender and familial dynamics which presently exists among heterosexual Black men and Black women. In fact, these gaps have widened and worsened. Dianne Stewart's *Black Women, Black Love* is a confirmation of this. Again, the conclusions of her work contradict the thesis of patriarchal domination that is upheld by feminist thought in the United States. The patriarchal thesis does not explain the unprecedented fragmentation and disintegration in Black American life, especially among heterosexual Black men and women. With respect to the work of Dianne Stewart, it does not explain why large numbers of heterosexual Black women, the main preoccupation of her book, are chronically single and unmarried.

In light of what I have outlined above, I am calling for a complete purging of demonic thinking with respect to Black masculinity, heterosexuality, and anti-Blackness. The *demonic imaginary* is responsible for the decimation of heterosexual relationships between Black men and women. This *demonic imaginary* has wreaked havoc on the lives of heterosexual Black men. The purging that I am calling for is a confrontation with the fears and mythologies which have been projected, in the past and the present, upon Black American men. The demonic accounts of heterosexuality which have been popularized by the late feminist bell hooks and other feminists and gender theorists of her ilk are now trite. These accounts, which have become standard by elites of all sorts, are reproduced and manufactured to no end and stand as major impediments to Black empowerment in the United States. As purveyors of a *demonic imaginary*, they are not exhaustive accounts of heterosexual interactions and relationships between Black men and Black women. They obscure the very real productive and healthy interactions that exist in real time between both groups. Their ongoing persistence only foments greater antagonism between heterosexual Black men and Black women. More significantly, this *demonic imaginary* adds fuel to the institutional mechanisms that criminalize Black men and sentence them to social death. For this reason, greater investment and energy must be dedicated to a more global picture of heterosexuality and heterosexual interactions which are devoid of demonic myths. This picture takes seriously present conditions as well as conditions in the past. It confounds and goes beyond the excesses of those who insist that heterosexual Black men as a group are categorically evil. The purging that I am calling for demands a complete re-evaluation and re-assessment of the Black condition in the United States. A rethinking and reconsideration of the Black American narrative is what is needed. Dianne Stewart's work is one effort that seeks to accomplish this. Though significant, Stewart's work does not go far enough in confronting, engaging, and, more importantly, purging the *demonic imaginary*.

RITUALS OF DEATH: PERFECTIONISM, CIVILIZATION, AND THE DEMONIC

From the standpoint of this chapter, the *demonic imaginary* is largely responsible for the lamentations that drive Dianne Stewart's work. The *demonic imaginary* is not only a destructive entity in relation to heterosexual relations, it is a criminalizing force which contributes to literal and social death among heterosexual Black men. The *demonic imaginary* with respect to heterosexual Black masculinity is not only a criminalizing force which sentences heterosexual Black men to literal and social death, but it is also an imaginary that is driven by a perfectionistic impulse which seeks to eliminate Black heterosexuality as a scourge in the world. As such, this perfectionism is anti-human and anti-life in nature. As anti-human, anti-life, and destructive, it erects and creates more problems than it seeks to resolve. As it has been indicated in this chapter, this deadly perfectionism is fraught with the baggage of history. This history is American and, by extension Western in its proportions. I am referring to a history of past efforts, in America and especially in the West, to civilize societies and cultures within North America and outside of the West.[16] This perfectionism is more recognizably associated with the history of slavery and colonialism, a history characterized by an effort to civilize populations deemed savage. What stands out in this history is the long process through education, religion, and overall conquest to remake populations in the image of dominate and normative European groups. This was the quest to make Africa, the subcontinent of India, South America, the Caribbean, and other regions and continents in the world in the image of European nations. The Spanish, the Portuguese, the French, the Dutch, and the British, are among those historical groups which sought to remake the world in their image. Our contemporary world is still reeling from the effects of their activities less than two centuries ago. The history of the United States, its laws, and institutions is a continuum on this historical scale. In North America, the history of Native or Indigenous populations and that of enslaved Africans is one place where Anglo-Saxon social engineering reigned supreme.[17] Anglo-Saxon social engineering, perfectionism, led to disaster in the past and it remains a disastrous force in the present. From the standpoint of this book and chapter, all forms of gender ideology in the United States bear the traits, features, and consequences of Anglo-Saxon perfection.[18] The history of Anglo-Saxon Progressive movements, from the early twentieth century to the present, are rife with the negative effects of perfection. The Temperance Movement, the Eugenics Movement, and the creation of the modern welfare state are among the examples where the consequences of Anglo-Saxon perfectionism have been damaging and irreversible. These movements were all undertaken under the guise of enlightenment and civilization. More deeply, the birth of the prison in the United States and the rise of the prison industrial complex (PIC) at the end of the twentieth century are heirs of Anglo-Saxon perfectionism. In profound respects, the entire American project is a project in and of Anglo-Saxon perfection. The quest for perfection lies at the heart of the Anglo-Saxon American identity. Where this analysis is concerned, all forms of politics across the political spectrum as well as social engineering in the United States are tainted with this perfectionistic impulse.

HETEROSEXUAL BLACK MEN AND THE CIVILIZING PROJECT OF THE UNITED STATES

In the 2020s, the quest to civilize groups and populations that are deemed savage, primitive, and criminal is still alive. Heterosexual Black men as a group are targets of this civilizing project. To add clarity to what I have suggested in this chapter, a broad spectrum of ideologies and actors which include liberals, leftists, feminists, and White nationalists fuel the engine of this civilizing regime. In the summer of 2020, the murder of George Floyd at the hands of a law enforcement officer in Minneapolis was a mass-mediated illustration of Anglo-Saxon perfectionism under the guise of civilization. George Floyd was a symbolic victim of what I have referred to as the *demonic imaginary* and its consequences for heterosexual Black men. As a symbol of the *demonic imaginary*, the manner in which George Floyd was policed, arrested, and eventually killed by an American law enforcement agent exposed, through social media, the civilizing and perfectionistic impulse in the United States. It exposed the manner in which Black men like George Floyd are expunged, for civilizing purposes, from the fabric of American society. They are removed from society for the purposes of cleansing, to remove a stain or taint from American civilization, to free America from its Black and male imperfections. His spectacled death, recorded on video and released via social media, was a horrific pedagogical moment regarding the nature and logic of anti-Blackness with respect to Black men. In the aftermath of his death, the global public became aware of the details of his life, his outsider status, his membership as one Black man among millions whose entire existence was stigmatized and limited by a *demonic imaginary*.[19] The bulk of George Floyd's adult life was marred by criminalization, being entangled by the streets and America's criminal justice system. What the world learned about his experience as a criminalized adult Black man speaks volumes to the concerns of this chapter and book. A life that was impacted by poverty, drugs, unemployment, jail, and prison, a man who fathered children, George Floyd belonged to a generation of Black men born after the 1970s which was not empowered through the achievements and aftermath of the Civil Rights and Black Power Eras.[20] He was not among that segment of Black Americans that was targeted for full-blown incorporation. He was a living and breathing product of unincorporated Black America. As such, George Floyd bore the marks of the politics and policies of law and order initiated by the presidential administration of Richard M. Nixon and later amplified through the administrations of Ronald Reagan and Bill Clinton. George Floyd came of age simultaneously with the emergence of the PIC and America's war on drugs. In terms of the broader American economy, George Floyd was also a casualty of the de-industrialization of the United States at the end of the twentieth century and the dawn of the twenty-first century. At present, the scholarship and activism of those who work in the arenas of prison abolition and criminal justice reform are illumined by George Floyd's life and subsequent death. Notwithstanding this context, at the time of his death, after the public became privy to the details of Floyd's life, after he was murdered and turned into a symbol of global dissent, George Floyd sought to transcend the many forces that plagued his life. A Black man in his late forties, George Floyd sought to move beyond and overcome his experiences with poverty, drugs, unemployment, jail, and prison. It was after his death that the global public learned that George Floyd wanted a better life. His pursuit of a better life compelled him to leave his home state of Texas and relocate to the state of Minnesota, a move where he could start over, begin again. In search of a rebirth, a different incarnation, in his mid-forties, such a move did not preclude the heavy weight of personal trauma and pain and the need to survive. This quest was integral to the inescapable details of his life. Like any human being with the weight of lived experience, the push for a new beginning was less than easy. The graphic manner in which George Floyd was murdered nullified his efforts. It completely censored and erased his desire for something more. George Floyd was only counted among the humans after his death. It was after his death that George Floyd was plausible as a member of American civilization, granted recognition among those civilizing agents who enforce the perfectionistic creed and civilizing project of the United States. Across the political spectrum from liberals to leftists to some feminists to some conservatives and actors, a Black man whose life had been implausible suddenly became legible. His life was legitimated only through death. In light of the concerns of this chapter and book, this is how the *demonic imaginary* and the civilizing project of the United States works. A Black man who is read through a *demonic imaginary* only meets the perfectionistic standards of civilization after a horrific death. This is what the world witnessed with the murder of George Floyd and it was characteristic of all the Black men and boys who were subject to some form of homicide (by law enforcement and private citizens) during *The Decade of Death (2012–2022)*. In light of the *demonic imaginary*, it is sobering to realize that the movement Black Lives Matter was preoccupied exclusively with the death of Black men and boys. The details of the deaths of Black men and boys, not the details of their lives prior to death, have been the unshakeable facts of this movement for justice. It is not lost on countless Black men and boys that they only matter, that their lives only have value, *after* they have been killed and removed from public view. Purging the *demonic imaginary* and the civilizing and perfectionistic impulse of the United States means disrupting and dismantling this project of civilization and perfection whose end is to remove Black men and boys from public sight even if it means death.

CONCLUSION

The present task of justice efforts that seek to overcome the legacies of anti-Blackness in the United States is the dismantling of those projects of civilization and perfection which seek to remove Black men and boys from open view. It means dismantling the ideas, mechanisms, and social conditions which are the playground of the *demonic imaginary*. It means a different conception of a human being as it bears upon heterosexual Black men that must emerge and take root. In the 2020s, our current conception of what counts as human and civilized is woefully inadequate. Such ideas belong to a bygone time and a worldview that is obsolete. Such ideas are embedded in a deep and long history of anti-Blackness in the United States and across the West. They bear the marks of slavery, the age of Jim Crow, and colonialism. They are the products of myths and the underside of religion and an entire world of ontological speculation. The American Christian tradition, informed by anti-Blackness, is the parent of this orientation.[21] In terms of this legacy, one only has to invoke the long history of anti-Blackness in the United States, especially its legal expression from the Supreme Court cases involving Dred

Scott (1854) and Plessy versus Ferguson (1896), to the murders of Emmet Till (1955) and Trayvon Martin (2012).

The most profound and arduous challenge connected to this demand to purge the demonic is the correction and rehabilitation of social, political, and religious thinking which has contributed to the problems outlined above. To echo the earliest concerns of this book expressed in chapter one, the greatest impediments to confronting the conditions of anti-Blackness, death, and jail is a crisis of imagination. It is worth repeating again, this crisis of imagination is specific to elite intellectuals and high-profile activists who fashion themselves as experts on the Black American condition in the United States. The sources of their expertise tend to be alien from the conditions that the vast majority of Black Americans face, particularly Black men. As I have indicated in chapter 1, intersectional feminism, postmodern theory, and queer theory—ideas that drove the movement Black Lives Matter—were mainly constructed behind the walls of elite colleges and universities. Unlike the ideas that drove Black activism from the 1950s to the 1970s, these perspectives are not organic outgrowths of a creative engagement with the conditions and circumstances that plague the majority of Black Americans in the 2020s. Prior to *The Decade of Death (2012–2022)*, these perspectives had not been tested in the public and were relegated to the elite subcultures of colleges and universities and the subcultures of the upper-middle class. However, it was during *The Decade of Death (2012–2022)* that the distance between the ideas and activism of elite intellectuals and activists was exposed and tested for all the world to see. In a word, elite intellectuals and activists failed the public testing of their ideas. Moreover, these perspectives were limited by their perpetuation and reinforcement of a *demonic imaginary* in relation to heterosexual Black men.

In the 2020s, the Black Lives Matter movement faces an arduous predicament. It is confronted with a crisis of legitimacy and imagination, which points to the demand to correct and rehabilitate historical, social, political, and religious thinking in relation to the Black American condition. As I echoed at the outset of this chapter and throughout its pages, the failures of the Black Lives Matter movement stemmed from its distance from the lived experiences of Black Americans, especially those who are not among America's elite. More significantly, it was disconnected from a political and cultural tradition of linked fates which existed prior to the 1970s, before the incorporation of a new Black middle class after 1980. The most efficient way to overcome this distance is to take seriously the present lived realities of Black Americans as they've been revealed during *The Decade of Death (2012–2022)* and to rethink or even abandon those perspectives which were born and nurtured outside of and apart from Black America, unincorporated Black America in particular. This means that elite intellectuals and activists who claim to care about and have investments in the present and future prospects of Black America have serious work to do. The work that they have to do is soul-searching and soul-wrenching. What this means is that this class of experts must hold a mirror to itself and ask probing questions about its existential, ideological, and political commitments. In the 2020s and beyond, the principal means of doing this is to engage *The Decade of Death (2012–2022)* and all of the lessons that it has taught us and currently teaches us about the Black American condition in the United States.

NOTES

1. Martin Luther King Jr., *Where Do We Go From Here: Chaos Or Community?* (Boston: Beacon Press, 1968).

2. Victor Anderson, *Beyond Ontological Blackness: An Essay in African American Religious and Cultural Criticism* (New York: The Continuum Publishing Company, 1995).

3. Manning Marable, *The Great Wells of Democracy: The Meaning of Race in American Life* (New York: Basic Civitas Books, 2002).

4. Eugene Robinson, *Disintegration: The Splintering of Black America* (New York: Anchor Books, 2011).

5. Cornel West and Christa Buschendorf, *Black Prophetic Fire* (Boston: Beacon Press, 2014).

6. See Orlando Patterson's *The Ordeal of Integration: Progress and Resentment in America's Racial Crisis* (New York: Basic Civitas, 1997).

7. See Elijah Anderson, *Black in White Space: The Enduring Impact of Color in Everyday Life* (Chicago and London: University of Chicago Press, 2020).

8. Dianne M. Stewart, *Black Women, Black Love: America's War on African American Marriage* (New York: Seal Press, 2020).

9. See Ronald B. Neal's Troubling the Demonic: Anti-Blackness, Black Masculinity, and the Study of Religion in North America, in *The Routledge Handbook on Religion, Gender, and Society* (London and New York: Routledge Press, 2021), Chapter 29.

10. Nathan Hare and Julia Hare, *The Endangered Black Family: Coping with the Unisexualization and Coming Extinction of the Black Race* (San Francisco: Black Think Tank, 1984).

11. Stewart's account of Black Marriage during and immediately after the era of enslavement is outlined in Chapter 1, Jumping the Broom: Racial Slavery and America's Roots of Forbidden Black, and Chapter 2, Slow Violence and White America's Reign of Terror, pp. 15–106. Both chapters outline the legal, cultural, and ideological barriers which impeded the formation of traditional households under these conditions. Stewart uses the concept of patriarchy, casually, in relation to its popular usage in the twenty-first century, in analyzing this history. Patriarchy as a category is undefined and appears to be out of place in light of the heightened levels of volatility involved in forming, maintaining, and sustaining traditional households

among the enslaved and those who were newly emancipated. It is a stretch to suggest that patriarchal households were an uninterrupted constant in the face of hostile historical conditions. The very histories which Stewart invokes contradict the very category she uses in reading this history.

12. Stewart's accounts of the welfare state and mass incarnation in Chapter 3, Love and Welfare: Johnnie Tillmon and the Struggle to Preserve Poor Black Families and Chapter 4, Black Love in Captivity: Mass Incarceration and the Depletion of the African American Marriage Market, pp. 107–80, outline the legal and economic barriers to heterosexual relationships in the twentieth and twenty-first centuries. Stewart's analysis and conclusions about the precarious nature of Black households under these conditions confound and trouble the very idea of patriarchy among Black Americans.

13. See bell hooks, *We Real Cool: Black Men and Masculinity* (New York and London: Routledge Press, 2004).

14. The hugely influential and widely read sociologist, William Julius Wilson, was a major voice during this era. Concerns about the welfare state, crime, family disintegration, and the impact of deindustrialization on the economic prospects of Black men in American cities were voiced in a major way in his 1996 book, *When Work Disappears: The World of the New Urban Poor* (New York: Alfred A. Knopf, 1996).

15. Orlando Patterson, *Rituals of Blood: The Consequences of Slavery in Two American Centuries* (New York: Basic Civitas Books, 1998). Also see Orlando Paterson's foundational work on slavery in world history, *Slavery and Social Death: A Comparative Study* (Cambridge: Harvard University Press, 1982).

16. For a recent account of the civilizing apparatus of Western societies, see Kwame Anthony Appiah's *The Lies That Bind: Rethinking Identity* (New York: Liverlight Publishing Corporation, 2018). Also see Charles H. Long's essays on religion and Western culture, *Significations: Signs, Symbols, and Images in the Interpretation of Religion* (Philadelphia: Fortress Press, 1986).

17. See Roxanne Dunbar-Ortiz's *Not A Nation of Immigrants: Settler Colonialism, White Supremacy, and a History of Erasure and Exclusion* (Boston: Beacon Press Books, 2022).

18. For a historical account of Anglo-Saxonism and its centuries-long cult of perfectionism, see Nell Irvin Painter's *The History of White People* (New York and London: W. W. Norton & Company, 2010).

19. For an early account of the details of the life of George as they were revealed during the summer of 2020, see Charles Holmes, He Shook the World: George Floyd's Houston Legacy in *Rolling Stone Magazine*, July 2020, 48–49.

20. For an extended, long account of George Floyd's tumultuous life, as told by his family members and those who knew him personally, see Robert Samuels and Toluse Olorunnipa of The Washington Post, *His Name Is George Floyd* (New York: Viking Books, 2022).

21. See Anthony B. Pinn's, *Terror and Triumph: The Nature of Black Religion 20th Anniversary Edition* (Minneapolis: Fortress Press, 2022).

Chapter 8

The Saga Continues

Cruel and Unusual Punishment, State-Based Fatherhood, and the Rage for Order in the United States

As I conclude this book, I must remind the reader of the political, moral, and intellectual commitments that birthed its contents. I write as a scholar and Black man who is deeply affected by the traditions of Black American freedom that existed prior to and up until the assassination of Martin Luther King Jr. In this book, I refer to such politics as the linked fate tradition. As I stated elsewhere, Black Americans were once bound together by a common struggle against a White society that was utterly hostile to them. This shared struggle and fate was largely inescapable. Throughout this book, I have maintained that this linked fate tradition was disrupted after the 1970s. With the incorporation of select elements within Black society into the edifice of White American capitalism, the ties that once bound Black Americans collectively were destroyed. For this reason, the notion of a "Black Community" in the United States is more of an abstract philosophical proposition than an existential reality. More than anything, this was made evident during *The Decade of Death (2012–2022)* and the Black Lives Matter movement. The decades-long fragmentation of Black America was made explicit in this moment. The politics that came out of this moment, Black Lives Matters, proved to be alienated from and dismissive of the indigenous traditions of linked fates that preceded it. Also, in terms of political mobilization, organization, political analysis, and sustained commitment, Black Lives Matter proved to be an inferior alternative to the indigenous history of struggle and the traditions that characterized late twentieth- century efforts toward racial justice. Among many things, *The Decade of Death (2012–2022)* was a moratorium on politics in Black America and whether such politics can effectively improve the quality of life among those Black Americans who have not been incorporated into the mainstream of White capitalist America. Based on the concerns of this book,

I do not think the most recent expression of politics, particularly Black Lives Matter, has the power to propel Black Americans, especially that sector of Black America which has not been incorporated into the mainstream White capitalist America, into the future. In fact, I am convinced that such politics will contribute to greater fragmentation, stagnation, and inertia among all Black Americans.

The Decade of Death (2012–2022) occurred against a backdrop of backlash, a right-wing reaction to the presidency of Barack Obama, economic shifts, and population change in the United States.[1] This backlash has been the recent expression of long-held sentiments, going back to the 1960s, that the United States was undergoing high levels of de-stabilization. The selective incorporation of Black Americans after the 1970s heightened this sensibility on the political right. Hence, a politically conservative rage for order has characterized right-wing politics for the last five decades.[2] However, it was with the presidency of Barack Obama that this demand for order reached a crescendo. The murder of seventeen-year-old Trayvon Martin in 2012 at the hands of a private citizen in Sanford, Florida, was the moment that the rage for order in the United States became visibly lethal. Since the death of Trayvon Martin, we have consistently seen this demand for order.[3] During *The Decade of Death (2012–2022)* not only was Black Lives Matter limited in dealing with this rage for order, but political liberalism and its derivatives among feminists and leftists proved to be impotent in standing up to and overturning this backlash. As this chapter is being written, it does not appear that political liberalism and its derivatives have the weight, muscle, and resolve to eclipse the political right. This state of affairs is a necessary consideration for any politics concerned about death and jail, the concerns of this book. How one goes about improving the quality of life for those Black Americans who are not incorporated into White capitalist America must take current realities seriously. To this end, the rage for order cannot be ignored. It must be engaged for what it is.

MAKE AMERICA GREAT AGAIN

The Supreme Court of the United States has been at the center of the rage for order in America. Across the political spectrum, it has been the battleground for the future of law and policy in the United States. It stands as a litmus test of ideals of freedom and justice in the United States. As the highest decision-making body in the United States, the jurisprudence of the Supreme Court is a commentary on the current state of public life in America and what constitutes a good society.[4] Since the Obama presidency, the dominant view of the Supreme Court has been regulatory and restrictive in nature.

With a conservative majority, it has propagated a highly restrictive view of the rights of citizenship, a perspective that seeks to regulate and even erase what is perceived as an excess of civil liberties.[5] From this perspective, civil liberties, under liberal jurisprudence have so run amok that within the American public there is now a pervasive view of citizenship rights that exceeds the view of rights outlined in the United States Constitution. The rights of Black Americans, the rights of women, the rights of LGBTQ+ people, and the rights of criminals have been prominent in this perceived over-expansion of rights. In simple terms, from the standpoint of the political right, political liberalism since the 1970s has gone too far in promoting the rights of citizens at the expense of responsible citizenship.[6] For the political right, political liberalism has done too much in treating the law as a mechanism for solving what is regarded as intractable social problems. From this view of the law, the excessive promotion of rights has created problems which the law was not intended to solve.

The conservative majority on the Supreme Court and its assault on liberalism has far-reaching implications for the future of freedom, responsible citizenship, and law in the United States. Its view of law and order is deeply rooted in visions of jurisprudence which existed prior to the 1970s. It is far-reaching, touching law and order during the antebellum era. In this vision of human freedom and responsibility, under the law, the US Constitution is understood in relation to the most anti-Black and anti-democratic periods in US history. Such history includes centuries of slavery and close to a century of Jim Crow.[7] This history remains a blemish on the American project. The political utopia of the political right is essentially nostalgia for a time that was seemingly characterized by order, a respect for law, authority, and pervasive social norms which governed society. This vision has no room for innovations in law and no place for law as a tool of social engineering. In this vision, there is zero tolerance for criminality and lawbreaking behavior.[8] In this worldview, punishment is intended to be swift, severe, and impactful.

LAW, ORDER, AND PUNISHMENT

As this chapter is being written, in 2022, very few citizens of the United States can imagine the world of law and order that existed prior to the 1970s. Very few citizens can imagine what it was like for Black Americans who went unrecognized as US citizens up until 1965. The law-and-order regime of prior eras did not protect Black Americans from threats of violence and terrorism by other citizens, White citizens in particular. It is important to invoke this history of law and order as it affected Black Americans. In a current moment such as ours, where the details of the history of the United States are being debated in public, those parts of American history that entail the legal disenfranchisement of Black Americans need to be remembered. Nostalgia for this history among the conservative majority on the Supreme Court and among political conservatives, those who hold political office and those who hold no political office, deserves attention too.

Criminal justice has been the major pillar of the decades-long rage for order in the United States. In reaction to political liberalism and its perceived weakening of longstanding social norms and traditions of civility, laws, decorum, and most particularly family life in America, the political right has maintained a stance on criminal justice which has been unrelenting.[9] It has been so forceful that liberal politicians, over the decades, have surrendered to its demands (e.g., former US president Bill Clinton, current US president Joe Biden, and Vice President Kamala Harris).[10] As a consequence, the United States has consistently, over decades, led the world in human incarceration. The American reputation for punishment, aggressive law and order which regulates society, is upheld as the most effective and necessary means to preserve domestic safety and America's dominance in the world. As such, criminal justice is tied not only to domestic peace but also national security. For this reason, the US war on terrorism since September 11, 2001, has been allied with the American criminal justice system in maintaining law and order in America and across the globe. In a word, the demand to protect American institutions and to protect American citizens from threats within and beyond the borders of the United States drives an endless rage for order.[11] The American court system (local, state, and federal) and the US Supreme Court have affirmed this mechanism of policing, punishment, and safety. The gravity of law and order has produced many critics among citizens, including some academics and some politicians and activists. However, such criticism has been limited in scaling back or halting this behemoth of law and order. In every decade since the late 1960s when the rage for law and order became the cornerstone of right-wing politics in America, the rage for order has asserted its hold on American life. The rage for law and order is most aggressively asserted during moments of political tumult when there is a clash between American citizens and the institutions of law and order in the United States. Such was the case during *The Decade of Death (2012–2022)*. It represents the most recent moment within the twenty-first century where the rage for order reared its public face. The summer of 2020, when mass protests took place in the United States and around the world, in response to threats of safety on the part of private citizens and law enforcement, resulting in the catastrophic deaths of Black citizens, crystalized the clash between Black citizens and the rage for order. Occurring within the backdrop of the COVID-19 pandemic, the rage for order was given new life. *The Decade of Death (2012–2022)*, including the mass protests of Summer of 2020 and the impact of the COVID-19 pandemic, made the most vulnerable citizens in the United States targets of longstanding anxieties, fears about safety, which have historically driven the engine of law and order in America.[12] As I have indicated throughout this book, *The Decade of Death (2012–2022)* exposed those aspects of Black American society which have not been incorporated into the mainstream of White American capitalism. It has also disclosed public fears held across the American public of this unincorporated population of Black Americans, perceptions which have resulted in death. If the American past is a good indicator of the future, the administrators of law and order may once again double down on perceived threats to public safety and national security. This means that aggressive criminal justice, whose main instrument is incarceration through jails, detention centers, and prisons, will present itself as a solution to perceived threats to public safety. Consistent with the history of prisons in the United States, human warehousing may eclipse alternative forms of justice and mechanisms designed to address societal problems which are not limited to jail and detention. In a possible future, we may find ourselves in a situation where human warehousing grows in proportions which surpasses the current state of incarceration in the United States. From the standpoint of this book, this is a morbid prospect that cannot be overlooked. This law-and-order politics cannot be upheld as the final solution to longstanding social, economic, and racial problems.

The possible expansion of the prison industrial complex as it is driven by the rage for order presents serious problems in relation to the role of the state in American life. It raises questions about the role and extent of the powers of the state in relation to citizens. The American criminal justice system and its punitive apparatus is one of the least-regulated and policed institutions in the United States. In the past and in the present, it has been culpable for the abuses of power at the hands of the state.[13] Unlike other governmental entities, it has functioned at a variety of levels, especially at the level of state government, without strong mechanisms of checks and balances. Jails, detention centers, and prisons have not been subject to public mechanisms of oversight and policing that prevent abuses of governmental authority from running rampant. The history of incarceration is fraught with instances of tyrannical authority tied to violations of civil and human rights. Violations of the Eighth Amendment of the US Constitution, Cruel and Unusual Punishment, have been at the center of incarceration in the United States.[14] Because significant distance exists between the general American public and the worlds of jail, detention centers, and prisons, mass concern and demand for checks and balances are virtually nonexistent. The lack of massive public scrutiny of the prison allows the abuse of governmental power to exist. This fact is part of the critique of the prison industrial complex (PIC) on the part of academics, activists, and citizens. The abuse of power, tyranny, has also been voiced by those who have been warehoused within the carceral system, former and current prisoners. An entire body of prison writings exists which exposes the abuses of power, the lack of checks and balances, which are characteristic of an unregulated and unpoliced public institution.[15]

Not only does the PIC stretch the powers of the state that contribute to tyrannical abuse, it fails to ultimately solve the problem of public safety purported by the law and order regime. Human warehousing does not ultimately address the social problems that lead to incarceration; it merely relocates the people who are connected to those problems. The weight of those problems do not disappear once people are incarcerated. In fact, in too many instances, what the incarcerated people bring with them prior to detention is amplified by containment.

CLARENCE THOMAS, UNINCORPORATED BLACK AMERICA, AND THE RAGE FOR ORDER

What I am calling unqualified power and authority on the part of the law-and-order regime in the United States is boldly supported and affirmed by the conservative majority on the US Supreme Court. If there is a single representative on this court whose jurisprudence is representative of this tyrannical authority, it is the Supreme Court Justice, Clarence Thomas. Clarence Thomas, who is the longest-serving Supreme Court justice in the history of the United States, is famous for his judicial opinions and rulings at the level of criminal justice.[16] During his three decades on the court, Thomas has demonstrated a bold deference to state and federal agencies responsible for the arrest, prosecution, and sentencing of persons accused of crimes. His legal decisions have been hostile to incarcerated individuals who have brought legal suits against prison officials, prosecutors, judges, and appellate courts, charging these entities with violations of civil and human rights. Thomas has ruled against incarcerated people who claimed that their Eighth Amendment rights have been violated. Thomas has also ruled against incarcerated individuals who've claimed that their Fourth Amendment, Fifth Amendment, and Sixth Amendment rights were violated at the time of their arrest and during the time that they were adjudicated through criminal courts. Prison inmates who suffered violence at the hands of correctional officials and individuals whose rights were violated through search and seizures and individuals who were denied due process by prosecutors and judges have been accorded no sympathy in Thomas' rulings in their respective cases. Thomas has also upheld death sentences which have been contested in capital cases, murder. Through a strict and conservative interpretation of the US Constitution, Thomas has upheld lower court rulings. Under Thomas' criminal jurisprudence, no incarcerated person or individual charged with contested crimes have successfully won his judicial favor. In Thomas' rulings, prosecutorial actions, judicial decisions, and correctional officials were consistently found innocent of legal misconduct. State and federal courts have been found just in their original dealings with incarcerated individuals and individuals arrested and prosecuted for crimes. In these cases where the circumstances of individuals, the events surrounding their cases and legal claims, and the biographical facts of their lives were entered into court records, such facts did not warrant consideration in his rulings. The letter of the law, as Thomas understands it, has more gravity than the narratives around these respective cases. Key to Thomas' rulings is his originalist interpretation of the US Constitution as well as his own moral and political philosophy related to criminal actions.[17] It is the latter part of his reasoning, steeped in Catholicism and a Catholic understanding of character, morality, and punishment and his views related to race, class, and conduct in the United States, which illuminate his overall approach to criminal justice. As the product of a particular era in America, coming of age under Jim Crow and living through the political tumult of the 1960s and 1970s, Thomas' approach to the law is as much biographical as it is legal.[18] It is tied to a tradition of conservatism and Black nationalism which has marked his life and consciousness. Thomas holds views about criminal justice and the condition of Black Americans in the United States which do not regard the US Constitution, American law, and politics writ large as guaranteeing Black Americans cosmic justice in America. In other words, the courts and politics alone should not be the vehicles which determine the fates of Black Americans.[19] In contrast to the power of the law and the state, the futures and fates of Black American lie in the hands of Black Americans themselves. In relation to criminal justice, Black Americans must avoid the entanglements of the criminal legal system if and when they engage in criminal activity. When and if such behavior takes place, the law cannot and should not save Black Americans. In fact, the law, when punitive, is justified in all of its actions when and if Black Americans are found guilty of violating the law. More importantly, this punitive understanding of the law is held up as beneficial to Black Americans and their efforts toward greater freedom in the United States. From Thomas' view, criminal punishment as a deterrence from criminal behavior is integral to the health of Black Americans. From this perspective, criminal justice is a stern parent, a punitive father, that ensures that his children engage in right conduct. This is the ethical view of punishment which gives free rein to prosecutors, judges, and courts to behave as they see fit and is legal in relation to incarcerated individuals and individuals charged with crimes. Hence, Clarence Thomas's view of criminal justice, which is paternalistic in nature, is tied to the regime and reign of law and order in the United States. This view of law and order as a paternal authority, a punitive father, is provocatively articulated by Corey Robin in his 2019 book, *The Enigma of Clarence Thomas*, where punitive patriarchy and criminal justice go hand in hand.[20] Robin comes to this conclusion based on his reading of Thomas' autobiographical writings, speeches, and judicial opinions. More than any source, Clarence Thomas' 2007 memoir, *My Grandfather's Son*, supports Robin's perspective. *My Grandfather's Son* is an autobiographical testament to the links between Thomas" lived experience as a Black man from the US South, his generational perspective on the Black American condition in the United States, his inheritance as a Roman Catholic, and his legal philosophy as a Supreme Court Justice.[21] More than anything, the de facto and de jure patriarchal authority of the world that shaped him is inseparable from the patriarchal authority which the criminal justice system and the PIC represent.

In light of the jurisprudence of Clarence Thomas, which includes his record of opinions on criminal cases, the law-and-order regime in the United States can be understood as a mythical father, an all-powerful and all-knowing tyrannical force whose role it is to discipline and punish wayward children. This father is a legal imposition on a society and its citizens who, for whatever reason, were denied or deprived of such a figure in life. Moreover, this father is necessary in a society and culture where the traditional role of a father and fathers has been diminished or erased, a society which has removed discipline and order as necessary stabilizing forces. This father is a response to the limits and failures of liberalism in social, cultural, and legal affairs. For a Supreme Court justice such as Clarence Thomas and for those on the political right, it is the removal of the father and his traditional role that is restored and reinforced through criminal justice and the overall law-and-order regime.

The mythical father as it relates to law and order is most pronounced at the level of the state. Prosecutors, judges, and correctional officials at the state level whose authority is connected to criminal courts, jails, detention centers, and prisons carry out this role with unmitigated power and authority. They are endowed with the power of the law and the state to correct undisciplined children. In this capacity, individuals who are arrested, charged, and prosecuted with crimes are infantilized. They are reduced to a form of childhood and adolescence and are subjected to unrelenting discipline, order, and control. With such power, levels of authority which strip individuality, eliminate choice, restricts opportunity, and demand unquestioned conformity circumscribe the lives of those under the grip of the punitive regime. This type of authority, under the auspices of the state, mirrors a communist regime. As such, punishment nullifies any and every effort at rehabilitation which promotes full-blown adulthood and the kinds of maturity across the stages of life. For this very reason, it is not unusual for individuals whose lives have been or are entangled by the criminal justice system to leave and return to this system upon release as individuals whose development as human beings has been arrested. As I write, thousands of individuals who've experienced this system are unable to function as free individuals in American society. Their ability to participate in society apart from criminal supervision is compromised by the carceral state. Reduced to a primitive state by the law-and-order regime, the fate of these individuals is a profound contradiction to deeply held American values, particularly the creed of democratic exceptionalism which is propagated by political authorities in the United States. It is a profound contradiction to the manner in which America exists in the global imagination as a bastion of enlightenment and cosmopolitan freedom in the world. This contradiction ensures that the law and order regime is far from an apparatus of deterrence where criminal conduct is concerned. In fact, the opposite is achieved where the infantilization of individuals who are arrested, charged, and prosecuted for crimes remain captive to this system. In light of this reality, few individuals are able to exit this punitive authority without returning to its paternalistic control. As I indicated above, the details of the infantilizing nature of the law-and-order regime are well documented in the writings of incarcerated and formerly incarcerated people. The writings of prisoners and ex-prisoners housed mainly in state prisons across the United States, across generations, illuminate the forms of patriarchal tyranny and arrested development that prisoners are subjected to. The prison writings of Wilbert Rideau, Albert Woodfox, Yusef Salaam, Shaka Shakur, Sanyinka Shakur, Huey P. Newton, Eldridge Cleaver, George Jackson, Malcolm X, and many others, all point to the dehumanizing nature of patriarchal prison authorities and the overall criminal justice system. Such infantilizing authority has also been depicted endlessly in media through television series, documentaries, and motion pictures. Any close observer of this media can identify the infantilizing and tyrannical patriarchal authority at work in the criminal justice system and especially the American prison.

As I have indicated earlier, those who are most vulnerable to the regime of law and order in the United States are those Black Americans who have not been fully incorporated into the mainstream of White capitalist America. Those Black Americans who were casualties of *The Decade of Death (2012–2022)* and the unincorporated Black spaces that produced them are most threatened and preyed upon by the law and order regime.[22] In light of this reality, it is important to note that the vulnerable nature of unincorporated Black America is in no way shared with the majority of Americans, citizens, who have been fully incorporated into the mainstream of White capitalist America. The law- and-order regime is very selective in the manner in which it exacts its apparatus of discipline and punishment. The most incorporated citizens in the United States are largely protected from and immune to the horrors of the law-and-order regime, cruel and unusual punishment. In profound ways, the selective nature of the law-and-order regime is borne out in the who, why, what, and where, related to those individuals who are punished. The details of unincorporated Black America and the manner in which it is subject to incessant policing disclose the selective nature of law and order in the United States.

As stated earlier, the law-and-order regime is a paternalistic patriarchal authority whose power is unchecked and unregulated. It is selective in nature in how it is applied. It is a tyrannical father whose job it is to keep his children in line. For an administrator of law and order such as the Supreme Court justice, Clarence Thomas, the child that is most in need of this type of discipline is male. In light of the autobiography and jurisprudence of Clarence Thomas, it is the male child, the son, the Black son, in particular, who needs tyrannical patriarchal authority to ensure he becomes a law-abiding citizen and an overall productive member of society. Hence, the Black American male who strays from the dictates of the law and does harm to society figures prominently in this patriarchal vision of authority. In general, males of all stripes are most vulnerable to law-breaking and criminal activity. However, the Black male is the most vulnerable male in US society to the entanglements of the criminal justice system. If such a male is not disciplined early on in the life cycle before such entanglements take place, then such discipline must be imposed upon him if and when he violates criminal law. This discipline is not solely meant for public safety for society in general; it is intended for the present and future health of Black Americans as they exercise freedom in American society. In this selective view in how punishment is applied, a profound commentary is made upon Black masculinity and law and order in the United States. It speaks in significant ways about patriarchal authority and the myth of the father with respect to discipline, punishment, and Black masculinity. With respect to Clarence Thomas, it touches upon widely known facts about his personal autobiography and the powerful role that patriarchal authority played in his life and development, at the hands of a mythical Black man, his grandfather, and the reverence he has for such authoritarian figures. In telling a passage from his memoir, *My Grandfather's Son*, Clarence Thomas articulates this view of patriarchal authority with respect to his own life and the condition of Black Americans:

> What I cared about more than anything else, I decided, was the condition of blacks in Savannah and across America. The only way I could hope to find personal fulfillment was to spend the rest of my life trying to make their lives better, and to do so in a manner that was consistent with the way Daddy had raised me. As a young radical, I had found it easy to cloak my belief in the necessity of black self-reliance in the similar-sounding views of Malcolm X

and the Black Muslims. It wouldn't be so easy now. To unhesitatingly proclaim the rightness of Daddy's way of life would be to court some kind of ridicule to which Thomas Sowell was being subjected. Once I, too, had fallen into the trap of condemning as Uncle Tom those black people who thought the way he did. I knew the same ridicule would greet me if I took his side-but I also believed he was right. Though I feared the consequences of saying so publicly, I knew that someday I would have to confront that fear.[23]

Thomas' autobiographical convictions about patriarchal authority (his grandfather is the reason why death and jail were not his fate) are best understood and amplified in relation to decades of social policy and social debate about the role and presence of fathers in the lives of children and families, in particular those that are Black, since the 1970s. Clarence Thomas has held a view shared by many on the political right and some who are not conservative in their politics that Black Americans have been impeded in their quests for freedom as a consequence of the absence or disappearance of mythical patriarchs in Black American life. For this reason, Black Americans, especially Black males, have been overrepresented in America's jails, detention centers, and prisons. Again, for Clarence Thomas, criminal justice and incarceration are not the problem. The problem is the absence of the mythical patriarch who sets his sons straight. The law-and-order regime is simply a replacement for this missing mythical patriarchal figure. Once this missing patriarchal figure is restored in ordinary life, the mythical carceral father will no longer be needed as a legal and punitive imposition by the law-and-order regime.

It cannot be overstated that the mythical patriarch which is implicated in Clarence Thomas' vision of discipline and punishment and that of the law-and-order regime writ large is a reaction to and a rejection of liberal jurisprudence and the effects of liberalism on civility and order in the United States. More specifically, it is a gross rebuke of the effects of liberalism on America's Black population. Although Black Americans as a group have supported political liberalism and many of its social and cultural derivatives, such affirmation on the part of Black Americans is frowned upon and regarded as a major impediment to Black American freedom and advancement. For Clarence Thomas, the acceptance of liberalism among many Black Americans has been misguided and is abject in its impact on Black Americans. Moreover, it is a deep betrayal of Black American traditions of survival which were more beneficial (before the liberalization of Black America) to quests for Black freedom in America than liberal creeds. The amplification of law and order through the mythical patriarch is intended to break the hold and influence of liberalism on Black American life. What this means is that the possible expansion of the carceral state in the present and the future is a necessary means of overturning the effects of liberalism on Black Americans.

From the standpoint of this book, cruel and unusual punishment is a haunting force whose long-term impact on Black America, unincorporated Black America in particular, is unknown.

In a word, the mythical patriarch as an administrator of law and order in the United States and a figure who rebukes the effects of liberalism in the United States presents a morbid scenario in the present and the future, which should cause alarm. It presents a dire state of affairs for new and emerging generations, particularly unincorporated Black males, which is frightening in its prospects. Since the 1970s, we have witnessed at least two generations that have been caught up in the law-and-order regime. The generational effects of their punishment have produced movements of criminal justice reform and prison abolition. The tyrannical abuse of power at the hands of the state has driven these movements for justice. Cruel and unusual punishment as the sole means of addressing the perceived effects of liberalism on new and emerging generations is less than likely to reverse the unintended effects of liberalism on unincorporated Black America, especially unincorporated Black males. It is difficult to see the emergence of a Black American situation that is positively affected by the de facto patriarch of law and order. More specifically, I do not see the rise of mythical patriarchal figures, imagined by Clarence Thomas, intended to supplant the negation of fathers and fatherhood, associated with the scourge of liberalism, in ordinary Black American life, especially unincorporated Black America.

PROTEST IS NOT ENOUGH: THE MYTHICAL FATHER AND UNINCORPORATED BLACK AMERICA

At the outset of this chapter, I expressed grave doubts about the ability of present-day justice movements to effectively address the lot of Black America, especially those elements in Black America which have not been incorporated into the mainstream of White capitalist America. These doubts are based on the distance between these movements and the traditions of linked fates which once characterized African American struggles in the United States. They are also based on the real force of the law-and-order regime in the United States, its logic and influence on the political right. The Black Lives Matter movement which appeared simultaneously with *The Decade of Death (2012–2022)* proved to be impotent in its efforts to address the ongoing legacy of anti-Blackness in the United States. Its detachment from the wisdom of Black traditions has been borne out at the level of organization, ideas, and commitment. Its fundamental weakness was that its sources and motivations were not indigenous to the conditions which form unincorporated Black America. More significantly, it proved to be no match for the punitive power of the state, the law-and-order regime in America. Fortunately, the Black Lives Matter movement was not subjected to the levels of punishment, at the hand of the state, which brought to a halt Black American protest movements and organizations that emerged during the 1950s and 1960s. The clash between citizens and the law-and-order regime during *The Decade of Death (2012–2022)* is not comparable to the contest between citizens and the state during the 1950s and 1960s. Federal law enforcement agencies such as the FBI and prosecutors and judges at the state level ushered in a program of criminal convictions, deaths, and long-term incarceration for dissent citizens, especially those who were Black Americas.[24] The 1950s and 1960s produced an era of martyrdom, human sacrifice, at the hands of the state which was not replicated during *The Decade of Death (2012–2022)*. This aggressive move of the law-and-order regime is responsible for the build-up of jails, detention centers, and prisons all over the United States, the PIC. The law-and-order regime demonstrated that it had zero tolerance for Black American protest. For this reason, protest movements among Black Americans were stifled and discouraged for more than three decades. Present-day justice movements as they are currently configured are simply found wanting in relation to a present and future reassertion of the rage for order in the United States. What is more, these justice movements, as they are currently configured, have the potential for further instigating the law-and-order regime whose primary targets are unincorporated Black America. As such, contemporary justice movements put a target on the backs of Black Americans as they pursue their visions of justice in America. The clash between citizens and the state during the summer of 2020, as America dealt with the COVID-19 pandemic, is one major instance of this. White Americans among leftists, liberals, and even conservatives who seized upon this moment to engage in spectacled dissent, engaging in vandalism, the defacing of public and private property, and confronting the police in sections of unincorporated Black America, only heightened resentment and animus toward such Black Americans on the part of the law-and-order regime. Simply stated, when White anarchists on the far left such as Antifa exploit moments of Black American dissent to promote their political agenda, they make Black Americans vulnerable to the strong arm of the state, the law-and-order regime. When other groups among liberals and leftists, feminists and LGBTQ+ groups, do the same, it only heightens the vulnerable nature of unincorporated Black Americans. Compounded by this are White nationalists who exploit these moments to engage in anti-Black acts of racism in relation to unincorporated Black America. At the end of these moments of protest, dissent, and spectacled activity, Black Americans are left to bear the weight of backlash in relation to the law-and-order regime. To the degree that this continues, unincorporated Black Americans pay the price exacted by the administrators of state punishment in America. The

White Americans who heighten Black vulnerability are simply immune to the strong arm of the state. In the end, unincorporated Black Americans remain avatars for those conservative and right-wing forces at the highest levels of American society who point to unincorporated Black America as evidence of the excesses of liberalization in America. As was the case during the 1950s and 1960s, unincorporated Black Americans will continue to be blamed for the perceived lack of civility, safety, and stability in American life. To the degree that contemporary justice movements exploit the Black American situation in the United States for their own political purposes, the rage for order will be amplified exponentially. As long as the condition of unincorporated Black America is exploited by the above White interests, limits are placed on real and substantive interventions with the goal of addressing the legacy of anti-Black racism in America and improving the quality of life among unincorporated Black America. There is simply too much at stake where interventions are concerned to allow contemporary justice movements led by White leftists and liberals to obstruct a better present and future for unincorporated Black Americans. Overcoming this problem which has been outlined, calls for specific and real attention to those conditions which form unincorporated Black Americas. An unqualified, unmitigated, and uncensored approach to unincorporated Black America is imperative. Such an approach involves an engagement with law and policy as they affect the lives of unincorporated Black America and are tied to the rage for order in the United States.

THE PRISON BEYOND THE PRISON: POVERTY MANAGEMENT AND UNINCORPORATED BLACK AMERICA

In chapter one of this book, I pointed to the significance of Michelle Alexander and her groundbreaking 2010 book *The New Jim Crow: Mass Incarceration in the Age Colorblindness*.[25] One of the contributions of this work was the connections it made between the welfare state and the state-driven world of social services for poor people and the entire edifice of mass incarceration: jails, detention centers, and prisons. Both the welfare state and the bureaucracy of mass incarceration are the primary vehicles for managing poverty in the United States. All efforts to engage the condition of unincorporated Black America are confronted with the inescapable and unrelenting reality of poverty management in the United States. Huge swaths of unincorporated Black Americans are managed by the welfare state and the same state apparatus that governs the welfare system also governs the criminal justice system. The welfare system of the United States, as it is administered by individual states, is the primary entity that controls and manages those Black

Americans who are not in the criminal justice system, who are on the outside of the mainstream White capitalist America. The Black Americans who are under the administrative arm of state welfare managers, which includes social workers, are the most vulnerable Black Americans to the law-and-order regime. These unincorporated Black Americans exist in close proximity to those unincorporated Black Americans who are actually caught up in the criminal justice system. Their proximity to each other and interactions are the breeding grounds for de facto and de jure incarceration. Those unincorporated Black Americans under the welfare state who receive state-funded housing, food stamps, and benefits for children and youth, live under high levels of paternalistic authority via the state.[26] They live in spaces bound by high levels of poverty and crime and are subject to excessive police surveillance. These are the spaces which were exposed during *The Decade of Death (2012–2022)*. These spaces are the playgrounds for academic sociology and media entities obsessed with race, poverty, and crime in the United States. Under state control, through its apparatus of welfare, social work, and child protective services, the ability of unincorporated Black Americans to enter the mainstream of White capitalist America is constrained. Built within the administrative apparatus of the welfare state are the policies and practices which govern it, ensuring that the arrested mobility of unincorporated Black Americans is maintained and preserved. Policies pertaining to children and families and policies pertaining to education and employment work in a colonial fashion which heighten the vulnerabilities of unincorporated Black Americans to the punitive arm of the law-and-order regime. In explicit terms, too many members of unincorporated Black America live under a state-run system of poverty management and social control whose logic and administration do not move unincorporated Black Americans beyond this administrative authority. Bad practices and poorly constructed policies are what characterize this poverty management system. Working in concert with the punishing apparatus of the law-and-order regime, poverty management, under the auspices of the state, is decisively paternalistic in its imperatives, enforcing an infantilized condition among unincorporated Black Americans. Similar to the punishment arm of the law-and-order regime, this management system is nothing more than a system of containment, a prison beyond the prison. This prison beyond the prison is among the many problems related to mass incarceration which appears in the work of Michelle Alexander. It is also given serious coverage in the work of political scientist Marie Gottschalk whose 2015 book, *Caught: The Prison State and the Lockdown of American Politics*, lays out the entire economy of poverty management (particularly the prison) and the conditions that breed the prison beyond the prison in America. This prison beyond the prison feeds actual prisons, jails, and detention centers in the United States.[27] For example, an American city such as Baltimore,

Maryland, is a major instance of poverty management and its relationship to mass incarceration in the United States. Baltimore, Maryland, has stood out in terms of racial politics in the United States. Baltimore, Maryland, is over-represented in journalism and popular culture where of poverty management under state-supervised welfare systems and criminal justice police, under the law-and-order regime, converge. Media productions, inspired by professional journalism, over the last twenty-five years, by Home Box Office (HBO) such as *The Corner*, *The Wire*, and *We Run this City* are testaments to this condition. During *The Decade of Death (2012–2022)*, the political scientist Keenga-Yamahtta Taylor outlined the condition of Baltimore, Maryland, in her book *From #BLACKLIVESMATTER to Black Liberation*.[28] At a more literary and autobiographical level, Baltimore resident, writer, and college professor, D. Watkins, laments this state of affairs in his book, *We Speak for Ourselves: A Word from Forgotten Black America*.[29] If you are an unincorporated Black American in Baltimore, Maryland, your life is confined to a prison beyond a prison and such a life is vulnerable to the brick-and-mortar American prison. The marriage between state- administered poverty management and the intake and management of prison, jails, detention centers is abhorrent. It is a major impediment to the elimination of anti-Black racism in the United States.

Unfortunately, what I am calling the prison beyond the prison or poverty management in relation to unincorporated Black America, has not received the same attention as the general problem of mass incarceration or the prison industrial complex. The prison beyond the prison or poverty management is implicated in the work of those who promote prison abolition and criminal justice reform. However, the entire colonial and administrative apparatus of poverty management in the United States has not been identified as a major impediment to overcome. Apart from efforts to reform the welfare state at the end of the 1990s and the early 2000s, the logic and edifice of poverty management as a problem has been relatively ignored. In contrast, the welfare state has been largely defended by those who see themselves as agents of justice in the United States.[30] Distinct from those efforts to reform welfare more than two decades ago, the defenders of the welfare state have done so with little to no examination of its practices and policies which amplify the condition of unincorporated Black America. In this regard, the contemporary welfare state is not imagined as a colonial entity, paternalistic in nature, which exists as a system of containment, a prison, in the United States. As a colonial state-funded and operated system with administrators, policies, and practices, the contemporary welfare state demands as much interrogation as the prison, especially as its function as a proxy to and feeder of the American prison. The questions of who administers the welfare state and how it is administered are just as important as who administers the punishment arm of the law-and-order regime in the

United States. Identifying the colonial nature of this system of poverty management exposes the manner in which it constrains and impedes the ability of unincorporated Black America to enter the mainstream of White capitalist America. Specific attention to how its logic is applied to unincorporated Black America illuminates how it works as a mechanism of management and control.

As I have indicated above, what I am calling the prison beyond the prison or poverty management is not a part of mainstream efforts of justice in the United States. It is not even treated as a problem that contributes to the condition of unincorporated Black America. Although the examination that I am calling for is not mainstream, the colonial concerns that animate this interrogation are far from new. The colonial questions that have been raised here have been raised before, during other periods in history when the welfare state began to expand in the United States. During the late 1960s and early 1970s, the expansion of the welfare state and its absorption of unincorporated Black America drew the attention of Black American critics who raised concerns about its paternalistic impositions on unincorporated Black America. How the welfare state presented itself as a colonial imposition in relation to Black Americans was identified as a problem. The colonial nature of this imposition was heightened by the logic of the state and how it imagined and managed Black Americans. At that time, the logic of the state was deeply animated by racist mythology pertaining to Black Americans at the level of the family. This is where the paternalistic imperatives of the state were amplified and unregulated. A view of Black families as deficient as the consequence of wayward, unemployed, and criminal Black men fueled the policies and practices of those who administered welfare, poverty managers, at the time.[31] This view was compounded by policies and practices which promoted the dissolution of families where adult men, particularly fathers, were members of households. Through policies and practices, welfare administrators enforced a system, existent to this day, which incentivized families headed exclusively by women. Since the 1970s, the incentivization of households headed exclusively by women has characterized the welfare state. This household which is headed exclusively by women is at the very heart of poverty management and the colonial control of unincorporated Black America. In 2006, the nature of this system and its exclusive focus on unincorporated Black households led exclusively by women was documented in the edited volume by professor of social work, Ronald B. Mincy, in *Black Males Left Behind*.[32] During the Obama Era, the political historian, James T. Patterson, gave further documentation to the birth, evolution, and negative consequences of this five-decade enterprise in his 2010 book, *Freedom Is Not Enough: The Moynihan Report and America's Struggle Over Black Family Life from LBJ to Obama*.[33]

The incentivization of unincorporated Black households headed exclusively by women, the cornerstone of poverty management in the United

States, has, over the decades, had ruinous effects on unincorporated Black America. Researched and studied endlessly by sociologists, other academics, and journalists, such households exist at a huge distance from those households which are associated with those Americans and parts of America which are fully incorporated into the mainstream of White capitalist America. The latter households, which are not colonial subjects of the state, are the antithesis, in terms of mobility and development and most significantly, wealth, of the women-led households of unincorporated Black America. The latter households are largely protected from and immune to the surveillance arms of the state.[34] An entire arsenal of incentives integral to participating in the mainstream of White capitalist America confounds the world of incentives, engineered by state-based poverty management, which rewards, promotes, and maintains households led by women in unincorporated Black America. If there is a single reason why the welfare state is worthy of serious questioning and interrogation, this reason lies in the gaps that it produces between households that are under its authority and households which are independent of its colonial machinations. The major difference, evident in the gaps between the two, is that households in parts of America that are fully incorporated into White capitalist America are not exclusively led by women.

At the level of the household, the gaps between unincorporated Black America and Americans who are fully incorporated into the mainstream of White capitalism have been widely documented. One recent study, undertaken by the Brookings Institute, which magnifies the gaps between these divergent households is the work of economist Richard Reeves in *Dream Hoarders: How the American Upper Middle Class Is Leaving Everyone in the Dust, Why That Is a Problem, and What to Do About It*.[35] In general, there is no controversy in citing the differences between households that are unincorporated and households that are fully incorporated in the edifice of American capitalism. However, when distinctions are drawn between these two distinct households which elevates one household over the other, or that one household is regarded as superior to the other, that is where controversy, contestation, and debate ensue. This happens at the political level among those defenders of the welfare state who have used the welfare state and/or state-managed and funded households led exclusively by women to advance a set of political interests. The household led exclusively by women, as it is managed and funded by the state, welfare, has been very useful for the said political program. Explicitly, second-wave feminists have politicized households led by women, controlled and funded by the state, to bolster the aims of feminism. In doing so, second-wave feminism has guarded the welfare state, its role as a poverty manager, and colonizer of unincorporated Black America, from criticism. To the degree that second-wave feminism has defended the welfare state, it reinforces and amplifies the condition of unincorporated

Black America and the marriage between poverty management and the criminal justice system. Among the prominent feminist defenders of the welfare state is the political philosopher, Nancy Fraser. Her promotion of state-managed and funded households led by women is figured prominently in her collection of essays, *Fortunes of Feminism: From State-Managed Capitalism to Neoliberal Crisis*.[36] Former US Senator, secretary of state, and US presidential candidate Hillary Clinton is also among a generation of feminists who also supported state-based poverty management as it relates to female-headed households during her political career. Her political support for state-based poverty management is taken up in Liza Featherstone's edited volume, *False Choices: The Faux Feminism of Hillary Rodham Clinton*.[37] Michelle Alexander, who has been cited in this book, has also written about the relationship between Hillary Clinton and poverty management in the United States. This analysis appeared in *The Nation Magazine* in 2016 when Hillary Clinton ran, for the second time, for the US presidency. This essay, *Why Hillary Clinton Doesn't Deserve the Black Vote*, was an updated and condensed rearticulation of arguments she made in *The New Jim Crow: Mass Incarceration in the Age of Colorblindness*.[38] In a word, over the course of decades, the relationship between the prison beyond the prison and the actual prison has been nurtured by second-wave feminism. Where unincorporated Black Americans are concerned, second-wave feminism has been hostile to the proposition that fully incorporated Black American households, led by men and women, are better than unincorporated Black households led exclusively by women. Second-wave feminism has been hostile to any proposition and political effort which seeks to replace the incentive structure of the welfare state, which is oriented toward unincorporated Black households led exclusively by women, with something else like a two-parent household or bring it closer to the incentive structure that fuels households that are fully incorporated in the mainstream of White American capitalism. To the degree that feminism defends the welfare state and its logic, it should be counted among the poverty managers and colonizers of unincorporated Black America.

The welfare state is fundamentally a system of containment and surveillance (or policing) which aligns it with and assists the nature, purpose, and function of the prison industrial complex. It is essentially paternalistic, patriarchal, and punitive in its orientation and execution. The way in which it is currently structured and managed is antagonistic to any kind of robust anti-racist politics. If a new wave of crime policies emerge in the near or not-too-distant future, the welfare state will continue to serve as a feeding ground for prison capitalists in America. An engagement with the welfare state as a poverty manager and colonizer is necessary for any politics which seeks to thwart cruel and unusual punishment, the state-based father, as the final solution for unincorporated Black America.

NOTES

1. See the chapter, How to Be a Black President, in Michael Eric Dyson's, *The Black Presidency: Barack Obama and the Politics of Race in America* (Boston and New York: Mariner Books, 2016), pp. 1–32.
2. See the chapter, "The Political Theology of Mass Incarceration," in Joshua Dubler and Vincent W. Lloyd's, *Break Every Yoke: Religion, Justice, and the Abolition of Prisons* (New York: Oxford University Press, 2020), pp. 65–103.
3. See the chapter, "White Fear, in Eddie S. Glaude Jr.'s *Democracy in Black: How Race Still Enslaves the American Soul* (New York: Crown Publishers, 2016), pp. 71–92.
4. With a solid conservative majority, enabled by the one-term presidency of Donald J. Trump, the future judicial decisions of the Supreme Court and their impact on jurisprudence in the United States have created a moral panic among liberals, leftists, and feminists. The New Republic magazine captured these concerns in a recent article on the Chief Justice of the Supreme Court, John Roberts, and his leadership role in a conservative court. See Matt Ford, The Chief Justice Who Isn't, in *The New Republic*, November 2022, pp. 13–19.
5. See Michael Eric Dyson.
6. For an account of the major critiques of liberalism over the last half-century, see Patrick J. Deneen, *Why Liberalism Failed* (New Haven and London: Yale University Press, 2018).
7. For a classic account of this history, especially as it pertains to the disenfranchisement of Black Americans, see C. Van Woodward, *The Burden of Southern History* (Baton Rouge: Louisiana State University Press, 1960).
8. See David M. Oshinsky, *Worse Than Slavery: Parchman Farm and the Ordeal of Jim Crow Justice* (New York: Free Press Paperbacks, 1996). Also see Theodore Rosengarten, *All God's Children: The Life of Nate Shaw* (Chicago: The University of Chicago Press, 1974).
9. See Glenn C. Loury, Pamela S. Karian, Tommy Shelby, and Loic Wacquant, *Race, Incarceration, and American Values* (Cambridge and London: The MIT Press, 2008).
10. See Joshua Dubler and Vincent W. Lloyd.
11. See James Braxton Peterson, *Prison Industrial Complex for Beginners* (Danbury: For Beginners, LLC, 2016).
12. See National Review (Special Edition): Law and Disorder: America's Crime Crisis and What to Do About It, Vol. LXXIII, No. 18 (October 4, 2021).
13. See Angela Y. Davis, Ed. *Policing the Black Man* (New York: Pantheon Books, 2017). Also see Marie Gottschalk, *Caught: The Prison States and the Lockdown of American Politics* (Princeton and Oxford: Princeton University Press, 2015).
14. See Melynda J. Price, *At the Cross: Race, Religion, and Citizenship in the Politics of the Death Penalty* (New York: Oxford University Press, 2015). Also, see Mark Lewis Taylor, *The Executed God: The Way of the Cross in Lockdown America* (Minneapolis: Fortress Press, 2001).

15. See Albert Woodfox and Leslie George, *Solitary: Unbroken by Four Decades in Solitary Confinement. My Story of Transformation* (New York: Grove Press, 2019); Wilbert Rideau and Ron Wikberg, *Life Sentences: A Story of Rage and Survival Behind Bars* (New York: New York Times Books, 1992); Wilbert Rideau, *In the Place of Justice: A Story of Punishment and Deliverance* (New York: Alfred A. Knopf, 2010); Yusef Salaam, *Better Not Bitter: Living on Purpose in the Pursuit of Racial Justice* (New York and Boston: Grand Central Publishing, 2021).

16. See Kevin Merinda and Michael Fletcher, *Supreme Discomfort: The Divided Soul of Clarence Thomas* (New York: Broadway Books, 2007); Corey Robin, *The Enigma of Clarence Thomas* (New York: Metropolitan Books, 2019).

17. Myron Magnet, *Clarence Thomas and the Lost Constitution* (New York and London: Encounter Books, 2019).

18. Clarence Thomas, *My Grandfather's Son* (New York: HarperCollins Publishers, 2007).

19. See A Question of Will in chapter 6 of *My Grandfather's Son*, pp. 121–150.

20. Robin, *The Enigma of Clarence Thomas*.

21. Thomas, *My Grandfather's Son*.

22. See Benjamin Crump, *Open Season: The Legal Genocide of Colored People* (New York: HarperCollins Publishers, 2019).

23. See Thomas, *My Grandfather's Son*, pp. 118–119.

24. See Huey P. Newton, *Revolutionary Suicide* (New York: The Penguin Group, 1973); Joshua Bloom and Waldo E. Martin, Jr., *Black Against the Empire: The History and Politics of the Black Panther Party* (Berkeley, Los Angeles, and London: University of California Press, 2013).

25. Michelle Alexander, *The New Jim Crow: Mass Incarceration in the Age of Colorblindness*, 10th Anniversary Edition (New York and London: The New Press, 2020).

26. See Mechthild Nagel's article on the relationship between punishment and child protective services, Policing Families: The Many-Headed Hydra of Surveillance, Newsletter, The American Philosophical Association, Vol. 12, No. 2 (Spring 2018), pp. 2–7.

27. Marie Gottschalk, *The Prison State and the Lockdown of American Politics* (Princeton and Oxford: Princeton University Press, 2015).

28. Keeanga-Yamahatta Taylor, *From #BLACKLIVESMATTER to Black Liberation* (Chicago: Haymarket Books, 2016).

29. D. Watkins, *We Speak for Ourselves: A Word from Forgotten Black America* (New York, London, Toronto, and New Delhi: Atria Books, 2019).

30. See Nancy Fraser, *Fortunes of Feminism: From State Managed Capitalism to Neoliberal Crisis* (London and New York: Version, 2013).

31. See James T. Patterson, *Freedom Is Not Enough: The Moynihan Report and America's Struggle for Black Family Life in the United States from LBJ to Obama* (New York: Basic Books, 2010).

32. Ronald B. Mincy, Ed. *Black Males Left Behind* (Washington, DC: The Urban Institute Press, 2006).

33. Patterson, *Freedom Is Not Enough.*

34. See Richard V. Reeves, *Dream Hoarders: How the American Upper Middle Class Is Leaving Everyone Else in the Dust, Why That Is Problem, and What to Do About It* (Washington, DC: Brookings Institute Press, 2017).

35. Ibid.

36. Fraser, *Fortunes of Feminism.*

37. Liza Featherstone, Ed. *False Choices: The Faux Feminism of Hillary Rodham Clinton* (London and New York: Verso Books, 2016).

38. Michelle Alexander, Why Hillary Clinton Doesn't Deserve the Black Vote, *The Nation*, February 29, 2016; *The New Jim Crow.*

Conclusion
Shut Up and Dribble

During *The Decade of Death (2012–2022)*, America witnessed a revival of activism among professional athletes. Among those athletes who were politically vocal in this period was basketball superstar LeBron James. As Lebron James became vocal about the racial climate of the United States, including the treatment of Black citizens at the hands of the police, he became the target of criticism by media elites. One such media elite was Laura Ingraham who is a political commentator at Fox News. From the perch of Fox News, Laura Ingraham, in commenting on the political outspokenness of LeBron James, stated that LeBron James should stick to being a professional basketball player and leave politics alone. Ingraham famously stated that LeBron James should just, "shut up and dribble." Laura Ingraham vocalized a strong consensus within conservative media outlets and among elite sports journalists in corporate media regarding the separation between politics and professional athletics. In this view, professional athletes such as LeBron James should not use their celebrity to make political statements, especially as it relates to matters of race and overall anti-Blackness in America. In their view, professional athletes should "stay in their lane" and confine their energies exclusively to the terrain of sports. This view is held and espoused despite a significant history and tradition of Black American athletes (e.g., Muhammad Ali, Kareem Abdul-Jabar, Jim Brown, Bill Russell, Arthur Ashe, et. al.) who have engaged in political activism and have been vocal about civil and human rights in the United States. What the media personality Laura Ingraham said to NBA superstar LeBron James spoke volumes not only about the disdain toward political dissent in relation to Black professional athletes but it also speaks to a larger consensus regarding the political voices of Black men writ large. This disdain which exists in the world of sports also lives in the world of academia where an unspoken rule exists that demands quietism among Black men who are scholars in the humanities and social sciences. Black men who are scholars in the humanities and social sciences are subject to censure in relation to postmodernism and identity politics which are standard in these arenas. When it comes to Black men who are scholars, there is an unspoken rule that the normativity of postmodernism and identity politics in the humanities and social sciences is above scrutiny and interrogation, that their necessity in the everyday world is universal, addressing all of the social problems, especially anti-Black racism, in the United States. The aim of this book, *Beyond Death and Jail*, has been to contest this consensus in academia. My contestation of this consensus happens at a time when academic voices similar to mine, Black men, are pushing for alternatives to postmodern and identitarian approaches to anti-Black racism in the United States. Such scholars include professors Tommy J. Curry (The University of Edinburgh, Scotland) and T. Hasan Johnson (University of California, Fresno). These scholars, along with myself, are thinking differently about anti-Black racism, especially as it relates to Black masculinity in America. This work is undertaken in the face of the universal demand for quietism, to "shut up and dribble." After *The Decade of Death (2012–2022)* this demand for quietism is no longer tolerable. More significantly, the demand for censure is anti-progressive and is fundamentally an impediment to the production and advancement of knowledge in service of justice. If there is a single thing that I hope this book accomplishes, it is that more voices emerge which go against the orthodoxies which I have outlined in its pages. As I have stated throughout various parts of this text, new perspectives and new approaches to anti-Blackness and unincorporated Black America are needed in the twenty-first century.

Bibliography

Alexander, Michelle. *The New Jim Crow: Mass Incarceration in the Age of Colorblindness*, 10th Anniversary Edition. New York and London: The New Press, 2020.
———. Why Hillary Clinton Doesn't Deserve the Black Vote. *The Nation*, February 29, 2016.
Ambedkar, B.R., Arundhati Roy, and S. Anand. *Annihilation of Caste (The Annotated Critical Edition)*. London and New York: Verso Books, 2016.
American Legends, Special Issue: Kamala Harris. New York: Centennial Media LLC, 2021.
Anderson, Elijah. *Black in White Space: The Enduring Impact of Color in Everyday Life*. Chicago and London: The University of Chicago Press, 2022.
———. *The Cosmopolitan Canopy: Race and Civility in Everyday Life*. New York and London: W. W. Norton & Company, 2011.
Anderson, Kristin J. *Modern Misogyny: Anti-Feminism in a Post-Feminist Era*. Oxford and New York: Oxford University Press, 2015.
Anderson, Victor. *Beyond Ontological Blackness: An Essay in African American Religious and Cultural Criticism*. New York: The Contiuum Publishing Company, 1995.
Appiah, Kwame Anthony. *The Lies That Bind: Rethinking Identity*. New York: Liveright Publishing Corporation, 2018.
Armstrong, Karen. *A History of God: The 4,000 Year Quest of Judaism, Christianity, and Islam*. New York: MJF Books, 1993.
———. *Islam: A Short History*. New York: Modern Library Books, 2002.
Arvin, Maile, Eve Tuck, and Angie Morill. Decolonizing Feminism: Challenging Connections between Settler Colonialism and Heteropatriarchy. *Feminist Formations*, Vol. 25, No. 1 (Spring 2013), pp. 8–34. Published: John Hopkins University Press. JSTOR: https://www.jstor.org/stable/43860665.
Baker Jr., Houston A. *Betrayal: How Black Intellectuals Have Abandoned the Ideals of the Civil Rights Era*. New York: Columbia University Press, 2008.
Baker-Fletcher, Garth Kasimu. *Xodus: An African American Male Journey*. Minneapolis: Fortress Press, 1996.

Baker-Fletcher, Garth Kasimu, Ed. *Black Religion after the Million Man March.* Maryknoll: Orbis Books, 1998.

Ball, Molly. Finding Kamala Harris. *Time Magazine*, October 19, 2019.

Banks, Ralph Richard. *Is Marriage for White People? How the African–American Marriage Decline Affects Everyone.* New York: Plume, 2011.

Barber II, William J. and Jonathan Wilson-Hartgrove. *The Third Reconstruction: How a Moral Movement Is Overcoming the Politics of Division and Fear.* Boston: Beacon Press, 2016.

Bartlett, Tom. When a Theory Goes Viral: Intersectionality Is Now Everywhere. Is It a Good Thing? *The Chronicle of Higher Education*, May 21, 2017.

Beck, Koa. *White Feminism: From the Suffragettes to Influencers and Who They Leave Behind.* New York, London, Tokyo, Sydney, and New Delhi: Atria Paperback, 2021.

Bell, Derrick. *And We Are Not Saved: The Elusive Quest for Racial Justice.* New York: Basic Books, Inc., 1987.

———. *Faces at the Bottom of the Well: The Permanence of Racism.* New York: Basic Books, Inc., 1992.

———. *Silent Covenants: Brown v. Board of Education and the Unfulfilled Hopes for Racial Reform.* Oxford: Oxford University Press, 2004.

Bernstein, Brittany. Black Lives Matters Removes Language About Heterosexual Nuclear Family Website. https://www.news.yahoo.com/black-lives-matter-removes-language-185621063.html?fr=sycrp-catchall.

Berry, Daina Ramey and Kali Nicole Gross's. *A Black Women's History of the United States.* Boston: Beacon Press, 2020.

Bijan, Stephen. Rebel Without a Pause: Killer Mike and the Return of the Politically Engaged Rapper. *The New Republic*, January/February 2016, pp. 52–55.

The Black Lives Matter Global Network, the official website (https://www.blacklivesmatter.com).

Blain, Keisha N. *Until I am Free: Fannie Lou Hamer's Enduring Message to America.* Boston: Beacon Press, 2021.

Bloom, Joshua and Waldo E. Martin, Jr. *Black Against the Empire: The History and Politics of the Black Panther Party.* Berkeley, Los Angeles, and London: University of California Press, 2013.

Boyd, Todd. *The New H.N.I.C.: The Death of Civil Rights and the Reign of Hip Hop.* New York and London: New York University Press, 2003.

Branch, Taylor. *Pillar of Fire: America in the King Years, 1963–1965.* New York: Simon Schuster, 1998.

Brooks, David. Listening to Ta-Nehisi Coates While Driving White, Op-Ed. *The New York Times*, July 12, 2015.

Butler, Judith. *Gender Trouble: Feminism and the Subversion Identity.* New York and London: Routledge Classics, 2006.

———. Merely Cultural. *Social Text*, No. 52/53 (Autumn–Winter, 1997), Queer Transexions of Race, Nation and Gender, pp. 265–277. Published: Duke University Press. JSTOR: https://www.jstor.org/stable/466744.

Butler, Paul. Black Male Exceptionalism? The Problems and Potential of Black Male Focused Interventions. *Du Bois Review*, Vol. 10, No. 2 (2013), pp. 485–511. W.E.B. Dubois Institute for African and African American Research.

———. *Chokehold: A Renegade Prosecutor's Thoughts on How to Disrupt the System*. New York: The New Press, 2017.

Butterfield, Fox. *All God's Children: The Bosket Family and the American Tradition of Violence*. New York: Vintage Books, 1995.

Chetty, Raj, Nathan Hendren, Maggie R. Jones, and Sonya R. Porter. *Race and Economic Opportunity in the United States*. Washington, DC: The Brookings Institute, March 2018.

Coates, Ta-Nehisi. *The Beautiful Struggle: A Memoir*. New York: Spiegal & Grau, 2008.

———. *Between the World and Me*. New York: Spiegal & Grau, 2015.

———. The Black Family in the Age of Incarceration. *The Atlantic*, October 2015.

———. The Case for Reparations. *The Atlantic*, June 2014.

———. *We Were Eight Years in Power*. New York: One World, 2017.

Cobb, Jelani. Where Is Black Lives Matter Headed? *The New Yorker*, March 14, 2016, pp. 34–40.

Cole, Johnetta B. and Beverly Guy-Sheftall. *Gender Talk: The Struggle for Women's Equality in African American Communities*. New York: One World Books, 2003.

Coleman, Monica A., Ed. *Ain't I a Womanist Too? Third Wave Womanist Thought*. Maryknoll: Orbis Books, 2013.

Collins, Patricia Hill. *Black Feminist Thought*, 2nd Edition. New York and London: Routledge Press, 2000.

———. *Black Sexual Politics: African Americans, Gender, and the New Racism*. New York: Routledge Press, 2004.

Cone, James H. *A Theology of Black Liberation: Twentieth Anniversary Edition*. Maryknoll: Orbis Books, 2008.

Cone, James H. and Gayraud S. Wilmore. *Black Theology: A Documentary History, Volume 2: 1980–1992*. Maryknoll: Orbis Books, 1993.

———. *Martin & Malcolm: A Dream or a Nightmare*. Maryknoll: Orbis Books, 1993.

Connell, R.W. *Masculinities*, 2nd Edition. Berkeley and Los Angeles: University of California Press, 2005.

Cooper, Brittney C. *Beyond Respectability: The Intellectual Thought of Race Women*. Urbana, Chicago, and Springfield: University of Illinois Press, 2017.

———. *Eloquent Rage: A Black Feminist Discovers Her Superpowers*. New York: St. Martin's Press, 2018.

Cose, Ellis. *The Envy of the World: On Being a Black Man in America*. New York: Washington Square Press, 2002.

Crenshaw, Kimberle. Mapping the Margins: Intersectionality, Identity Politics, and Violence Against Women of Color. *Stanford Law Review*, Vol. 43, No. 6 (July 1991), pp. 1241–1299. Published by *Stanford Law Review*. https://www.jstor.org/stable/1229039.

Crump, Ben. *Open Season: The Legal Genocide of Colored People.* New York: Harper Collins Publishers, 2019.

Cullors, Patrisse and Darnell L. Moore. Black Lives Matter/Black Life Matters: A Conversation with Patrisse Cullors and Darnell L. Moore. *The Feminist Wire*, December 1, 2014. https://thefeministwire.com/2014/12/black-lives-matter-black-life-matters-conversation-patrisse-cullors-darnell-l-moore/.

Curry, Tommy. *The Man-Not: Race, Class, Genre, and the Dilemmas of Black Manhood.* Philadelphia: Temple University Press, 2017.

Dailey, Jane. *White Fright: The Sexual Panic at the Heart of America's Racist History.* New York: Hatchet Book Group, Inc., 2020.

Davis, Angela J., Ed. *Policing the Black Man.* New York: Pantheon Books, 2017.

Davis, Angela Y. *Are Prisons Obsolete?* New York: Seven Stories Press, 2003.

———. *Women, Race, and Class.* New York: Vintage Books, 1981.

Day, Keri. *Religious Resistance to Neoliberalism: Womanist and Black Feminist Perspectives.* New York: Palgrave Macmillan, 2016.

De Beauvoir, Simone. *The Second Sex.* New York: Vintage Books, 2011.

Deneen, Patrick J. *Why Liberalism Failed.* New Haven and London: Yale University Press, 2018.

Douglas, Kelly Brown. *Sexuality and the Black Church: A Womanist Perspective.* Maryknoll: Orbis Press, 1999.

———. *Stand Your Ground: Black Bodies and the Justice of God.* Maryknoll: Orbis Books, 2015.

Dubler, Joshua and Vincent W. Lloyd. *Break Every Yoke: Religion, Justice, and the Abolition of Prisons.* New York: Oxford University Press, 2020.

DuBois, W.E.B. *The Gift of Black Folk: The Negroes in the Making of America.* Garden City Park: Square One Publishers, 2009.

Dunbar-Ortiz, Roxanne. *Not a Nation of Immigrants: Settler Colonialism, White Supremacy, and a History of Erasure and Exclusion.* Boston: Beacon Press Books, 2022.

Duncan, Jason K. *John F. Kennedy: The Spirit of Cold War Liberalism.* New York and London: Routledge, 2014.

Dyson, Michael Eric. *The Black Presidency: The Politics of Race in America.* New York: Mariner Books, 2017.

———. *Making Malcolm: The Myth and Meaning of Malcolm X.* New York and Oxford: Oxford University Press, 1995.

———. *Race Rules: Navigating the Color Line.* New York: Addison Wesley Publishing Company, 1996.

Fanon, Frantz. *Black Skin, White Masks.* New York: Grove Press, 1952.

Farley, Edward. *Good & Evil: Interpreting a Human Condition.* Minneapolis: Augsburg Fortress Press, 1990.

Featherstone, Liza, Ed. *False Choices: The Faux Feminism of Hillary Rodham Clinton.* London and New York: Verso Book, 2016.

Fluker, Walter Earl. *The Ground Has Shifted: The Future of the Black Church in Post-Racial America.* New York: New York University Press, 2016.

Foner, Philip S., Ed. *The Black Panthers Speak.* Chicago: Haymarket Books, 2014.

Ford, Matt. The Chief Justice Who Isn't. *The New Republic*, November 2022.
Forman Jr., James. *Locking Up Our Own. Crime and Punishment in Black America.* New York: Farrar, Straus, and Giroux, 2017.
Franklin, John Hope. *From Slavery to Freedom: A History of African Americans.* Columbus: McGraw-Hill, 2010.
Fraser, Nancy. *Fortunes of Feminism: From State Managed Capitalism to Neoliberal Crisis.* London and New Yok: Verso, 2013.
Fulton, Sybrina and Tracy Martin. *Rest in Power: A Parent's Story of Love, Injustice, and the Birth of a Movement.* New York: Spiegal and Grau, 2017.
Garza, Alicia. A Herstory of the Black Lives Matter Movement. *The Feminist Wire*, October 7, 2014. https://thefeministwire.com/2014/10/blacklivesmatter-2/.
Glaude Jr., Eddie S. *Democracy in Black: How Race Still Enslaves the American Soul.* New York: Crown Publishers, 2016.
Golden, Marita. *Wild Women Don't Wear No Blues.* New York: Anchor Books, 1993.
Gottschalk, Marie. *Caught: The Prison State and the Lockdown of American Politics.* Princeton and Oxford: Princeton University Press, 2015.
Griffith, D.W. *The Birth of a Nation.* Epoch Producing Corporation, 1915.
Guha, Ramachandra, Ed. *Makers of Modern India.* Cambridge and London: The Belknap Press of Harvard University Press, 2011.
Guy Sheftall, Beverly, Ed. *Words of Fire: An Anthology of African American Feminist Thought.* New York: The New Press, 1995.
Halper, Evan. Political Education. *The Los Angeles Times: Special Education: Vice President Kamala*, New York, 2021.
Harding, Vincent. *Martin Luther King: The Inconvenient Hero.* Maryknoll: Orbis Books, 1996.
Hare, Nathan and Julia Hare. *The Endangered Black Family: Coping with the Unisexualization and Extinction of the Black Race.* San Francisco: Black Think Tank, 1984.
Hart, William David. *Afro-Eccentricity: Beyond the Standard Narrative of Black Religion.* New York: Palgrave Macmillan, 2011.
———. *Black Religion: Malcom X, Julius Lester, and Jan Willis.* New York: Palgrave McMillan, 2008.
Holmes, Charles. He Shook the World: George Floyd's Houston Legacy. *Rolling Stone Magazine*, July 2020.
hooks, bell. *We Real Cool: Black Men and Masculinity.* New York and London: Routledge, 2004.
Hooks, Bell, Michele Wallace, Andrew Hacker, Jared Taylor, Derrick Bell, Ishmael Reed, Nathan Hare, Rita Williams, Cecilia Caruso, Carl H. Nightingale, Jim Sleeper, Elsie B. Washington, Yehudi Webster, Kenneth S. Tollett, Sr. and Cecil Brown. The Crisis of African American Gender Relations. *Transition*, No. 66 (1995), pp. 91–175. Published by: Indiana University Press on Behalf of the Hutchins Center for African and African American Research at Harvard University. JSTOR: https://www.jstor.org/stable/2935286.
Hudson-Weems, Clenora. *Africana Womanism: Reclaiming Ourselves*, 5th Edition. London and New York: Routledge, 2020.

Irving Painter, Nell. *The History of White People*. New York and London: W. W. Norton & Company, 2010.

Jackson, Emily. Catharine MacKinnon and Feminist Juris Prudence: A Critical Appraisal. *Journal of Law and Society*, Vol. 19, No. 2 (Summer, 1992), pp. 195–213. Published by: Wiley on behalf of Cardiff University. JSTOR: https://www.jstor.org/stable/1410220.

Jackson, Sherman A. *Islam and the Blackamerican: Looking Toward the Third Resurrection*. New York: Oxford University Press, 2005.

Johnson, T. Hasan. *Solutions for Anti-Black Misandry, Flat Blackness, and Black Male Death: The Black Masculinist Turn*. Oxford: Routledge, 2023.

Jones, Bomani. State of America: Ta-Nehisi Coates. *Playboy Magazine*, July/August 2016.

Jones, Feminista. *Reclaiming Our Space: How Black Feminists Are Changing the World from Tweets to the Streets*. Boston: Beacon Press, 2019.

Jones, William R. *Is God a White Racist?: A Preamble to Black Theology*. Boston: Beacon Press, 1988.

Kavka, Martin. *Jewish Messianism and the History of Philosophy*. Cambridge: Cambridge University Press, 2004.

King, Jr. Martin Luther. *Stride Toward Freedom: The Montgomery Story*. Boston: Beacon Press, 1958.

———. *Where Do We Go From Here: Chaos or Community?* Boston: Beacon Press, 1968.

———. *Why We Can't Wait*. Berkeley: Signet Classics, 1964.

King, Deborah K. Multiple Jeopardy, Multiple Consciousness: The Context of Black Feminist Ideology. *Signs*, Vol. 14, No. 1 (Autumn, 1988), pp. 42–72, *The University of Chicago Press Journals*, JSTOR (https://www.jstor.org/stable/3174661).

Knott, Kim. *Hinduism: A Very Short Introduction*. Oxford: Oxford University Press, 2016.

Kornegay Jr., EL. *A Queering of Black Theology: James Baldwin's Blues Project and Gospel Prose*. New York: Palgrave McMillan, 2013.

Lightsey, Pamela. *Our Lives Matter: A Womanist Queer Theology*. Eugene: Pickwick Publications, 2015.

Lofton, Kathryn. *Oprah: The Gospel of an Icon*. Berkeley: The University of California Press, 2011.

Long, Charles H. *Significations: Signs, Symbols, and Images in the Interpretation of Religion*. Philadelphia: Fortress Press, 1986.

Los Angeles Times. Special Edition: Vice President Kamala Harris. New York: Meredith Premium Publishing, 2021.

Lott, Eric. *The Disappearing Liberal Intellectual*. New York: Basic Books, 2006.

Loury, Glenn. *The Anatomy of Racial Inequality*. Massachusetts and London: Harvard University Press, 2002.

Loury, Glenn C., Pamela S. Karian, Tommie Shelby, and Loc Wacquant. *Race, Incarceration, and American Values*. Cambridge and London: The MIT Press, 2008.

Magnet, Myron. *Clarence Thomas and the Lost Constitution*. New York and London: Encounter Books, 2019.

Marable, Manning. *The Great Wells of Democracy: The Meaning of Race in American Life*. New York: Basic Civitas Books, 2002.

———. *Race, Reform, and Rebellion: The Second Reconstruction and Beyond in America*, 3rd Edition. Jackson: University Press of Mississippi, 2007.

Marbury, Herbert Robinson. *Pillars of Cloud and Fire: The Politics of Exodus in African American Biblical Interpretation*. New York: New York University Press, 2015.

Mason, Melanie. *A Place in History, Los Angeles Times: Special Edition: Vice President Kamala Harris*. New York: Meredith Premium Publishing, 2021.

Mason, Melania and Michael Finnegan. *A Mixed Record on Police Reform, Los Angeles Times, Special Edition: Kamala Harris*. New York: Meredith Publishing Group, 2021.

McDougal, Serie. *Black Men's Studies: Black Manhood and Masculinities in the U.S. Context*. New York, Bern, Berlin, Brussels, Vienna, Oxford, and Warsaw: Peter Lang, 2020.

McLanahan, Sara, Ron Haskins, Irvin Garfinkel, Ronald B. Mincy, and Elisabeth Donahue. *Strengthening Fragile Families*. Princeton, NJ: Policy Brief Fall 2010, The Future of Children, Princeton-Brookings.

Menand, Louis. *The Metaphysical Club: A Story of Ideas in America*. New York: Farrar, Straus, and Giroux, 2001.

Merinda, Kevin and Michael Fletcher. *Supreme Discomfort: The Divided Soul of Clarence Thomas*. New York: Broadway Books, 2007.

Michaels, Walter Benn. *The Trouble with Diversity: How We Learned to Love Identity and Ignore Inequality*. New York: Metropolitan Books, 2006.

Miller, Monica. *Religion and Hip Hop*. New York and London: Routledge, 2013.

Mincy, Ronald B. *Black Males Left Behind*. Washington, DC: The Urban Institute Press, 2006.

Moses, Wilson Jeremiah. *Black Messiahs and Uncle Toms: Social and Literary Manipulations of a Religious Myth*. University Park: The Pennsylvania State University Press, 1982.

———. *The Golden Age of Black Nationalism, 1850–1925*. New York: Oxford University Press, 1978.

Moynihan, Patrick. *The Negro Family: The Case for National Action*. Office of Policy Planning and Research, United States Department of Labor, March 1965.

Nagel, Mechthild. Policing Families: The Many Headed Hydra of Surveillance. *Newsletter, The American Philosophical Association*, Vol. 12, No. 2 (Spring 2018), pp. 18–26.

The Nation. New Orleans: Ten Years Later. August 31/September 7, 2015.

National Review (Special Edition). Law and Disorder: America's Crime Crisis and What to Do About It. Vol. LXXIII, No. 18 (October 4, 2021).

Neal, Ronald. *Democracy in 21st Century America: Race, Class, Religion, and Region*. Macon: Mercer University Press, 2012.

———. Savior of the Race: The Messianic Burdens of Black Masculinity; Jesus Traditions and Masculinities in World Christianity. *Exchange: Journal of Missiological and Ecumenical Research*, Vol. 42, No. 1 (2013), pp. 1–17.

———. Troubling the Demonic: Anti-Blackness, Black Masculinity, and the Study of Religion in North America. *The Routledge Handbook on Religion, Gender, and Society*. London and New York: Routledge Press, 2022, Chapter 29.

Nelson, Sophia A. *Black Women Redefined: Dispelling Myths and Discovering Fulfillment in the Age of Michelle Obama.* Dallas: Benbellla Books, 2011.

Newman, Michelle Louise. *White Women's Rights: The Racial Origins of Feminism in the United States.* New York and Oxford: Oxford University Press, 1999.

Newton, Huey P. *Revolutionary Suicide.* New York: The Penguin Group, 1973.

Nielson, Erick and Andrea Dennis. *Rap on Trial: Race, Lyrics, and Guilt in America.* New York: The New Press, 2019.

Obama, Michelle. *Becoming Michelle Obama.* New York: Crown Books, 2018.

Oshinsky, David M. *Worse Than Slavery: Parchman farm and the Ordeal of Jim Crow Justice.* New York: Free Press Paperbacks, 1996.

Paris, Peter J. *Virtues and Values: The African and African American Experience.* Minneapolis: Fortess Press, 2004.

Patterson, James T. *Freedom Is Not Enough: The Moynihan Report and America's Struggle for Black Family Life in the United States from LBJ to Obama.* New York: Basic Books, 2010.

Patterson, Orlando. *Backlash.* Transition, No. 62 (1993), pp. 4–26. Published by Indiana University Press on behalf of the W.E.B. DuBois Institute. JSTOR: https://www.jstor.org/stable/2935200.

———. *Rituals of Blood: The Consequences of Slavery in Two American Centuries.* New York: Basic Civitas Books, 1998.

———. *Slavery and Social Death: A Comparative Study.* Cambridge: Harvard University Press, 1982.

———. *The Ordeal of integration. Progress and Resentment in America's Racial Crisis.* New York: Basic Civitas Books, 1997.

Perkinson, Robert. *Texas Tough: The Rise of American's Prison Empire.* New York: Metropolitan Books, 2010.

Peterson, James Braxton. *Prison Industrial Complex for Beginners.* Danbury: For Beginners, LLC, 2016.

Pinn, Anthony B. *Terror and Triumph: The Nature of Black Religion, 20th Anniversary Edition.* Minneapolis: Fortress Press, 2022.

Powers, Bernard. *Black Charlestonians: A Social History 1822–1885.* Fayetteville: University of Arkansas Press, 1994.

Price, Melynda J. *At the Cross: Race, Religion, and Citizenship in the Politics of the Death Penalty.* New York: Oxford University Press, 2015.

Raboteau, Albert J. *Slave Religion: The invisible Institution in the Antebellum South.* Oxford: Oxford University Press, 2004.

Radford Reuther, Rosemary. *The Radical Kingdom: The Western Experience of Messianic Hope.* New York: Harper & Row, 1970.

Reed, Adolph, Jr. Nothing Left: The Long Slow Surrender of American Liberals. *Harper's Magazine*, March 2014.

Reed, Ishmael. *Airing Dirty Laundry.* New York: Addison Wesley Publishing Company, 1993.

Reeves, Richard V. *Dream Hoarders: How the American Upper Middle Class Is Leaving Everyone Else in the Dust, Why It Is a Problem, and What to Do About It.* Washington, DC: The Brooking Institution, 2022.

———. *Of Boys and Men: Why the Modern Male Is Struggling, Why It Matters, and What to Do About It.* Washington, DC: Brooking Institution Press, 2022.

Richardson, Riche. *From Uncle Tom to Gangsta: Black Masculinity and the U.S. South.* Athens and London: The University of Georgia Press, 2007.

Richie, Beth E. *Arrested Justice: Black Women, Violence, and America's Prison Nation.* New York and London: New York University Press, 2012.

Rideau, Wilbert. *In the Place of Justice: A Story of Punishment and Deliverance.* New York: Alfred A. Knopf, 2010.

Rideau, Wilbert and Ron Wikberg. *Life Sentences: A Story of Rage and Survival Behind Bars.* New York: Times Books, 1992.

Robin, Corey. *The Enigma of Clarence Thomas.* New York: Metropolitan Books, 2019.

Robinson, Eugene. *Disintegration: The Splintering of Black America.* New York: Anchor Books, 2010.

Robinson, Nathan. *Super Predator: Bill Clinton's Use and Abuse of Black America.* West Somervile: Current Affairs Press, 2016.

Rosengarten, Theodore. *All God's Children: The Life of Nate Shaw.* Chicago: The University of Chicago Press, 1974.

Rosin, Hannah. *The End of Men/ And the Rise of Women.* New York: Riverhead Books, 2013.

Rowan, Carl T. *Dream Makers, Dream Breakers: The World of Justice Thurgood Marshall.* Canada: Little, Brown & Company, 1993.

Roy, Arudhanti. *Capitalism: A Ghost Story.* Chicago: Haymarket Books, 2014.

Sabo, Don, Terry A. Kupers, and Willie London, Eds. *Prison Masculinities.* Philadelphia: Temple University Press, 2001.

Salaam, Yusef. *Better Not Bitter. Living in Purpose in the Pursuit of Racial Justice.* New York and Boston: Grand Central Publishing, 2021.

Samuels, Robert and Toluse Olorunnipa. *His Name Is George Floyd.* New York: Viking Books, 2022.

Sartre, Jean-Paul. *Being and Nothingness.* New York: Washington Square Press, 1992.

Scheck, Barry and Peter Neufeld. *The Fight Against Wrongful Convictions, Time Magazine* (Special Edition). New York: Time Inc, Books, 2017.

Senghor, Shaka. *Writing My Wrongs: Life, Death, and Redemption in an American Prison.* New York: Convergent Books, 2013.

Sidanius, Jim and Felicia Pratto. *Social Dominance: An Intergroup Theory of Hierarchy and Oppression.* Cambridge University Press, 1999.

Smith, Barbara, Ed. *Home Girls: A Black Feminist Anthology.* News Brunswick, New Jersey, and London: Rutgers University Press, 2000.

Smith, Robert C. *We Have No Leaders: African Americans in the Post-Civil Rights Era.* New York: State University of New York Press, 1996.

Smith, Jamil. Killer Mike's Battle Rhymes. *Rolling Stone Magazine*, Issue 1341, July 2020.

Smith, Lillian Smith. *Killers of the Dream. See Killers of the Dream.* New York and London: W. W. Norton & Company, 1949.

Sneed, Roger A. *Representations of Homosexuality: Black Liberation Theology and Cultural Criticism.* New York: Palgrave Macmillan, 2020.

Sperber, Jonathan. *Karl Marx: A Nineteenth Century Life.* New York: Liveright Publishing Corporation, 2013.

Spillers, Hortense J. Mama's Baby, Papa's Maybe: An American Grammar Book. *Diacritics*, Vol. 17, No. 2, Culture and Countermemory: The "American" Connection (Summer, 1987), pp. 64–81.

Stackhouse, Max L. *Walter Rauschenbusch: The Righteousness of the Kingdom.* New York: Abingdon Press, 1978.

Staples, Robert. *Black Masculinity: The Black Man's Role in American Society.* San Francisco: The Black Scholars Press, 1982.

———. Change in Black Family Structure: The Conflict Between Family Ideology and Structural Conditions. *Journal of Marriage and Family*, Vol. 47, No. 4 (November 1985), pp. 1005–1013. National Council on Family Relations. https://www.jstor.org/stable/352344.

———. The Myth of the Black Matriarchy. *The Black Scholar*, Vol. 1, No. ¾, IN MEMORIUM: W.E.B. DuBois (January–February 1970), pp. 8–16. Published by Taylor & Francis, Ltd. https://www.jstor.org/stable/41163415.

Starkey, Caroline and Emma Tomalin, Eds. *The Routledge Handbook of Religion, Gender, and Society.* Oxford and New York: Routledge, 2022.

Steele, Shelby. *A Bound Man: Why We Are Excited About Obama and Why He Can't Win.* New York: Free Press, 2008.

Steinem, Gloria. After Black Power, Women's Liberation. *New York Magazine*, April 4, 1969.

Stevenson, Bryan. *Just Mercy: A Story of Justice and Redemption.* New York: Spiegel and Grau, 2017.

Taylor, Keeanga-Yahmatta. *From #BLACKLIVESMATTER to Black Liberation.* Chicago: Haymarket Books, 2016.

Taylor, Mark Lewis. *The Executed God: The Way of the Cross in Lockdown America.* Minneapolis: Fortress Press, 2001.

Thomas, Clarence. *My Grandfather's Son.* New York: Harper Collins Publishers, 2007.

Traister, Rebecca. *All the Single Ladies: Unmarried Women and the Rise of an Independent Nation.* New York: Simon & Schuster Paperbacks, 2016.

The Trump Presidency: A Damage Report. *The Atlantic Monthly*, October 2017, Vol. 320, No. 3.

Von Drehle, David, Jay Newton Small, and Maya Rhodan. Murder, Race, and Mercy: Stories from Charleston. *Time Magazine*, November 23, 2015.

Wallace, Michele. *Black Macho and the Myth of the Superwoman.* London and New York: Verso Classics, 1999.

Wallace-Wells, Benjamin. The Hard Truths of Ta-Nehisi Coates. *New York Magazine*, July 12, 2015.

Warren, Calvin L. *Ontological Terror: Blackness, Nihilism, and Emancipation.* Durham and London: Duke University Press, 2018.

Washington, Booker T. *Up From Slavery.* New York: Signet Classics, 2000.

Washington, James, Ed. *Martin Luther King, Jr.: I Have a Dream: Writings and Speeches That Changed the World.* New York: Harper Collins Publishers, 1986.

Watkins, D. *We Speak for Ourselves: A Word from Forgotten Black America.* New York, London, Toronto, and New Delhi: Atria Books, 2019.

Wehelive, Alexander G. *Racial Assemblages, Biopolitics, and Black Feminist Theories of the Human.* New York: Duke University Press, 2014.

West, Cornel. *Brother West: Living and loving Out Loud.* New York: Smiley Books, 2009.

———. *Democracy Matters: Winning the Fight Against Imperialism.* New York: Penguin Books, 2005.

———. *Prophesy Deliverance: An Afro–American Revolutionary Philosophy.* Philadelphia: The Westminster Press, 1982.

West, Cornel and Christa Buschendorf. *Black Prophetic Fire.* Boston: Beacon Press, 2014.

West, Traci C. *Disruptive Christian Ethics: When Racism and Women's Lives.* Philadelphia: Westminster John Knox Press, 2006.

Williams, Delores S. *Sisters in the Wilderness. The Challenge of Womanist God-Talk.* Maryknoll: Orbis Books, 1996.

Wilmore, Gayraud, Ed. *Black Men in Prison: The Response of the African American Church: A Book for Induvial and Congregational Study.* Atlanta: The ITC Press, 1990.

———. *Black Religion and Black Radicalism: An Interpretation of the Religious History of African Americans*, 3rd Edition. Maryknoll: Orbis Books, 1998.

Wilson, William Julius. *When Work Disappears: The World of the New Urban Poor.* New York: Alfred A. Knopf, 1996.

Wood, Mark David. *Cornel West and the Politics of Prophetic Pragmatism.* Urbana and Chicago: University of Illinois Press, 2000.

Woodfox, Albert and Leslie George. *Solitary: Unbroken by four Decades in Solitary Confinement. My Story of Transformation and Hope.* New York: Grove Press, 2019.

Woodward, C. Vann. *The Burden of Southern History.* Baton Rouge: Louisiana State University Press, 1960.

———. *The Strange Career of Jim Crow, Commemorative Edition.* Oxford: Oxford University Press, 2001.

Yancy, George, Ed. *Cornel West: A Critical Reader.* Malden: Blackwell Publishers, 2001.

Young III, Ulysses Josiah. *James Baldwin's Understanding of God: Overwhelming Joy and Desire.* New York: Palgrave McMillan, 2014.

Zakaria, Rafia. *Against White Feminism: Notes on Disruption.* New York: W. W. Norton & Company, Inc., 2021.

Zweigenhaft, Richard L. and G. William Domhoff. *Diversity in the Power Elite*, 3rd Edition. Landham, Boulder, New York, and London: Rowman Littlefield, 2008.

Index

abolitionism, 19–21, 111–13, 126–27
Abrahamic religions, 35–36
activism, 27–35
affirmative action, 87–93
Alexander, Michelle, 5–7, 34, 113–14
Ambedkar, BR, 22
Amendments, U.S. Constitution, 156
Americas most wanted victims, 74–78
Anderson, Victior, 133
Anglo Saxon perfection, 141–45
Angola, 20
anti-Black misandry, 72, 111
anti-Blackness, 5–7, 17–19, 27–35, 45–48, 71–74, 153, 162

backlash, 152
Baker, Ella, 53
Baldwin, James, 27
Baltimore, 166
Bell, Derrick, 127
Biden, Joe, 95, 154
bifurcation, 88–93
The Birth of a Nation, 121
Black churches, 49–52
Black families, 88–93
Black family life, 72–74, 80–82, 164–69
Black feminism, 87–88, 93–103, 122–24, 141–44, 147–49
Black Girl Magic, 86–87

Black liberation theology, 75–78
Black Lives Matter, 27–33, 57–59, 103, 147–49
Black Male Exceptionalism, 116–20
Black male feminist, 113
Black Males Left Behind, 167
Black Male Studies, 80–82
Black male youth, 69–74
Black masculinity, 5–17, 67–78
The Black Panther Party for Self Defense, 32–33
Black Power, 30–32
Boyd, Todd, 50
Brahmin elites, 115–16
The British Empire, 115–16
Brown, John, 22
Brown v. Board of Education, 32, 128
Butler, Paul, 113

capitalism, 85–87
charisma, 49–52
The Charleston Massacre, 31–33, 46–49
Chokehold, 111–16
Christian elites, 55–57
Christianity, 45–49, 57–59, 75–76
Christianity, Constantinian, 75–76
civilizing projects, 144–45
civil rights, 32–33, 128
The Civil Rights Act of 1964, 33, 128

The Civil Rights Act of 1965, 33, 128
The Civil Rights Movement, 32–35, 45, 52–57
The Civil War, 119
Cleaver, Eldridge, 79, 159
Clinton, Bill, 154
Clinton, Hillary, 125, 169
Coates, Ta-Nehisi, 27–32
Cohen, Cathy, 103
Cole, Johnetta B., 123
Coleman, Monica A., 87
colonial elites, 113–16
colonialism, 85–87, 113–16
commodification, 85–88
Cone, James H., 40, 75
conservatives, 151–56
Cooper, Brittany, 103
The Corner, 166
Cose, Ellis, 7–8
COVID-19, 154–55
Crenshaw, Kimberle, 103, 125–28
criminal justice system, 11, 13–16, 124–29, 153–56, 162–69
The crisis of imagination, 6–7, 16–23, 147–49
Critical Race Theory, 127
cruel and unusual punishment, 151–56
cultural studies, 16
Curry, Tommy J., 23, 80

Davis, Angela J., 13
Davis, Angela Y., 87, 103
Day, Keri, 87
The Decade of Death, 6–7, 68–69, 86–87, 111, 133–36, 151–52
The Demonic Imaginary, 5–7, 69–71, 98–103, 112–13, 135
Dennis, Andrea L., 111
disintegration, 113–15
diversity and inclusion, 77–78, 126
Douglas, Frederick, 58
Douglas, Kelly Brown, 87
DuBois, W. E. B., 53, 58, 89
Dyson, Michael Eric, 16, 56

Eighth Amendment, U.S. Constitution, 156
Emanuel African American Episcopal Church, 48–51
The Enigma of Clarence Thomas, 158
Eulogy, Barack Obama, 5, 46
exceptionalism, 87, 93

family structures, 71–74, 89–93
fathers, 71–74, 156–64
the fear of Black masculinity, 94–106, 111–20
Featherstone, Liza, 169
female headed households, 71–74, 164–69
feminists, 88—93, 117–20
Ferguson, MO, 58
fetishizing Black women, 93–94
Floyd, George, 145–47
Fluker, Walter, 69
Foreman, James Jr., 23, 114
Fraser, Nancy, 169

Garvey, Marcus, 35, 53
gender ideology, 136–41
Gottschalk, Marie, 34
Guy-Sheftall, Beverly, 87, 123

Hamer, Fannie Lou, 97
Hare, Nathan and Julia, 137
Harris, Kamala, 95–97, 154
Hart, William D., 60–61
heterosexual Black men, 135–41
high brow intellectuals, 16–19
Hill-Collins, Patricia, 87, 103
Hindu Caste System, 115–16
hip hop, 19–21, 78–79, 111
Historically Black Colleges and Universities (HBCUs), 95
hooks, bell, 8–12, 87, 141–44
Hurricane Katrina, 38–39

identity politics, 16–19, 93–106, 147–49, 151
incorporation, 85–93, 124–27
India, 85–86, 115–16
intersectionality, 103, 116–20, 128

Jackson, George, 159
Jarrett, Valerie, 126
Johnson, Lyndon B., 33
Jones, William R., 45–46, 62

Kennedy, John F., 33
Killer Mike, 78
King, Jr. Martin Luther, 45, 54

law and order, 151–56
law schools, 111–13
LGBTQ+, 67–71, 138–41
liberalism, 27, 33–35, 88–93, 124–27
Lightsey, Pamela, 67
Lil Boosie, 20–21
linked fates, 88–93, 133–35, 151–52
Louisiana State Penitentiary, 20

Malcolm X, 79
Manning, Marable, 133
Marshall, Thurgood, 53
Martin, Trayvon, 5–7, 147–49
mass incarceration, 28–30, 37–39, 152–56
Mays, Benjamin Elijah, 56
McDougal, Serie, 80
messianic ideology, 27–28
messianic religion, 27–28, 35–37, 48–49, 54–57
metaphysics, 11–12
misandry, 111
Morrison, Toni, 87
Moynihan, Daniel Patrick, 88–90, 167

The Nation of Islam, 72
The New Jim Crow, 5, 113–16, 164, 169
Newton, Huey P., 159
Nielson, Erik, 111
nongovernmental organizations (NGOs), 85–87

Obama, Barack, 34, 46–48
Ontological Blackness, 133
ontological problems, 37–39

patriarchal authority, 8–12, 101–4, 141–44, 156–64
Patterson, James T., 167
Patterson, Orlando, 15–16, 142–44
perfectionism, 144
Perkinson, Robert, 34
Pickney, Clementa, 47
Pinn, Anthony B., 79
Plessy v. Ferguson, 128
policing Black men, 11–15, 123–28
popular culture, 78–80
postmodernism, 16–19, 127, 147–49
the power elite, 74–78
presidential elections, 95–98, 125–27
Prison abolitionism, 19–23, 111–13, 124–29, 164–69
the prison industrial complex (PIC), 5, 113, 153–56
prison writings, 159
prophetic Christianity, 75–78
prosecutorial misconduct, 111–13
prosecutors, 111–13
The protection of women, 120–22

racial mythology, 28–32, 120–22, 144, 147
radical feminism, 98–103, 121–24
The Rage for Order, 151–56
Ransby, Barbara, 124
Rap on Trial, 111
rappers, 78–80
redemptive suffering, 27–28, 45–49
Reed, Adolph, 29
Reed, Ishmael, 15
Reeves, Richard, 168
religious studies, 67–69, 81–82
Rideau, Wilbert, 159
Robin, Corey, 158
Robinson, Eugene, 113
Rose, Tricia, 87
Roy, Arundhati, 85–86

Sanders, Bernie, 78
Shakur, Sanyinka, 159
Sneed, Roger, 67

the social gospel, 56
South Carolina, 48–51
The Southern Christian Leadership Conference (SCLC), 45
Staples, Robert, 15
Stewart, Dianne, 136–41
summer 2020, 145–49, 154
Summers, Larry, 17–18
super predator, 8

Taylor, Keenga-Yamahtta, 166
terrorism, 48, 154
theology, 67
Thomas, Clarence, 156–62
tribalistic Black womanhood, 93–106
tribalistic extremists, 95–104
Truth, Sojourner, 58
Tubman, Harriet, 124

unincorporated Black America, 156–69
The U.S. Supreme Court, 152–62

Walker, Alice, 87
The War on Drugs, 5–7
Washington, Booker T., 58
Watkins, D., 166
The welfare state, 164–69
Wells, Ida B., 58
We Real Cool, 8–11
We Run This City, 166
West, Cornel, 16–18, 21, 75–78
West, Traci, 67
White capitalist America, 86
White Christian South, 49
White interests, 86–101
White nationalism, 120
White redeemers, 120
White ruling class, 85–88
Williams, Delores S., 87
The Wire, 166
womanism, 67, 87
women's rights, 88–93
Woodfox, Albert, 159
world religions, 59–62

About the Author

Ronald B. Neal is an associate professor of religion in the Department for the Study of Religions at Wake Forest University, Winston-Salem, NC. Professor Neal is the author of *Democracy in 21st Century America: Race, Class, Religion, and Region*. His teaching and research are in the areas of African American religious history and culture, critical theories of religion, religion and politics, gender studies in religion, and religion and popular culture.